Forthcoming

British Industry since 1945
Margaret Ackrill

Foreign Policy since 1945
Anthony Adamthwaite

The Conservative Party since 1945
John Barnes

Town Planning in Britain since 1900
Gordon Cherry

Electoral Change since 1945
Pippa Norris

Sport in Britain since 1945
Richard Holt and Tony Mason

Class and Inequality in Britain
Paul Keating

Parliament since 1945
Philip Norton

British Youth Cultures
William Osgerby

The Labour Party since 1945
Eric Shaw

Terrorism since 1945
Paul Wilkinson

Local Government since 1945
Ken Young and Nirmala Rao

*Indicates title now out of print.

The series *Making Contemporary Britain* is essential reading for students, as well as providing masterly overviews for the general reader. Each book in the series puts the central themes and problems of the specific topic into clear focus. The studies are written by leading authorities in their field, who integrate the latest research into the text but at the same time present the material in a clear, ordered fashion which can be read with value by those with no prior knowledge of the subject.

**THE INSTITUTE OF CONTEMPORARY
BRITISH HISTORY**
50 Gordon Square, London WC1H 0PQ

The British Economy since 1945

Economic Policy and Performance, 1945–1995

Second edition

Alec Cairncross

BLACKWELL
Publishers

First published 1992
Reprinted 1993, 1994
Second edition published 1995

Blackwell Publishers Ltd
108 Cowley Road
Oxford OX4 1JF

Blackwell Publishers Inc.
238 Main Street
Cambridge, Massachusetts 02142
USA

British Library Cataloguing in Publication Data
A CIP catalogue record for this book is available from the British Library.

Library of Congress Cataloging-in-Publication Data
Cairncross, Alec, Sir, 1911–
    The British economy since 1945: economic policy and performance,
1945–1995 / Alec Cairncross. – 2nd ed.
    p. cm. – (Making contemporary Britain)
Includes bibliographical references and index.
ISBN 0-631-19961-6
    1. Great Britain—Economic conditions—1945– 2. Great Britain—
Economic policy–1945–   I. Title. II. Series.
HC256.5.C257   1995
338.94′009′045—dc20   95-17554
                                                       CIP

Printed in Great Britain by Hartnolls Limited, Bodmin, Cornwall
This book is printed on acid-free paper

Contents

Figures

Tables

General Editor's Preface

The Institute of Contemporary British History's series *Making Contemporary Britain* is aimed directly at students and at others interested in learning more about topics in post-war British history. In the series, authors are less attempting to break new ground than presenting clear and balanced overviews of the state of knowledge on each of the topics.

The ICBH was founded in October 1986 with the objective of promoting the study of British history since 1945 at every level. To that end, it publishes books and a quarterly journal, *Contemporary Record*; it organizes seminars and conferences for school students, undergraduates, researchers and teachers of post-war history; and it runs a number of research programmes and other activities.

A central theme of the ICBH's work is that post-war history is too often neglected in British schools, institutes of higher education and beyond. The ICBH acknowledges the validity of the arguments against the study of recent history, notably the problems of bias, of overly subjective teaching and writing, and the difficulties of perspective. But it believes that the values of studying post-war history outweigh the drawbacks, and that the health and future of a liberal democracy require that its citizens know more about the most recent past of their country than the limited knowledge possessed by British citizens, young and old, today. Indeed, the ICBH believes that the dangers of political indoctrination are higher where the young are *not* informed of the recent past.

Alec Cairncross's volume is the first in the series exclusively on economic policy, filling a notable gap because no single book has yet been published which adequately explores all aspects of Britain's post-war economic policy and performance.

There can be no author better qualified to write this book than Alec Cairncross, because none have straddled so well, for so long, the twin worlds of academic life and economic adviser to government. A university lecturer in economics before the war, he came into government service during the war, and has since been at the heart of both, culminating in his post as Chief Economic Adviser and an indian summer of literary creativity in the last ten years.

The book is a remarkably clear assessment of the apparatus of economic policy-making, policy-instruments and outcomes, which will be read with profit by specialists and those new to the subject.

The second edition of Alec Cairncross's book brings the story up to 1995. It allows him to include key economic events such as Britain's withdrawal in 1992 from the Exchange Rate Mechanism, and also to debate the extent to which the 1990s have seen an economic recovery. The new edition confirms the book's status as not just the most up-to-date but also the most accessible introductory text to Britain's economic history since 1945.

Anthony Seldon

Preface to First Edition

There are few up-to-date one-volume economic histories of the whole post-war period for this or any other country in print. There are symposia with contributions covering particular aspects of policy and performance and indeed two such symposia for the United Kingdom have been published. But there does not exist a full-scale chronological account of developments in the United Kindom over the whole period, nor — what would seem to me highly desirable — a series of studies for each of the main industrial countries treating in detail their experience in seeking to manage their economy since 1945.

It was for this reason that I took in hand, at the suggestion of Anthony Seldon, the preparation of such a study for the United Kingdom. It is not designed to advance a thesis or test a theory but aims to provide a rather matter-of-fact account of developments from the point of view of an economist who has spent some time in the business of economic management and a much longer time thinking and writing about it.

The discussion is deliberately confined to macro-economic developments, largely ignoring the extent to which these were shaped at the micro-economic level and at the risk of encouraging the common illusion that differences in economic performance mainly reflect macro-economic government policy. It would have been impossible to do justice to all aspects of policy and performance over so long a period within the space available.

I am very conscious of the book's defects. Even when micro-economic developments are excluded, it is not easy to marry an adequate exposition of the sequence of events with comment and analysis that brings out the full significance of these events. It is also difficult, particularly in the later years, to confine the discussion to the United Kingdom and avoid constant reference to pressures and trends originating elsewhere. Much that happens in the United Kingdom can only be understood as part of the story of what is taking place in the world economy.

I have prefaced the history with some account in chapter 1 of the ideas that influenced or aspired to influence developments over the period: the issues that stirred controversy whether anything came of it or not; whether they related to policy and what governments ought to do or were matters of theory and the interpretation of market behaviour.

Chapters 2–6 provide a narrative history of the period divided roughly into decades except that chapter 2 covers only the first five years of the transition to a peace-time economy and chapter 6 takes in 1979 to cover the whole of the Thatcher era. History cannot, of course, be parcelled into decades without exaggerating the discontinuities that this implies. But there *were* marked differences in the preoccupations of successive decades that this treatment brings out.

Each of these chapters is prefaced by a short overview before entering on a detailed account. A table in each overview sets out the year-to-year changes in the main economic aggregates over the decade so as to show the fluctuations in the growth of GDP and in its principal components. It would be a mistake to attach too much weight to any of the figures in these tables but they do convey more vividly than prose can do, a picture of the underlying trends and the ups and downs accompanying them.

The book concludes in chapter 8 with a brief survey of some of the main changes over the period.

Preface to Second Edition

The main changes in this new edition are the inclusion of a new chapter sketching the events of recent years and the factors at work in the 1990s, and a fairly extensive revision of the survey of the past fifty years that concluded the previous edition.

With the important exception of the first and last chapters, the book is still chronological in treatment. Where there is a single author this is the natural way to convey and explain the development of events. But of course it cannot be done in a single chapter and chapters have to end somewhere. I have elected to break up the period into decades, recognizing that any such division is open to objection as distorting the continuity of history. Nevertheless successive decades since 1950 do appear to be fairly easily differentiated from one another and to provide natural breaks in the narrative provided there is no attempt to set too precise limits to each decade or confine the discussion to events falling exactly within the decade.

In a book as short as this, it is necessary to be selective in the topics covered. For this reason I have in general limited myself to macroeconomic policy (although by no means exclusively as the first and last chapters should bear out). My aim has been to convey a clear understanding of the development of macroeconomic policy and I have given priority to this although I am well aware that many aspects of macroeconomic policy (those directed towards faster economic growth, for example) are highly dependent on success at the micro level.

In other words, the book does not attempt to be more than an introduction to the history of the period and survey the broad changes in policy and outcome over the past half century.

Acknowledgements

My thanks are due to Anthony Seldon for encouraging me to undertake this study and for many useful suggestions. I am also grateful to Andrew Britton for allowing me to see the manuscript of his *Macroeconomic Policy in Britain 1974–87* prior to publication. I have drawn heavily on the work of the National Institute of Economic and Social Research in several chapters. I am also greatly indebted to Nuffield College Library for access to statistical material and grateful to Mr E. A. Doggett of the Central Statistical Office for help in bringing the figures in table 6.2 up-to-date.

In chapter 1 I have reproduced some passages at pp. 21–8 from my Chichele Lecture of 1988, subsequently published in the *Royal Bank of Scotland Review* for September 1988 as 'Britain's Industrial Decline'. Chapter 2 is a reproduction, with minor amendments, of my contribution to Crafts, N.F.R. and Woodward, N. (eds.) *The British Economy since 1945*. I am indebted to the Royal Bank of Scotland and Oxford University Press respectively for agreement to their appearance in this volume.

Mrs Anne Robinson, as always, has performed miracles with my scribbles. But my heaviest obligation is to my wife for bearing uncomplainingly with the long silences of composition.

Alec Cairncross

1 Changing ideas on policy and performance

The economic history of the recent past can be written either as an attempt to explain what happened and why, or it can concentrate on what the government was trying to do and what success it had. Either way the historian is dependent on a set of ideas: about how the economy works and the likely sources of the changes observed; and about the aims of policy and how these aims can be achieved. The ideas themselves are constantly changing as new economic theories evolve, new policies are introduced and new ways of giving effect to policies are devised.

It may be useful to start, before we plunge into the detail, by looking at some of the ideas that have dominated controversy since the war over how the economy behaves and how economic policy has affected that behaviour. There are difficulties under both heads which it is well to recognize. Our knowledge of the workings of the economy is imperfect and even the facts themselves are often in dispute. Although we have far more information, particularly statistical information, about the economy than ever before, much of it is of limited reliability, subject to amendment years afterwards, inconsistent and open to different interpretations. We cannot take for granted that we know the past. Similarly our knowledge of policy is often limited and the effects of policy are difficult to assess. It is easy to claim too much for policy when there is some broad accord between policy pronouncements and observed events and to neglect other factors that may have been of more importance.

Central economic planning

One of the first ideas to surface at the end of the war was that of economic planning. People had become used to planning in war-time; and since the war had ended in victory, they thought well of the planning that contributed to it (without much understanding of what planning involved). At that time, too, the state was in a dominant position, spending half the national income and exerting great influence on economic activity through the many controls surviving from the war. There were strong grounds for continuing many of the controls for a while as a means of making the best of scarcities that were likely to disappear as the economy reverted to peace-time pursuits. Planning would then be a transitional process involving the co-ordination of controls with a limited life during the reconversion from war to peace.

Advocates of central planning did not see it as transitional. They wanted an adaptation to peace-time use of war-time methods of budgeting and programming. Their ideas, however, were some-what vague and never crystallized into a design for indicative planning for economic growth such as the French evolved, and which formed the basis for the National Plan when enthusiasm for planning was re-kindled in the early 1960s. The one common feature in most expositions of central planning was distrust of market forces and an almost entire absence of any reference to the price mechanism.

There was clearly a difference between planning in war-time and in peace. When the unquestioned objective was to win the war, only the state could co-ordinate economic activity so as to serve that purpose and it could make use of whatever controls were required. When the aim was to rebuild economic prosperity and allow the public the freedoms they associated with peace, it was more difficult to justify the compulsions acceptable in war. In a consumer-driven society the state might have important func-tions but it was not indispensable to the co-ordination of economic activity when this could be left to the price mechanism with such supplementary action by the state as was thought desirable.

What made many people lean towards central planning was a sense of the inadequacies of the supply side of the economy such as have been well described in Correlli Barnett's *Audit of War*.

There was an urgent need for industrial reconstruction in which the state might play a leading role. The governing idea would be, as in France, modernization; and planning would consist primarily of an investment programme concentrated on the leading industries and financed largely from public funds. Many historians still think along these lines and look back on the early post-war years as a period of missed opportunities when there was no proper plan for reconstructing British industry under the auspices of the government. As will be suggested below, this view neglects the efforts the government made to plan for industrial recovery, the extent to which investment *was* planned and the real obstacles to modernization.

The only official publication explaining what economic planning entailed was the *Economic Survey 1947*. A preliminary section which we now know to have been drafted by Stafford Cripps divided planning into three elements. First there were long-term 'plans' for a few basic industries, the 'plans' amounting in practice to output targets (e.g. for coal and electric power). Then there were 'economic budgets' for the coming year showing how manpower might be redistributed between different industries and what changes the government hoped to see in the constituent elements of national income and expenditure. These would be supplemented, thirdly, by an analysis undertaken by a central staff of particular problems: the balance of payments, capital investment, shortages of all kinds. How these various elements were to be co-ordinated in a consistent plan and what was to determine the size and shape of the plan was left obscure.[1]

The one objective of economic policy in the years after 1945 that unified efforts to plan the economy was full employment. Planning for full employment began as soon as the war ended.[2] This kind of planning has since become identified with demand management through the use of monetary and fiscal policy but in the early years it was supported by various administrative controls operating directly on bottlenecks and shortages. If the balance of payments was in deficit, the government did not simply let the price of foreign exchange rise. It restricted imports, embarked on an export drive, and controlled the movement of funds out of sterling. Similarly, it dealt with a shortage of steel by a system of allocations, a shortage of butter by rationing, a shortage of building labour by licensing new building and assigning starting dates. The common element in all this was resort to administrative decisions instead of letting price increases do the job.

There were those who argued for the continuation of some at least of the controls as part of planning for full employment. Gaitskell, for example, put round a memorandum in January 1950 protesting against exclusive reliance on demand management through the use of financial pressures rather than direct controls. If scarcities and bottlenecks arose as employment expanded, he argued, they might threaten inflation and bring expansion to a halt before full employment was reached. At the level of income accompanying full employment excess demand might develop in particular localities, for particular commodities, for some groups of workers or some types of raw materials, for foreign exchange, and so on. In each case there would be a need to relieve the shortage by limiting or diverting demand if expansion was to continue. There might then appear to be a choice between letting prices rise, with awkward consequences, or halting expansion. With controls, Gaitskell argued, the choice could be avoided. As the more acute shortages inherited from war disappeared, it was possible that the dilemma might then be resolved and some of the controls become unnecessary. but the need for exchange control and import control to keep the exchange rate steady would go on indefinitely.[3]

What in fact happened was that the government sought to co-ordinate existing controls − over investment, imports, prices, etc. − so as to keep demand within the limits of available resources whether in the form of savings, dollars or manpower. This was done on the basis of advice from the Economic Section of the Cabinet Office and the Planning Staff in the Treasury without at first much public understanding of the new system of economic management. For example, the forecasts which formed the basis of demand management were not disclosed and no outside agency prepared economic forecasts until the end of the 1950s.

As the economy came back into balance and shortages diminished controls were gradually wound up and more weight attached to purely financial instruments such as the budget and bank rate. By 1950 most of the physical controls were on the way out but their life was extended by the outbreak of war in Korea and the rearmament that followed.

Historians have tended to look back on the immediate post-war years as a period of lost opportunity. Criticism has come partly from the left for the government's failure to intervene more vigorously to shake up British industry, and partly from the right for what is represented as squandering resources on the 'New Jerusalem' of the Beveridge Plan, the National Health Service, and the Welfare State.[4]

That British industry needed a shake-up was never in dispute. Its deficiencies were fully recognized in war-time and have been amply illustrated by subsequent events. The question was always: what could be done from the outside by a government with limited funds and industrial expertise? Great efforts were made under the Marshall Plan to familiarize managements and men with American productive methods but, so far as can be judged, to little effect.[5] The government did all in its power to facilitate a high level of investment but, as was to happen throughout the post-war period, the yield in additional output to higher investment was disappointing. Comparisons drawn with France and other continental countries make no allowance for the different mood and state of expectations in a country that ended the war victorious and with its economy largely intact. Little could have been done in the short run to restructure British industry and whether the government knew how to make it more efficient is open to question.

The 'New Jerusalem' thesis is badly out of focus. In the context of the early post-war years the increase in expenditure on the social services, although substantial, was not the main burden on the Exchequer. Expenditure on the social services, including education, health, housing, pensions, and unemployment benefit amounted in pre-war years to about £450=£500 million, or about £1000 million in terms of post-war prices, and had risen to about £1500 million by 1950. Expenditure on defence, which did not exceed £200 million until 1938, was never less than about £750 million after 1945, and rose again to over £1400 million in 1952–3. The food subsidies cost more than any of the social services, reaching nearly £500 million in 1949. Neither of these is mentioned in Correlli Barnett's attack on the 'illusions' of the post-war years. Moreover, of total expenditure on the social services, a large part did not fall on the taxpayer but on the (contributory) National Insurance Fund which by 1951–2 was running an annual surplus of nearly £600 million – 50 per cent more than the entire cost of the National Health Service.

If instead of the early post-war years the argument relates to the whole period since the war, then it is difficult to see why so much weight should be attached to expenditure on social welfare as a factor in industrial decline when such expenditure is known to fall short of the level in most other industrial countries.

Demand management

The set of ideas behind economic policy in the first thirty years after the war are often summarized as 'demand management'. It is true that policy concentrated more heavily on the demand side of the economy than on the supply side but each reacted on the other, an increase in supply adding to demand and an increase in demand eliciting more output. The selection of demand as the object of management rested on the Keynesian view that the running in any economy was made by the growth of effective demand and that stability or growth should be approached by operating on demand rather than supply. Planning for full employment, therefore, meant planning for a level of demand that would call forth the full potential of the economy. It was appreciated that if demand became excessive its impact would be increasingly on prices rather than on output or supply. It was also appreciated that prices might rise for reasons partly or wholly unconnected with demand such as a rise in import prices or pressure for higher wages.

An important concept was the pressure of demand on capacity. At low levels of pressure there would be unemployed resources and output would be below economic potential. At high pressure the margin of unused resources would disappear, output would cease to expand and additional demand would spend itself on driving up prices. It became clear, however, that there was a fairly broad band over which the pressure could alter with no sudden change in prices and that output adjustments to changing conditions were generally more easily made when pressure was relatively high than when it was low.

Demand management was at first rather crude and rested on estimates and forecasts that were subject to a wide margin of error. These forecasts related to the expected change over the coming year or so in the main aggregates making up the national income: consumer spending, government expenditure on goods and services, fixed investment, stockbuilding, exports and imports. Forecasting became increasingly sophisticated as economic statistics improved – particularly after quarterly estimates of the aggregates became available in 1957 – but it was always difficult to spot in advance the more important turning points. There were also problems of devising changes in fiscal or monetary policy to keep demand on an even course.

Variations in the size of the budget surplus came to be the main instrument of demand management and were accepted as such by Cripps in 1948–50 when he ran large budget surpluses sufficient to finance all or nearly all loan expenditure in the public sector and so reduce the danger of inflation. In the 1950s there was never any need to plan for a budget deficit; but the mere prospect of one produced such alarm in the Treasury that it was obviously not fully converted to demand management through the budget. It proved sufficient in those years to budget for comparatively small changes in the surplus of up to £150 million except in 1959 when a much larger reduction was made in the prospective surplus without quite pushing it into deficit. Demand was sufficiently resilient, not just in the United Kingdom, but all over the world, to make demand management far more a matter of holding down demand than of providing a budgetary stimulus.

There has been much controversy over the extent to which policy in the post-war years was 'Keynesian'.[6] Keynes himself would have had serious reservations about demand management. What he argued for was stabilization of investment, the main domestic source of instability, rather than of aggregate demand. He had doubts about the wisdom of stimulating consumer spending through budget deficits because of the temptations to which this exposed spendthrift Chancellors and preferred either to vary national insurance contributions or to have a separate capital budget that would allow loan-financed investment to be raised or lowered without affecting the ordinary budget. Keynes was also distrustful of elaborate economic forecasts and preferred to rely more heavily on hunch in judging what ought to be done to limit or expand demand.

Nevertheless the very idea of managing demand was profoundly Keynesian. In pre-war years he was always conscious of the gap between the actual level of output and the level of which the economy was capable. How large the gap had been was demonstrated in war-time; and the whole point of demand management, through the budget or in any other way, was to prevent such a gap from re-emerging. The danger was thought to be most acute in the early post-war years when it was feared that there might be a repetition of the 1921 slump and subsequent depression once the re-stocking boom that usually followed a war had passed its peak. These expectations were not fulfilled. Instead a long boom began that lasted throughout the world into the 1970s and swamped all minor hesitations and setbacks in this country or that until the final blowout in 1973. The boom made demand management easier but not superfluous. Indeed the boom itself owed something to demand management: the confidence that sustained investment throughout the period was nurtured by the conviction that governments would, if necessary, act to sustain demand.

Demand management was not, however, the same thing as economic management. As we have seen, an expansion in demand might press unevenly on particular parts of the economy and produce shortages in some parts and surpluses in others. There was an element of indeterminateness in wage behaviour so that wage costs might rise for reasons little connected with demand pressure. Then there were all the uncertainties of external pressures that could throw the balance of payments into deficit even when the economy was far from fully employed. There was thus a constant problem of adjustment so as to keep different elements in demand in line with one another as the aggregate increased and prevent awkward shortages from holding up expansion.

There was also a danger that concentration on demand, and particularly on short-term fluctuations in demand, might deflect attention from the long-term development of the supply side of the economy. This was the argument most consistently levelled against short-term demand management. It was labelled 'fine tuning' and attacked as neglecting the long-term growth in industrial capability for the sake of small temporary gains in the level of employment. If demand management *aggravated* fluctuations in demand, as some have urged, it might well have done harm to long-term growth.[7] But so far as this was so, the resulting fluctuations were no greater than in other countries;[8] and the more important effect was that business could count on intervention to prevent major swings in demand. Some of the methods used to stabilize aggregate demand, for example hire purchase restrictions, did destabilize components of total demand, such as demand for cars, and had a harmful effect on particular industries. But so far as demand management was successful, it is difficult to see why this should have had a negative effect on industrial efficiency across the board.

Demand management could not be, and never pretended to be, a substitute for action on supply. Nor did it ever exclude attempts to maintain a long-term perspective. But without short-term demand management that succeeded in maintaining a high level of output what was forfeited was not only output but employment and, most important of all, the pressure for adjustments that depression arrests and for innovations that depression postpones. No doubt there were other adjustments, for example in the attitudes and expectations of workers and their representatives, that depression helps to bring about; and such adjustments might be necessary if inflation was to be avoided. But there was also a danger, as the attitudes bred in the 1930s showed, that prolonged exposure to high unemployment might build up new resistances to healthy industrial relations that would survive into a period of ample demand.

In the early years after the war, demand management rested heavily on a budget surplus and until the 1980s fiscal policy continued to be the pillar of demand management. It also made use in those years of a long list of controls that were gradually removed. Among them were several that coped directly with balance of payments deficits: quantitative import controls, devices for promoting exports, exchange control. Others were financial: selective credit control, ceilings on bank credit, hire purchase restrictions. Others again were physical: building controls, consumer rationing, allocation of raw materials, etc. It was this wide range of controls that enabled inflation to be held in check, brought foreign trade into balance within three years, and underlay the dominance of exports and investment in access to resources in the early post-war years.

All of these controls have gradually been abandoned, most of them by the mid-1950s but some only in the Thatcher era: exchange control, direct limitation of bank lending, hire purchase controls. A substitution of financial for physical controls was a natural ingredient of post-war reconstruction, but was it desirable for the state to retreat so far? Did it make sense to renounce the use of the budget to control demand and regard its impact on government borrowing and *possibly*, therefore, on the money supply as taking precedence over its impact on demand, when borrowing and money matter only to the extent they affect demand?

External pressures

Planning was conceived of in terms of the domestic economy with little regard to international trade and finance. But it was precisely the pressures these exerted that dominated the economy and by which policy was most closely circumscribed. By way of illustration one need only point to the abandonment of the National Plan in the 1960s under the pressure of efforts to avoid devaluation.

In the early years some form of planning of international trade itself was difficult to avoid. Controls were used to limit imports, encourage exports and restrict capital movements. As the dollar shortage became acute the controls had then to be adapted to economize the use of dollars. This involved discrimination when the United States was campaigning against discrimination. It also meant inconvertibility when the Loan Agreement with the United States promised convertibility of sterling by mid 1947. Efforts were made to extend the use of sterling as an international currency in conditions under which there was simply too much sterling and too few dollars. Trade was conducted with non-sterling countries largely on a bilateral basis until the introduction of the European Payments Union in 1950. The limitations of planning in international trade had been demonstrated in the previous year when sterling (and most other currencies) were devalued against the dollar.

The ideas of this period are coloured by political aims: the efforts of the United States to assist in the recovery of Western Europe and encourage its economic integration as a bulwark against Communism; the acceptance of the need for Germany to play its part in European recovery; the resulting conversion of France from antagonism to German recovery to the vision of a united Europe built on Franco-German co-operation. In all this the United Kingdom, regarding itself as a world power with strong links to the Commonwealth and a 'special relationship' with the United States, could play only a limted part. It had spent the war helping to plan new institutions on a worldwide, not a regional, basis, traded mainly with other continents outside Europe, was conscious of its economic weakness, and feared that close links with Europe would weaken it still further.

The debates of the post-war years on external economic policy dwelt heavily on the problems of discrimination and inconvertibility. Once convertibility could be established, as happened at the end of 1958, discrimination between dollar and non-dollar sources of supply ceased to make sense. The limited convertibility of European currencies through the European Payments Union from 1950 to 1958 had already ended discrimination between member countries. But there were occasions in 1949 and again in 1952 when it seemed possible that the dollar and non-dollar worlds would fall apart and the prospect of worldwide multilateral trade disappear indefinitely.

In a world of controls there are always some who challenge the need for them. By the time the Conservatives took office in 1951 they were convinced of the need for greater market freedom. This was in keeping with their traditional views and found expression again in 1970 and even more in 1979. In 1951 they began by using import quotas to restrict imports in three successive cuts. This did not prevent them from voicing a determination to 'free the pound', i.e. allow it to float free of restrictions. Although they drew back from this in 1952, it was about this time that controversy began over the case for floating the pound. The idea had earlier been sponsored by the Economic Section (e.g. at the time of devaluation in 1949 and again as an anti-inflationary move early in 1951). Economists such as James Meade and Nicholas Kaldor wrote in favour of letting the pound float and official policy up to 1955 visualized the introduction of a float when the pound became convertible. In the 1960s, as it came to be thought that the pound was overvalued and that a fixed rate stood in the way of export-led growth, opinion in favour of floating gathered strength. Little was said about the drawbacks of floating or about the added danger of inflation if the pound floated downwards

The current of opinion moved more powerfully in favour of floating in the 1970s in a world of high inflation where it was difficult to hold to a fixed rate for almost any currency. The pound was allowed to float in June 1972 when there was still a surplus in the balance of payments but it was not long before all the other main currencies were also floating. The fashion gradually changed in the 1980s as inflation fell away and the repercussions of fluctuating exchanges were seen in a less favourable light. Pressure to join the European Monetary System accompanied argument for a stable rate of exchange based on the belief that such stability would assist stability of the domestic price level. Where thirty years previously devaluation had been seen as opening the way to economic growth, by 1990 it had become fashionable to regard devaluation as ineffective because more or less automatically offset by inflation and to contemplate without a qualm a regime where devaluation could never occur once a common currency replaced the national currencies of members of the European Community.

The issues in external economic policy were far from being confined to exchange rate policy. Whether the rate was fixed or floating, the balance of payments remained sensitive both to domestic and external pressures and the two could not be kept in balance merely by changes in the exchange rate, still less by exchange control. It was rare, except in the heyday of North Sea oil, for the balance of payments to be in healthy surplus. For most of the time it was chronically weak, precipitating recurrent exchange crises, periodic bouts of foreign borrowing and measures that fell short of outright subsidy to keep deficits at bay. Two major devaluations, one in 1949 and a second in 1967, had only temporary success in removing the external pressure; and if they did not occur oftener in the first twenty-five years it was largely because of the buoyant state of the world economy and the inflation of foreign incomes it promoted. After 1972 a long decline in the effective exchange rate began and continued for the next two decades apart from a brief but disastrous rise from 1978 to 1981.

The weakness of sterling put paid to its durability as an international currency but not to London's position as an international financial centre, thanks to its development of euro-dollar business. Once sterling was devalued for the second time 1967, and it was necessary to underwrite the value of balances held in London with the help of other central banks in the Basle Agreement of 1968, its pretensions as an international currency were difficult to take seriously. It is true that large sterling balances continued to be held especially when Arab money flowed in after the first oil shock at the end of 1973; but the inflow was followed by an embarrassing outflow in 1976 and sterling never regained the attraction it had once possessed.

Throughout the post-war period economic relations with Europe were of high importance. Britain took a prominent part in the establishment of the OEEC (Organisation for European Economic Co-operation) in 1948 by the countries benefiting from the Marshall Plan, but refrained from joining the European Economic Community and signing the Treaty of Rome in 1957. After the failure of an attempt to become associated with the Community in a European Free Trade Area in 1958 Britain entered into an organization with six other European countries calling itself EFTA or the European Free Trade Area. By 1961, however, it had been decided to seek entry to the EEC and after two rebuffs by the French, first in 1961 then in 1967, membership was finally negotiated in 1972 and took effect on 1 January 1973. British trade had already begun to change direction and even before entry, trade with the Community countries had grown from about one-tenth of the total in the early post-war years to nearly one-half in 1972.

Economic growth

Domestic economic policy can hardly avoid being about economic growth if it seeks to improve the standard of living. Economic statistics moreover show very clearly the growth in income and productivity from year to year. Nevertheless public discussion of economic growth was rare until the later 1950s when it seems to have sprung from a consciousness that other countries were growing faster than Britain. By the late 1950s the need to achieve a faster rate of growth had become a common theme of political debate.

At that stage it was widely thought that the cause of slower growth in Britain than elsewhere was low investment and stop-go, i.e. an oscillation of government policy between expansion in the interests of reducing unemployment and contraction once expansion tilted the balance of payments into deficit. But fluctuations in economic activity were not confined to the United Kingdom and were just as pronounced in countries growing much faster: except that, with a more steeply rising trend, a slowdown there did not completely arrest the growth of output. As for low investment, this was just as likely to be a *reflection* of slower growth and a less rapidly expanding market as its prime cause. In relation to the investment that *was* undertaken, the response in additional output was disappointing in comparison with the response elsewhere. Lower investment reflected a lower return: and what lay at the root of slower growth were the various factors making for a lower return to investment.

The conclusion drawn by those who attributed slower growth to stop-go was that the government should adhere to an expansionist policy, whatever the deficit in the balance of payments, and give more time for investment to respond. The higher productivity that was expected to result would then improve Britain's competitive position and wipe out the deficit, completing a virtuous circle of expanding output, higher investment, higher productivity, and further growth. Ideas of this kind were popular with ministers from 1960 onwards; and although when put into practice in a 'dash for growth' they were abandoned in face of a balance of payments crisis, they continued to be urged by those who attributed the abandonment to a failure of nerve.

Faster growth was also linked in the 1960s with the idea of planning. Partly this originated in the model presented by the French, who expounded the technique they used at a conference in London in the spring of 1961. It owed something also to the reaction against stop-go: planning, with its more extended horizon, was expected to bring a steadier growth in output and allow the economy to ride out temporary difficulties in the balance of payments or of other kinds.

These ideas made a deep impression on both the major parties. Under a Conservative government they led in 1961 to the creation of NEDC (the National Economic Development Council) which brought representatives of employers and workers into consultation with the government to consider what might be done to promote faster economic growth. This succeeded an earlier tripartite institution, the Economic Planning Board, which was set up in 1947 but had done comparatively little to affect the course of events and had no contact with the public.

Under the Labour government that followed in 1964 a new government department, the Department of Economic Affairs, was created with the specific aim of preparing a National Plan. The new department was intended to take responsibility for economic policy while the Treasury dealt with matters of finance but as had been shown in 1945–7, when a somewhat similar division was attempted, there is no easy way of separating finance and economics in a country relying heavily on financial instruments to give effect to economic policy. There were also ambiguities in the Plan itself. It consisted largely of a set of output targets designed to achieve a predetermined (higher) rate of growth in total output. But there was little reason to suppose that the targets would of themselves transform the performance of British industry and raise the rate of growth. The success of the Plan depended on the action taken to permit of its fulfilment; and government action, in face of the balance of payments difficulties with which it was wrestling, was likely to have quite the opposite effect. Those who prepared the Plan assumed that if necessary the pound would be devalued; but its completion coincided with deflationary measures to avoid devaluation and these measures were irreconcilable with the Plan's targets.

The abandonment of the Plan was accompanied by an end to policies aimed at some specific long-term rate of growth. Growthmanship, as Colin Clark called it, died in the 1960s.

Economic decline

It might appear logical, before embarking on policies to speed up economic growth, to investigate why the rate of growth in the United Kingdom was consistently below post-war rates on the continent in countries with widely different economic regimes. But most of the voluminous discussion of British economic decline and its causes came after the 1960s.

For many years after the war there was little or no consciousness of decline. On the contrary, it was a matter of satisfaction that a major depression such as followed the first world war had been avoided and that the national income was growing faster than ever before. That the main continental countries, starting from a far lower level because of the destruction and dislocation of war, should achieve high rates of growth occasioned little surprise or unease. It was not until the mid 1950s or later, when the continuation of rapid growth could no longer be seen as a short-term spurt to normality, that the idea of relative decline took root.

The contrast between British and continental experience is best illustrated in terms of labour productivity. At the end of the war this was far higher in Britain than in countries like France and Germany and in 1990 well below. Table 1.1 shows how these countries had caught up with Britain by about 1970 and how by 1984 Britain (and still more, France and Germany) was catching up with the United States in output per manhour.

Table 1.1   Real GDP per hour worked, 1938−1984 (UK = 100)

	UK	US	France	Germany	Italy	Japan
1938	100	143	84	78	70	36
1950	100	171	71	57	57	24
1960	100	174	86	89	70	34
1973	100	145	108	106	102	64
1984	100	124	121	112	101	69

Source: C. H. Feinstein, 'Economic growth since 1870: Britain's performance in international perspective', *Oxford Review of Economic Policy*, spring 1988

Table 1.2 shows relative decline from a different angle. Instead of levels of productivity it compares rates of growth in the years after 1948. Throughout the period up to 1985 output, employment, output per worker and the standard of living all grew at an appreciably slower rate in Britain with the single exception that at the end of the period, in 1979−85, output per worker grew at much the same rate in Britain as in the other member countries of the OECD as a group. In the years of rapid growth up to 1973, output per worker grew about 25 per cent faster in other OECD countries. After 1973, when growth slowed down, the margin at first narrowed and then disappeared. In absolute terms, however, the *level* of productivity remained higher in continental countries.

An even more striking indication of relative decline is the reduction in Britain's share of international trade in manufactures. This has fallen from about 25 per cent in a year like 1950 to about 8 per cent in the late 1980s. Whereas in, say, 1951 Britain's exports of manufactures were above the combined total for Germany, France and Japan they are now (in 1991) a mere one-sixth and below those of Italy. The fall has been more or less continuous from 1950 onwards. It was arrested in the 1980s; but imports of manufactures grew over the decade at a rate 50 per cent faster than exports, so that the excess of imports over exports was on an increasing scale. By 1989 it had reached nearly £19 billion.

The development and growth of this excess was one of several factors, producing a long-term decline in manufacturing employment in Britain. Since the post-war peak in 1966 the decline has been over 40 per cent and has reduced employment in manufacturing to less than a quarter of total employment compared with about 40 per cent at peak. The drop of nearly 4 million in employment in manufacturing from nearly 9 million to just over 5 million was offset only partially by an expansion in employment in services and other occupations so that unemployment reached a very high level. Some of this change, it is true, was common to most industrial countries in Europe, particularly after 1973. But the decline of manufacturing was more protracted and more pronounced in Britain than on the continent.

It should be emphasized that there has been no absolute decline − only a decline in comparison with the faster rate of growth

Table 1.2 Economic change in the United Kingdom and OECD, 1948–1989

| | Increase per annum in | | | | | | | |
| | Gross domestic product | | Civil employment | | Output per worker | | Prices[b] | |
	UK	OECD	UK	OECD	UK	OECD	UK	OECD
1948–51	3.1	7.0[a]	1.0	–	2.1	(5.9)[c]	3.8	–
1948–56	2.9	5.4[a]	0.9	–	2.0	(4.3)[c]	4.3	–
1956–73	3.1	4.5	0.3	1.0	2.8	3.5	4.5	4.0
1973–79	1.5	2.6	0.2	1.1	1.2	1.5	16.0	9.0
1979–85	1.2	2.3	–0.6	0.6	1.8	1.7	8.9	7.1
1985–89	3.7	3.5	1.6	–	2.1	–	5.4	3.5
1956–85	2.3	3.7	0.1	0.9	2.3	2.7	7.7	5.7

[a] OEEC.
[b] GDP deflator.
[c] OEEC; per inhabitant.

Sources: For all figures from 1956 to 1985, OECD; for UK 1948–56 and 1985–9 *Economic Trends Annual Supplement 1990*, *British Labour Statistics Historical Abstract*, National Institute *Economic Review*; for OEEC from 1948 to 1956 *General Statistics 1957* and OECD *National Accounts 1990*

elsewhere. Indeed, it would seem that in the 1980s Britain did better than her European neighbours. In the last five years of the decade (which include the boom of 1987–90) GDP did grow faster and so, too, did manufacturing productivity. But this largely reflected slower growth abroad rather than unusually fast growth in Britain. It is very doubtful whether the evidence is yet sufficient to warrant the conclusion that the relative decline has come to an end.

It also needs to be emphasized that relative decline is not something new dating from 1945. Economic historians are well aware that from at least as far back as 1870 there was some slackening in the British rate of growth and a quickening of growth elsewhere so that for much of the period before 1914 economic growth in Britain had fallen markedly short of growth in the leading industrializing countries such as Germany.[10] There is hardly a single failing of British industry as seen by modern critics that was not voiced with equal vehemence a century or more ago.

The causes of decline

Why has the decline occurred? Many different reasons have been given. Some writers stress the comparatively low level of investment in Britain. This seems more a symptom than a cause. The evidence suggests that additional investment effected a much lower increment in output in the United Kingdom than elsewhere, and this points to some deficiency in the way capital assets were used more than to a lack of investment. Sometimes the argument is narrowed to industrial investment, or even further to machine tools; but in periods when industrial investment rose substantially, as in the 1960s, it did not appear to transform the rate of growth. Even in the 1980s when fixed investment, expecially in plant and equipment, was much above the level in other decades, output per head measured over the economy as a whole remained obstinately at 1.8 per cent per annum – a rate well below previous experience up to 1973.

Other explanations point to the slow growth of British markets in the Commonwealth in the first two post-war decades compared with the faster growth of markets in Europe and the difficulty of redirecting British trade to markets in which competition was more severe. This was certainly of some importance but hardly accounts for such a long and obstinate decline.

Another common explanation, based on the weakness of the British balance of payments and failure of exports to hold their own against foreign competition, is the absence of export-led growth. In the early post-war years, however, when exports were increasing fast there is no evidence of faster growth than in later years when exports were lagging behind. In the years 1948–51, for example, when the worst of the shortages holding back production had passed, industrial productivity did not rise faster than 3 per cent per annum. In the 1980s, when industrial productivity grew at 4 per cent or more, exports performed relatively well but imports grew much faster so that it is hard to see how there was any net advantage affecting the growth of productivity. It is at least as plausible to look on rising exports as the fruit of growing productivity as vice versa. The truth, so far as exports are concerned, would seem to be that what makes for faster growth is the assurance of a strong balance of payments and the unlikelihood of a sudden check to demand because of balance of payments difficulties.

Most explanations of slower growth fasten on shortcomings either in management or in the typical British worker. A common theme is that managements are not sufficiently professional, lacking in a spirit of enterprise, out of touch with their workers, and so on. Or that British workers tend to be bloody-minded, easily bored, given to restrictive practices and badly trained. There is obviously some truth in this catalogue and there is a strong case for picking on human attitudes and skills as the central problem. But we have to be careful to get the question right. The question is not why labour productivity was lower in Britain but why it grew more slowly. The two questions are related but they are not the same. Extra effort, for example, will produced a once-for-all gain in productivity but unless increased progressively it will not raise productivity year after year.

For that what is required is more rapid change in some respect that enhances productivity: some improvement in process or produce, in technique, or equipment or material or organization or skill. All such change we label innovation, recognizing that it consists, not in invention and scientific breakthroughs, but in a day-to-day *commercial* endeavour to introduce improvements of one kind or another with a view to profit. New ideas and inventions create *opportunities* for innovation. But if the opportunities are to be used, the new discoveries have to be adapted to market requirements and this calls for quite different gifts and encounters quite different obstacles. A country with an outstanding record in scientific discovery may make a very poor showing when it comes to using the discoveries commercially.

Most discoveries are made abroad. From the point of view of a single firm all discoveries other than its own are made, so to speak, abroad. Much of the process of innovation, therefore, involves importation and domestication: the adaptation of a discovery to different circumstances of production and use. There has to be the ability to spot the potential of the discovery, to view it in relation to a different set of market requirements, to adapt it to the productive facilities available, and to co-ordinate all the various changes involved.

Innovation will be rapid where staffs are skilled at recognizing the possibilities for change and at handling the various changes required. It will be slow where these skills are lacking or where there is inertia or active opposition to change or a failure to make proper use of new equipment and techniques, or a disposition on the part of employees to skim off the prospective gains as the price of acquiescence in technical or organizational change. The obstacles to innovation are obviously greater, for example, in a country flushed with victory in war and confirmed in its faith in existing institutions and practices than in one that has been defeated, devastated or occupied. Where the disturbance has been less, the chances of a re-establishment of the status quo are obviously greater.

There will, of course, be some innovations where the gains are so large that they proceed as rapidly in Britain as elsewhere. There is evidence that in the adoption of major inventions the British record is not appreciably different from elsewhere. But major inventions form only a small part of the steady flow of improvements in design and method by which productivity is gradually increased.

It is change and innovation that yield rising productivity and an economy seeking to improve its rate of growth has to gear itself to welcome change and facilitate innovation. It is the obstacles to innovation whether in the labour force or in management or in any other form that account for slow growth.

Since there are many such obstacles both in Britain and in other countries, it is not easy to establish which of them accounts for the lag in productivity growth. It is impossible to identify some single factor that can by itself provide a complete explanation of Britain's relatively poor performance. Even if one could, the explanation would be unlikely to have the same force throughout the past hundred years. Moreover, an explanation that accounted convincingly for poor performance in one industry would have to be coupled with quite different explanations for others. The obstacles to innovation in the coal industry , the motor industry and nuclear power generation may differ widely. All one can hope to do is to run over some of the more plausible explanations of the divergence in performance in the more recent past and see which of them seems to hold water.

Some explanations focus on the industrial environment within which an innovator operates and point to the constraints which he cannot himself relax. These may be cultural or educational or economic. Other explanations confine themselves to the constraints within the enterprise making the innovation. These may limit the pace of innovation by dissipating the gains expected from it: through outright opposition to its introduction or failure to secure its use under optimum conditions; through higher wages to those who operate it or lower prices to the consumer or extra tax payments to the Exchequer.

A variety of cultural factors have been blamed. Sometimes it is alleged that innovation has been stifled by a decline in the industrial spirit through 'gentrification': a diversion of business talent into an attempt to mimic the aristocracy.[11] It is difficult to reconcile such an explanation with more *rapid* innovation since the second world war. More important, as is argued below, are the cultural influences that express themselves in weaknesses in the educational system: the aversion from relating education to the requirements of prospective employers; the English preference for training on the job rather than first engaging in study and training. It may also be true that the cultural environment helped to deflect talent away from manufacturing industry. But this may have been less an outcome of the educational system than of a sense that industry in Britain can easily turn into a dogfight best avoided by going into the professions or the City.

A cultural bias limiting the capacity of British managements to innovate, particularly in the metal and engineering trades, which form about half the manufacturing industry of the country, is a lack of high-grade engineers. Qualified engineers in Britain lack the prestige they enjoy abroad. In contrast to other industrial countries, few of the brightest university entrants have elected to study engineering and many of those who qualify prefer not to enter industrial employment. Thus for many years the engineering profession has failed to attract men of the highest calibre (to say nothing of women). But this is not just a matter of cultural bias or appropriate training. It reflects also the value British managements set on well-qualified engineers, and indeed on industrial training generally. So long as engineers are offered much higher salaries in the City, one can only conclude that industry does not rate their services very highly. In the same way if there is an aversion from industrial employment among graduates generally, the explanation is more likely to lie in low pay and the absence of demand than in the kind of education they have received.

Economic Constraints

Other explanations run in terms of economic constraints. Economists have argued, for example, that British experience demonstrates the ineffectiveness of competition in promoting industrial efficiency. Most British industries, it is suggested, stood in post-war years in need of extensive reorganization into larger units, able to take a long view and enjoy modern corporate management. Instead, they remained fragmented into sub-optimal units, each competing vigorously in price but unable, because of competitive pressures, to make the profits necessary for modernization of its equipment and adaptation of its products and processes. One can illustrate the process from the failure of Scottish steelmakers between the wars to agree on the replacement of their small and obsolete plants by a single integrated plant at Erskine Ferry. Competition in these circumstances neither drove plants out of business nor allowed them to make the profit necessary for modernization nor led to investment in a larger and more efficient plant making lower cost steel. Such investment would have been too risky in face of competition from existing units. On this showing, what British industry needs is restructuring into a few large and forward-looking units, with a management and market power to match, free to concentrate on planning for future development without the distractions of intense competition.

It is a prescription that many would endorse. Even in Victorian times economists would have agreed that efficiency in rail transport was not likely to be promoted by multiplying the number of competing railway systems. A single well-managed company may well prove a more successful innovator than a group of under-capitalized competitors. Nevertheless it is hard to believe that the path to more rapid innovation in Britain lies through the swallowing up of competitors into large monopolistic units. Experience with the nationalized industries hardly points in that direction. In any event, large units already play as important a role in British manufacturing industry as in Germany or other industrial countries. Whatever the workings of competition, it is not fragmentation into smaller units that distinguishes British industry; and where larger units are needed in the interests of efficiency, takeovers go at least some way to establishing them and to keeping managements on their toes.

An allied explanation of British backwardness is couched in terms of financial arrangements. It is argued that reliance for capital on share holders free to sell their holding at any time obliges industry to take a short-term view and aviod innovations involving heavy capital outlay. There is also a difficulty in raising capital for new ventures lacking an adequate track record. Financial agencies like the investment banks of continental countries would be more likely to arrive at a reasonable assessment of risk and stick to their judgement without looking for short-term capital gains. There is obviously some force in these considerations even if, as a matter of history, investment banks were a substitute for the kind of capital market that had come into existence in countries where the banks were able to confine themselves more narrowly to the provision of working capital. But lack of finance has rarely been a major complaint of British industry, even in periods like that before the first world war when scholars continue to assume that it must have been.[13] It is lack of demand for capital rather than lack of supply that has to be explained; and it is very doubtful whether lack of demand can be attributed to dependence on a host of shareholders rather than on a single backer.

There have also been wider influences at work in the international economy unfavourable to the United Kingdom. It has been true for at least two centuries that Britain supplied a particularly wide scatter of markets throughout the world while her continental neighbours tended to concentrate to a greater extent on the markets on their doorstep. This had two important consequences. One was that British exports fluctuated with the prosperity of primary producing countries overseas rather than with the prosperity of other manufacturing countries in Europe. In the post-war years this meant that British export markets expanded less rapidly than the European markets supplied by her continental neighbours, which were particularly buoyant as they recovered from the low levels of activity to which the war had reduced them. This of itself gave her competitors on the continent an advantage since productivity rises faster the more buoyant the markets supplied. In addition, the greater diversity of British markets made for a less specialized industrial structure with shorter runs and less scope for standardization. There was less possibility, therefore, of layouts using capital intensive methods to produce to a pre-arranged design and concentrating on improvement of the design so as to reduce production costs or keep pace with market requirements. In an area like Clydeside, for example, the industrial structure shaped by market pressure was such in the late 1940s that there was virtually no experience of series production. The engineering industries, although highly diversified, were confined almost exclusively to turning out one-off jobs like ships and locomotives and had little or no familiarity with line production such as is required in the manufacture of motor-cars, aircraft, and consumer durables of all kinds.

In the post-war years therefore large sectors of British industry laboured under a double disadvantage. On the one hand, their traditional markets abroad were not particularly elastic and were thrown open progressively to competitors previously excluded by preferential tariffs and other circumstances. On the other hand, their traditional layouts, staffs and mentalities were ill-adapted to the requirements of an age of mass production. British industry was over-supplied with skill, under-supplied with capital, and lacking in the kind of staff needed for rapid innovation.

Labour problems

Most observers, however, would point to none of these influences on industrial productivity as the prime source of British backwardness. They would be more likely to pin on constraints within the individual enterprise, notably inadequate training both of management and of workers and bad industrial relations. The need for better labour training has been argued convincingly by S. J. Prais and its importance to the level of productivity is obvious. In its effects on the rate of growth in productivity, however, it is perhaps a less important factor than the confrontational atmosphere in much of British industry.

The obstacles to innovation are greater when managements shrink from changes likely to produce disputes or find their time (the most important single input into innovation) absorbed in trying to settle disputes; or if there is such a large price tag attached to innovation by those who are asked to give effect to it that it is robbed of profit, which oozes away trying to placate or compensate them.

Labour difficulties have been particularly marked in British industry throughout the post-war period − not so much strikes as difficulties and tensions in the working day. There have been constant complaints of poor motivation of the labour force and lack of readiness to co-operate in changes of organization, equipment and productive methods (or, put differently, bloody-mindedness and militancy). Nor are such complaints new. They were probably at their height in the years before the first world war at a time, when, not surprisingly, labour productivity showed little or no improvement. Moreover, by common consent, labour relations in industry in Britain have been fundamentally different from those in our continental neighbours. We have thus an explanation of such generality and persistence that it can plausibly account for at least some of the continuing divergence between the growth of labour productivity here and abroad.

Labour attitudes do not provide the whole explanation. Other contributory factors include the influence of managerial inertia and inadequacy. Weak and incompetent managements, moreover, make their own contribution to bad labour relations in British industry. The two things interact. If managements show inertia and weakness it is sometimes in reaction to labour militancy and strength. Even when management is competent and respected, innovation may still be held back by labour attitudes. In most other industrial countries managements feel free to decide how best to use the services of their workers; but in Britain the use to which workers' time is put is far more frequently a matter of negotiation between them and their employers.

The lack of control over activities on the shop floor in British factories originated in the low level of investment in plant, the underdevelopment of management and supervisory staff and the general lack of direct co-ordination of the production process. Reliance came to be placed on incentive payments to maintain the pace of work rather than careful advance planning of tasks; and with this went a degree of 'labour independence' and an increase in labour bargaining power. Management economised on staff and capital but at the cost of a surrender of shop floor control.

This surrender of control has an impact on innovation extending well beyond the simple issue of militancy and strike-proneness. The example of the motor industry illustrates how the pace of innovation is affected by labour relations and labour attitudes. The report of the Central Policy Review Staff (the think tank) on the industry in 1975 showed that a much larger proportion of managerial time in Britain than on the continent went on handling industrial disputes and that the disputes themselves were liable to hold up or discourage efforts by the management to hasten technical change. In a comparison between a Ford factory in the United Kingdom and one in Belgium with exactly the same equipment, a *Sunday Times* article some years ago showed that the difference in output per head (which was considerable) could be traced largely to the frequency of breakdowns in line production. This in turn was traceable to a difference in work habits, the Belgian workers keeping track of the first signs of trouble and taking action at once to prevent it while the British workers were content to amuse themselves until a breakdown actually occurred and would only then spring into action to put things right. In such circumstances the impact on innovation is through the effect on investment decisions. These come to favour expansion in Belgium and the operation of economies of scale then widens the gap between productivity in Belgium and in Britain.

One might suppose that with the big multi-nationals there could be no marked difference from large foreign concerns in competence to effect technical innovation. But the lag seems to exist there too. The multi-nationals expand their business more rapidly in locations abroad: for example, Ford produces more and more for the British market in Spain or Belgium and tries to wind down what is left in Britain. A high and growing proportion of business profits comes from overseas activities. When introducing new products or new processes they tend to use foreign affiliates or branches as test-beds. They enjoy a more rapidly expanding market abroad, find that risk taking pays better, and have less difficulty in making changes in work practices. Productivity therefore rises faster.

The British government has sought throughout the post-war period to raise productivity in Britain, experimenting with all sorts of devices for that purpose. In the early years there were appeals to the war-time spirit, Anglo-American productivity teams, tripartite working parties in the consumer goods industries, and so on. In the 1950s came investment allowances and in the 1960s the National Plan, the Industrial Reconstruction Corporation, and the little Neddies attached to the NEDO. The 1970s continued the attempt to work out a successful industrial strategy and the vestiges of industrial policy — for example, in the shape of the National Enterprise Board — remained even in the 1980s. But the effect of all this effort on the growth of productivity is not easy to detect. The mood, attitudes and capabilities that govern the rate of innovation seem to have remained largely unaffected.

There is a widespread belief that other governments have done better. Perhaps they have. But the extent to which it has been government action that has produced high rates of growth in countries like France and Japan is greatly exaggerated. Both of these countries (and most others) were not trying to improve the rate of growth, like the United Kingdom, but to maintain a rate that was already high. They were climbing fast before the policies to which high growth is attributed were in place. Latterly there has been a marked slowdown.

Deindustrialization

One aspect of economic decline, which was at first thought to be peculiar to the United Kingdom, was the fall in manufacturing employment. By 1980 this had gone so far that it came to be described as deindustrialization although manufacturing output continued to expand. The share of manufacturing in GDP, however, declined more or less continuously and it gradually became clear that this decline was common in some degree to all the main industrial countries although the rate of decline varied from country to country.

At first there was a tendency to regard deindustrialization as the obverse of the growth of industry in the developing countries. But the exports of manufactures from developing to industrial countries were much too small to account for any large proportion of the deindustrialization in progress. The major factor was a change in consumer habits. Just as agriculture had taken a declining share in consumer spending, so also now did manufacturing, although much more slowly, while services took an increasing share.

Whatever the explanation, there was a continuing loss of jobs in manufacturing in Britain from 1966 onwards. As will be seen from table 1.3, the decline in manufacturing (in proportion to total employment) between 1960 and 1986 was greater in the United Kingdom than in any other industrial country. In 1960 the proportion had been much the same as in Germany; by 1986 it was 30 per cent less. Since labour productivity increased faster in

Table 1.3 Employment in manufacturing, 1960–1986 (% of total civilian employment)

	1960	1970	1980	1986
United Kingdom	36.0	34.7	28.4	22.5
United States	27.1	26.4	22.1	19.1
France	27.5	27.8	25.8	22.6
Italy	23.0	27.8	26.7	22.9
West Germany	37.0	39.4	34.3	32.2
Japan	21.5	27.0	24.7	24.7

Source: A. Dunnett, 'The role of the exchange rate in the decline of UK manufacturing', *The Royal Bank of Scotland Review*, March 1989

manufacturing than in the rest of the economy, the share of employment fell even further than the share of value added.

Controversies over economic growth and decline continued throughout the 1960s and early 1970s sinking into the background as larger and more urgent problems took priority in the second half of the 1970s. Some of these controversies are discussed in chapters 4 and 5 need only a passing mention here. Nicholas Kaldor, for example, regarded manufacturing as exercising a critical influence on the rate of growth of the entire economy and a shortage of labour as the major constraint on the growth of manufacturing productivity. A little later, Bacon and Eltis argued that slow growth was due to the excessive burdens imposed by the state on the taxpayer and the consequent pre-emption of scarce resources to meet welfare and other needs that lay outside the operation of market forces. Neither of these ideas need detain us here.

Inflation

As inflation accelerated in the 1970s (see figure 1.1) controversy

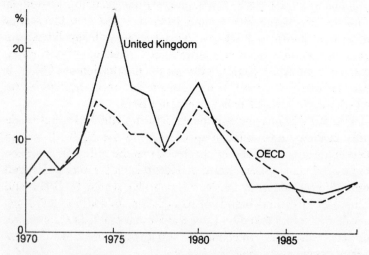

Figure 1.1   Inflation in the UK and OECD (Europe only), 1970–1990
(as measured by private consumption deflators)
Source: OECD, *Economic Outlook*, June 1990

became focused on a different issue: how was inflation to be brought under control. Demand management was thought to have failed, since even with a contraction in demand prices rose faster than ever before. There was little confidence in incomes policy when wages were rising at 30 per cent per annum. Government borrowing was on an increasing scale and widely assumed to be inflationary. The old idea that inflation consisted in too much money chasing too few goods began to take hold and offered a simple prescription for putting an end to a terrifying disorder. Leading figures in journalism and politics embraced the doctrines that came to be known as monetarism.

Monetarism

The controversies over macro-economic policy were comparatively limited in scope in the 1950s and 1960s. There were differences over the scale to which the public sector should grow, whether taxation should be higher or lower, what could be done to hold back inflationary increases in money wages. But there was agreement that demand management should be used to stabilize the economy; and even when talk of economic planning revived in 1960–1, it aroused little controversy, either between the parties or between informed observers. In comparison with any differences in those decades – over convertibility, relations with Europe, economic growth, incomes policy, or the devaluation of 1967 – it was not until the arrival of monetarism that really heated debate on the whole basis of policy came to a head.

The monetarist controversy began in the late 1960s but made little headway until inflation speeded up in the 1970s. It was in that decade, as explained in chapter 5, that the orthodox approach to demand management, based on Keynesian ideas, was challenged from different sides: by the New Cambridge school, by Bacon and Eltis, and by various brands of monetarism. In addition there was strong pressure, backed by Lord Kaldor and others in Cambridge, to seek refuge in protectionism and expand domestic demand behind quota restrictions on imports.

The latter line of argument, however appealing, failed on two grounds. As a remedy for unemployment it had to meet the objection that other countries also suffering from unemployment would be the victims of quota restrictions and were likely therefore to retaliate. Even if were true that total imports would rise again as activity expanded, no country could be sure that *its* exports would be restored to their former level. There was the further difficulty that no one could be sure when, if ever, the restrictions would be withdrawn and an obvious danger that the protection afforded would merely delay the adjustments eventually necessary. In short, in a worldwide recession such as followed the first oil shock it was not easy for any one industrial country to justify measures which, if effective, could with equal justification and effectiveness be taken by its trading partners.

Monetarist doctrine took a firmer hold. In its more extreme form it had few friends in the academic profession but appealed to politicians anxious to find a cure for inflation that did not bring them into conflict with the unions. It also found proselytes among leading financial journalists, including Nigel Lawson, Sam Brittan and Peter Jay, and in other quarters less equipped to argue the matter.

The monetarist thesis could be expressed most simply as follows. The demand for money varies with money incomes and is otherwise stable. If therefore the supply increases a fresh balance can only be established if money incomes rise in the same proportion. If output is unchanged, this implies a rise in prices (or a fall in the value of money) exactly equal to the increase in supply.

The essence of monetarist doctrine was that it shifted the emphasis from demand management to monetary management. It started from the proposition that 'inflation is always and everywhere a monetary phenomenon', with the plausible corollary that in the absence of a larger stock of money to 'validate' it, any initial rise in prices will necessarily reverse itself. If the supply of money doubled, prices would eventually double and no doubt if the supply of money were halved, prices would fall by 50 per cent. However plausible this was, it did not accord with recent experience. A shortage of money might reduce demand but this was much more likely to reduce employment than to reduce prices. This objection rarely troubled convinced monetarists who could put the fall in employment down to the folly of workers who priced themselves out of a job. When, however, workers did accept wage cuts on an economy-wide footing, the experience had usually been that prices were forced down by competition. The idea that *real* wages are settled by collective bargaining may be attractive; but it has little foundation.

As we shall see in chapter 5, problems arose in seeking to make monetarist doctrine operational. First of all, there was the question: what kinds of money matter? Should a broad definition be used so as to include all bank deposits, deposits in building societies, and all near-substitutes for money? Or should a narrow definition limiting money to what enters into ordinary day-to-day transactions be used? Some monetarists plumped for £M3 (now M3) and some for M1 or M0.[16] The number of possible definitions grew; there were large differences in behaviour between them; and those selected as targets were liable to behave differently or to produce changes in other monetary phenomena because of their new-found significance.

An even more important difficulty was the limited power that could be exercised over the stock of money. In the days of commodity money there was a determinate stock that could expand only if more money was minted. But in a world in which the stock of money was governed by bank lending on the one hand and how much money the public felt it needed on the other, there was no direct control over the total. The days when the banks preserved a fixed ratio between their liabilities (bank deposits) and reserves which in total the Bank of England could readily control, were long past. To reimpose control over the monetary base would impart a volatility to interest rates that was highly undesirable in a major financial centre. On the other hand, to use the only weapon at the Bank of England's disposal, its control over short-term interest rates, could have perverse effects since higher rates might induce the public to hold more money at those higher rates. And if the authorities concentrated on some narrow definition of money, such as currency in circulation, that was more intimately related to spending, they would find it hard to explain why a small fragment of the total stock should be singled out for control when there was no difficulty in swapping bank deposits for more currency. If on the other hand what was in question was not control but some indicator of change in the monetary situation, there were many other indicators conveying more important information.

A further problem was just how effective monetary control was.

Did the monetary weapons that actually existed, as distinct from hypothetical control of the monetary base, provide the most effective instrument for the management of the economy? The Radcliffe Committee had been sceptical. The record showed that, in the past, interest rates had chiefly been used to influence the flow of funds internationally with slower and less predictable repercussions on the domestic economy. Experience in 1989—90 bore out the view that high interest rates were indeed slow-acting in checking demand; and there could be no doubt that low rates were even slower in stimulating it. On the other hand, interest rates had the virtue that they could be moved instantly at any time and that they could be used without the need to seek the parliamentary approval that fiscal policy required.

There was never any question that monetary policy should *not* be used. So long as there was an exchange rate to be managed, whether fixed or floating, interest rates had to vary; and the more widely the balance of payments fluctuated, the vaster the flow of short-term funds across national boundaries, the more necessary it became to rely on monetary policy to keep fluctuations in the rate of exchange within reasonable limits.

Economic growth since the second world war

If we turn from ideas and policy to economic performance we can concentrate either on the short-term changes from year to year or on the long-term growth of the economy. Short-term changes are discussed at length in what follows but it may be useful to start with some idea of the magnitude of the fluctuations that occurred. These were greater in output than in employment but even in employment, as figure 1.2 shows, the fluctuations were not negligible. Up to the 1960s they were not such as to raise unemployment above half a million except briefly and rarely, and even in the 1960s unemployment was below half a million for most of the time and hardly ever above 600,000. But even in those two decades employment rose or fell several times by 300,000 or so in a year and could fall for three or four years running. After 1970 the fluctuations were much more severe and employment could fall from peak to trough, as in 1979—83, by

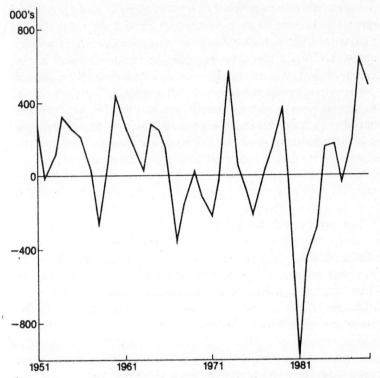

Figure 1.2 Change in employment (including self-employed) mid year
to mid year, 1951–1989
Source: *Economic Trends Annual Supplement 1990*

1¾ million. Apart from the fluctuations in those years, there was a
fall in employment in every year between 1974 and 1983 except
for a brief interlude in 1977–9, and unemployment remained on
a level almost unimaginable in the 1950s and 1960s, never falling
below 1½ million even in the boom of 1987–9.

When we turn to the long-term there are two major questions
to be addressed. One relates to the secular boom that continued
from the end of the war until 1973. Why did it last so long in
comparison with earlier booms and what brought it to an end?
The second relates to the slowdown that began after 1973 and
left behind a large residue of unemployment that showed no sign

of disappearing twenty years later. Why did the slowdown in the rate of productivity growth occur and why did so much slack in the form of unemployment persist? These are questions not just about the United Kingdom but about the world economy, for all countries had a somewhat similar experience. They cannot be answered in British terms alone: although the impact of world trends on Britain may have been modified in the particular circumstances in which Britain was placed or by the policies it adopted, it is the trends that most need explanation. How they affected the British economy is considered in chapters 5 and 6.

What prolonged the boom?

When we look back on what is now referred to as the Golden Age that ended in 1973 with the greatest international boom of the century it is natural to ask why experience after 1945 was so different from experience after 1918. Then there had been a brief boom in which prices rose steeply with decontrol, succeeded by a sharp recession in 1921. Industrial production fell by about 20 per cent, unemployment shot up to over 2 million, export prices were cut in half and it was not until 1927 that the pre-war level of production was recovered. In 1929 came a fresh downturn; and ten years later, at the outbreak of war, GDP was still less than 30 per cent above the level of 1913. The experience of thirty years of almost uninterrupted growth after 1945 contrasts, in the British case, with a period of almost uninterrupted depression that lasted well into the 1930s.

This contrast raises two rather different issues. First, how was it possible to avoid a deep post-war depression such as occurred in 1921? Second, why was the subsequent rate of growth so much faster than in the inter-war period? Both questions have to be looked at from an international point of view, not from the narrower angle of British experience.

It is easy to see why there was an initial recovery in production in 1945–7. This carried production up near to the level of 1938 in many European countries and in the British case above it. Producers and consumers had accumulated funds which they were unable to spend in war-time – and the war had lasted much longer than in 1914–18. Destruction had taken place on a vast scale all over Europe and there was an urgent need to make good the damage, especially to the transport system but also to housing and other structures. There were stocks to be built up to meet a different set of demands from those of war. In these respects the situation was similar to, but a good deal worse, than in 1918. Up to 1947, moreover, the role played by the United States had not differed greatly from the economic point of view except that it was still involved politically in Europe as an occupying power in Germany.

In 1947, however, the recovery threatened to come to an abrupt halt as a shortage of dollars developed all over Europe. The danger was illustrated most dramatically in the case of the United Kingdom which paid out $1 billion in a single month and like some other countries had fewer dollars at the end of 1947 than it had expended during the year. It was this danger of a halt to recovery that was defeated by Marshall Aid. Where in 1947 Europe had great need of imports that America and only America could supply, by the time Marshall Aid ceased, other sources of supply, including sources within Europe, had become available; and at the same time recovery had developed a momentum that carried it forward into the 1950s. Supplying Marshall Aid at the same time sustained activity in the United States when there was some danger of a relapse had external markets shrunk.

This view of Marshall Aid as providing a bridge across a threatened dip in economic activity contrasts with the view expressed at the time by many distinguished American economists who prescribed balanced budgets and devalued currencies as a sufficient remedy for Europe's problems.[17] It also treats as a major obstacle to European recovery what is dismissed by one economic historian as 'no more than technical'[18]: the difficulty of obtaining sufficient 'hard currency' after 1947 to meet the cost of imported food, materials, fuel and equipment indispensable to current levels of production.

In the British case there were simpler explanations why there was no relapse. The controls exercised by the government pushed back demand in a way that prevented a sharp, unsustainable peak and allowed pressure to continue over a longer period. Low rates of interest, although they drifted slowly up, also contributed to the prolongation of intense pressure.

Looking at the longer period, in which, by comparison with later years, employment hardly wavered, two factors help to account for the length of the boom. One was the expansion in the employed labour force that accompanied the move to full employment. This in itself added substantially to capital requirements since additional capacity had to be created to match the rise in employment. A second factor was the rise in productivity which raised incomes and hence consumption which in turn made additional capacity necessary. Most economists see investment producing higher productivity; but it can equally well be the other way round.

A third factor was housing. Although the population grew little in size, housing construction remained high throughout the entire period as households divided and each member sought separate accommodation. Housing was usually around 20 per cent of gross investment but a much higher proportion of net investment, since it had a much longer life than machinery and plant.

What caused the slowdown?

The slowdown in output is more easily explained than the slowdown in productivity growth. The boom of 1973 was peculiar in that the cyclical upswing in all the main countries synchronized, producing a steep rise in the price of international commodities (raw materials and foodstuffs) that was reinforced at the end of the year by a fourfold increase in the price of oil. These changes in price upset the balance of the world economy, with large surpluses in the oil-exporting countries and large deficits in the oil-importing countries. Increases in the price of inputs also produced increases in the price of outputs — so that inflation spread everywhere: from international to domestic prices; from domestic prices to wages; and from wages back again to prices. The dislocation produced by inflation and changes in the terms of trade were enough by themselves to arrest the boom and check production. A more powerful check was exerted by deflationary government policies. Alarmed by high, and in some countries, rising rates of inflation as well as by mounting external deficits, governments either took no action to check a downturn already in progress or adopted restrictive policies that cut demand still further.

When expansion was resumed, government policy remained inhibited by fear of reviving inflation. For the rest of the 1970s unemployment remained at a higher level than before and so also did inflation: neither sank back to its former level. With the second oil shock in 1979 the same kind of dislocation occurred with a new burst of higher inflation and higher unemployment in 1980–82 and again in the following years a drop in inflation and unemployment to levels that left both undesirably high.

While scarcities of primary materials in 1973, two oil shocks and government fears of inflation have played the major part there have been two other factors that may have contributed to the larger amount of slack in industrial economies in the 1970s and 1980s. One is the ending of undisputed American hegemony with an expanding American market exercising a strong pull on the rest of the world economy. In the 1950s America accounted for roughly half of world production and had no reason ever to be concerned over a balance of payments deficit. The tempo of world activity was set by the United States, backed by the powerful expansionary influence of European and Japanese reconstruction. In the 1960s, although there were tremors and latterly the inflation associated with the war in Vietnam, America was still in a dominant position and its expanding market still set the pace, while the binding together of the European Community helped to sustain it. By the 1970s, however, America was in a much weaker position, the world of Bretton Woods, with its fixed exchange rates under American leadership, had come to an end, and no other power took its place. The world economy lost momentum because no country had the strength (or indeed the inclination) to provide it.

Perhaps, secondly, there was another source of the loss of momentum. What had carried the industrial countries forward in the post-war years was largely the manufacturing sector. When that began to droop in the 1970s as a proportion of GDP, there was difficulty in absorbing the labour released from manufacturing. If the experience of the United Kingdom is anything to go by, the jobs that were lost were full-time jobs for men while the new jobs were for women and the self-employed or were part-time only. Thus the labour market was changing as manufacturing employment contracted and with each downturn the residue of men seeking full-time employment and unable to find it in other sectors of the economy steadily accumulated. In the 1930s it had taken a war to bring back into employment the nearly two million workers still unemployed in 1939. It might prove in the 1990s almost equally difficult to make inroads into a total equally formidable.

Many have tried to account for the slowdown in the growth of labour productivity. Denison, for example, examined numerous different explanations without being satisfied with any of them.[19] Others have concluded that the rise in raw material and oil prices played an important part. Many of the technical advances before 1973, for example, depended on cheap fuel and the efforts to economize on fuel after 1973 must have involved some handicap in labour productivity.[20] It is natural, however, to suspect that the main factor at work was the slowdown in production. Fast growth in output stretches the capabilities of the resources employed and can raise productivity while the presence of slack takes from industrial efficiency. Where short-term fluctuations in output occur what is known as Okun's Law applies: output rises more than in proportion to employment. The converse proposition may apply not only to a depression but to a prolonged slowdown: output is lost more than in proportion to employment.[21] A slowdown means less pressure to introduce improvements of all kinds that would increase output. There may be less money available for investment and development so that technology advances more slowly. On the other hand, if some capacity is forced out of business it is likely to include at least a proportion of the more inefficient firms and this raises the average efficiency or productivity of the surviving firms.

It is also possible that opportunities of improvement arose less frequently as the war receded, not just that they were less readily seized upon and introduced to the market place. When American methods of production were well ahead of Europe's there was, so to speak, a stock of opportunities to be drawn upon in the process of catching up. But once the process had brought about a substantial convergence, this source of growing productivity lost its former importance. Countries at the frontier of technology – and not just technology since organization is also involved – grow more slowly than those that have lagged behind.[22]

Whatever the explanation, the earlier pace of productivity growth was not recaptured. While there was some improvement in the second half of the 1980s, production in countries like France and Germany grew annually at only 2 per cent or so compared with 5 or 6 per cent in the 1950s and 1960s, and the growth in labour productivity was even lower. The one outstanding exception was manufacturing productivity in the United Kingdom where, in the exceptional circumstances of a major boom, the annual improvement in labour productivity exceeded the highest rate previously experienced. To the record of the 1980s we will return in chapter 6.

Notes

1 For a fuller account see Cairncross, *Years of Recovery*, ch. 11, 'The planned economy.'
2 Cairncross and Watts, *The Economic Section 1939–61*, pp. 121ff.
3 Cairncross, *Years of Recovery*, p. 329.
4 Correlli Barnett, *The Audit of War*, ch. 12.
5 J. Tomlinson, 'A missed opportunity: labour and the productivity problem 1945–51'.
6 A. Booth, 'The "Keynesian Revolution" in economic policy-making', *Economic History Review*, 1983; A. Booth, 'Defining a Keynesian revolution', *Economic History Review*, 1984; J. Tomlinson, 'A "Keynesian Revolution" in economic policy-making', *Economic History Review*, 1984; N. Rollings, 'The "Keynesian Revolution" and economic policy-making: a comment', *Economic History Review*, 1985; G. Peden, 'Keynes, the Treasury and British economic policy', 1988.
7 Bent Hansen, *Fiscal Policy in Seven Countries 1955–65*. Paris. OECD, 1969.
8 T. Wilson, 'Instability and the rate of growth', *Lloyds Bank Review*, July 1966, pp. 16–32.
9 Growth targets associated with expanding employment rather than higher productivity might still be set, however, as in the 'Barber boom' in 1972–4.
10 N. F. R. Crafts, 'Economic growth in France and Britain 1830–1910: a review of the evidence', *Journal of Economic History*, 1984, pp. 49–67.
11 M. J. Weiner, *English Culture and the Decline of the Industrial*

Spirit, 1850–1950 Cambridge: Cambridge University Press, 1981.

12 Notably in Elbaum and Lazonick, *The Decline of the British Economy*, Oxford: Oxford University Press, 1986.

13 Industrial investment expanded in those years while the rest of domestic investment, notably housing, fell away as capital flowed into investment abroad on an enormous scale.

14 S. J. Prais and K. Wagner, 'Some practical aspects of human capital investment: training standards in five occupations in Britain and Germany', NIESR *Economic Review*, August 1983. 'Schooling standards in England and Germany', ibid., May 1985; S. J. Prais and H. Steedman, 'Vocational training in France and Britain: the building trades, ibid., May 1986; S. J. Prais, 'Education for productivity: comparisons of Japanese and English schooling and vocational preparation', ibid., Feb. 1987. These and other articles are reprinted in *Productivity, Education and Training* 1990 issued by the National Institute of Economic and Social Research.

15 W. Lewchuk in Elbaum and Lazonick (eds), *The Decline of the British Economy*.

16 See Appendix 3, 'Definitions of money'.

17 They included F. D. Graham, G. Haberler and 'less rigidly' Jacob Viner and Fritz Machlup (C. P. Kindleberger, *Marshall Plan Days*, 1987, pp. 65, 159, 248).

18 A. S. Milward, *The Reconstruction of Western Europe*, 1984, p. 55.

19 E. F. Denison, *Accounting for Slower Economic Growth*, 1979.

20 M. Bruno, 'World shocks, macroeconomic response and the productivity puzzle', in R. C. O. Matthews (ed.), *Slower Growth in the Western World*, 1982, p. 89, assigns 60 per cent of the fall in productivity growth to the rise in raw material prices.

21 R. C. O. Matthews, 'Introduction', in R. C. O. Matthews (ed.), *Slower Growth in the Western World*.

22 The process of catching up is discussed in M. Abramovitz, *Thinking about Growth*, 1989.

Further Reading

In addition to the works listed above, the following should also be consulted:

Beveridge, W. H. 1944. *Full Employment in a Free Society*, London: Allen & Unwin.

Blackaby, F. (ed.) 1979. *Deindustrialisation*, London: Heinemann.

Cairncross, F. (ed.) 1981. *Changing Perceptions of Economic Policy*, London: Methuen.

Dow, J. C. R. and Saville, I. D. 1990. *A Critique of Monetary Policy* (2nd edn), Oxford: University Press.

Durbin, E. 1985. *New Jerusalem: the Labour Party and the economics of democratic socialism*, London: Routledge.

Feinstein, C. H. 1988. 'Economic growth since 1970: British performance in international perspective', *Oxford Review of Economic Policy*, spring.

Friedman, M. 1968. 'The role of monetary policy', *American Economic Review*, March.

Kaldor, N. 1971. 'Conflicts in national economic objectives,' *Economic Journal*, March.

Laidler, D. 1981. 'Monetarism: an interpretation and an assessment', *Economic Journal*, March.

Maddison, A. 1982. *Phases of Capitalist Development*, Oxford: Oxford University Press.

Matthews, R. C. O. (ed.) 1982. *Slower Growth in the Western World*, London: Heinemann for NIESR.

Meade, J. E. 1955. 'The case for variable exchange rates' and 'Flexible exchange rates', Howson, S. (ed.), in *The Collected Papers of James Meade* vol. III, London: Unwin Hyman.

Robinson, E. A. G. 1967. *Economic Planning in the United Kingdom: some lessons*, Cambridge: Cambridge University Press.

Tomlinson, J. 1991. 'Productivity policy', in Mercer, H., Rollings, N. and Tomlinson, J. (eds), *Labour Governments and Private Industry*, Edinburgh: Edinburgh University Press.

Official reports

1942 *Social Insurance and Allied Services* (Beveridge Report), Cmd 6404.
1944 *Employment Policy*, Cmd 6527.
1947 *Economic Survey*, Cmd 7046.

2 Reconversion, 1945–1950[1]

When the war with Germany ended in May 1945 the full serious-ness of the economic situation facing the United Kingdom was not widely appreciated. The strain of six years of war created expectations of better things when peace returned that it was not possible to fulfil.

The first and most compelling problem was how to pay for the imports indispensable to recovery. As Keynes put it, Britain was in danger of 'a financial Dunkirk', with total earnings of foreign exchange in the autumn of 1945 paying for only 40 per cent of expenditure abroad. This problem was aggravated by the dis-turbed state of the world, the need to maintain British troops in many different countries from Germany to Indonesia, and the growing distrust of Russian intentions both in Europe and in Asia. There was also in 1945–7 a worldwide shortage of food to add to procurement difficulties.

The domestic front also posed many awkward problems. The labour tied up in the armed forces and supply services, totalling nearly 9 million in June 1945, would have to be run down to a peace-time level so as to allow workers to be absorbed into civil employment without more than a brief transitional spell of unem-ployment. It was to be hoped also that the jobs they would find would be in the industries it was most important to staff.

In parallel with this, industry had to be converted from making munitions and army supplies to meeting civilian market require-ments at home and abroad and reconstructed with an eye to future international competition. Industries such as coalmining, textiles and building which had been contracted in war-time had now to be rapidly expanded while others which had expanded in war-time, especially the metal and engineering industries, were badly in need of an extensive overhaul.

A third domestic problem was the heavy arrears of maintenance and renewal throughout the economy, the extensive bomb damage to housing, and the further investment that would be required if there was to be enough capacity to allow the level of employment to be raised and the surplus manpower of pre-war days to be offered full employment. This would make it necessary to achieve a high rate of industrial investment, stockbuilding, and capital formation of all kinds.

How, fourthly, was this to be financed when consumers would be in no mood to save and had accumulated unspent funds in war-time which they would wish to bring into use as soon as the goods they wanted were on sale? Was there not a danger that the pressure of demand would become excessive and find vent in inflation? Would full employment not add to this danger by opening the door to wage inflation? In war-time various controls had helped to limit the rise in prices but no one contemplated their indefinite retention. There was thus yet another problem of dispensing with the controls without letting loose uncontrollable inflation.

These were all problems arising out of the war. But the world had changed and new aspirations had been born. These included not just full employment but social security on a comprehensive scale. The public looked to the government to implement the Beveridge Plan and usher in what is now referred to as the 'Welfare State'. On the international plane also, change was in the air and relations with the United States, the Commonwealth and Europe all needed reconsideration.

It fell to a new government elected in July 1945 shortly after the end of war with Germany and shortly before the end of war with Japan, to confront these problems and give expression to popular aspirations. It was the first Labour government to enjoy a clear majority and it intended to use that majority to carry through a full programme of legislation. Not much of its programme bore on the acute economic problems listed above. It was a social, not an economic revolution at which it aimed. Nationalization and full employment were its first concerns; but what was to be done with the industries nationalized, and how full employment was to be secured, had been given little consideration. Similarly, although there was much talk of planning, hardly any member of the government was sure what it meant except perhaps the continuation of physical controls. What dominated thinking as the government took office was the expectation of an early slump in the United States such as had occurred after the first world war. The danger of inflation was correspondingly discounted. Even the external situation, to which we now turn, appeared more manageable than it proved to be: there was little expectation of a worldwide shortage of dollars.

The external situation

Large changes had taken place in Britain's command over imports from abroad. Not only had the war wrought havoc in many parts of the world from which she drew her imports, so that supplies were much reduced, but other countries could now be expected to re-enter world markets and bid for the reduced supplies. More troubling still was Britain's impoverishment, indeed her near-bankruptcy, in the form of inability to settle accounts with her suppliers.

Firstly, there was a huge external debt such as no other belligerent had incurred: it was the largest external debt in history. The cumulative deficit in the balance of payments on current account from the outbreak of war to the end of 1945 amounted to £10,000 million; and although more than half of this had been met by the United States under lend-lease arrangements, not far short of £5,000 million had had to be found by borrowing in sterling or in dollars or by selling foreign investments.[2] Most of the borrowing was in sterling from poor countries like India and Egypt and reflected large military expenditures in those countries. It was this borrowing that gave rise to the chronic post-war problems of the sterling balances – funds held in London on short-term by foreign banks and official holders. At the outbreak of war these liabilities had been roughly equal to the gold and dollar reserves at about £500 million. At the end of the war they were over five times as great: not far short of £3500 million while the gold and dollar reserves were just over £600 million.

Secondly, the debt was still mounting. As Attlee told the House of Commons shortly after the Japanese surrender, British earnings from exports were currently no more than £350 million a year to which other receipts of foreign exchange might add a further £450 million in 1945. Total outgoings, on the other hand, including military expenditure abroad and the food and other supplies previously paid for by the United States, were running at the rate of £2000 million a year. This left a gap of £1200 million a year to be met by fresh borrowing abroad.[3]

The external deficit reflected the intensity with which resources had been mobilized for the prosecution of the war. Manpower had continued to be withdrawn from the export industries until, by 1944, the volume of exports had fallen to 30 per cent of its pre-war level. This was made possible by the provision of lend-lease aid by the United States and by extensive borrowing abroad. The resulting division of labour between the allies, while it was no doubt to the mutual advantage of Britain and America, left the British economy in a very exposed position when the war ended and lend-lease was suddenly withdrawn. Britain had counted on continued American financial support in virtue both of the heavy dependence on foreign aid that her role in allied strategy implied and of undertakings by Roosevelt to Churchill at the Quebec Conference in 1944. No such support was offered when lend-lease came to an abrupt end in August 1945.

Official forecasts suggested that the deficit in the balance of payments would continue for at least three years. Over those years a cumulative deficit of perhaps £1250 million was likely to be incurred before balance was restored. Even so, it would be necessary to keep the volume of imports below pre-war levels throughout and to regain the pre-war level of exports by the end of 1946. On a long-term view nothing less than a 50 per cent increase in exports — and more probably a 75 per cent increase — would do, and this would require a fivefold increase or more in volume in comparison with 1944.

A disproportionate rise in exports was required because of a third change in Britain's international accounts. In pre-war years exports had covered only 55 per cent of the cost of imports, the balance being largely met from a surplus on invisibles, mainly net shipping earnings and income from foreign investments (see table 2.1). These two items alone had paid for 35 per cent of the value of pre-war imports. In the war, however, half Britain's

Table 2.1   UK balance of payments, 1936–1938 and 1946
(£ million)

	1936–8 *(average)*	*1946* *(forecast)*	*1946* *(actual)*
Imports[a]	−866	−1300	−1063
Exports[a]	+477	+ 650	+ 960
Trade deficit	−389	− 650	− 103
Government expenditure overseas (net)[b]	− 7	− 300	− 223
Net income from overseas investments	+203 ⎫		+ 85 ⎫
Net income from shipping	+105 ⎬	+ 200[c]	+ 9 ⎬
Other invisibles	+ 44 ⎭		+ 2 ⎭
	− 44	− 750	− 230

[a] Import and export prices were assumed to be about double pre-war prices in the forecast in col. 2 and turned out to be slightly higher than this. Re-exports and imports for re-export are excluded from the figures in cols 1, 2 but not 3. Imports and exports of silver bullion and specie are excluded from col. 1.

[b] In col. 2 the figure relates only to war expenditure. In the *Annual Abstract of Statistics 1953* military expenditure overseas in 1946 is given as £374 million but if war disposals, etc. are deducted, the net figure works out at £210 million. The figure in col. 3 excludes interest paid or received by government.

[c] 200 in col. 2 refers to all 3 items in col. 1.

Source: col. 1 *Statistical Material presented during the Washington Conference Negotiations*, December 1945, HMSO, Cmd 6707; col. 2 Keynes, *Collected Writings*, vol. XXIV, Macmillan, 1979, p. 555; col. 3 *Economic Trends Annual Supplement*, 1981

merchant marine had been sunk, sales of investments abroad had exceeded £1000 million, and interest had to be paid on the large debts to other countries that had been run up. A large drop in invisible income was inevitable and the purchasing power of what was left over imports had been halved. It was to make up for this loss on invisibles that Britain would have to push up her exports. To do so would mean fighting for a higher share of world trade and remaining competitive once Germany and Japan recovered.

A further reason for seeking a big increase in exports was the need to cater for a larger working population and one that it was hoped would be more fully employed and more productive than in pre-war years. With a higher GNP there was likely to be a higher demand for imports and to pay for additional imports still more exports would be required.

The restoration of external balance faced yet another problem. The war had dislocated the economies of many other countries and left nearly all of them, like Britain, in deficit. Only the United States and Canada were in surplus. Other countries had to draw on their reserves or borrow abroad in order to sustain their imports; and the source to which one and all turned for additional supplies was North America. Such supplies, however, were obtainable only for dollars and a shortage of dollars grew out of the shortage of supplies.

The dollar shortage

In those circumstances what came to dominate Britain's international accounts was not the balance of payments deficit but the drain of gold and dollars from the reserves. There was ample sterling around the world to pay for exports from Britain; but if payment was made in sterling, Britain was no further on in finding the means to settle accounts with the United States, her principal supplier. Payment in other currencies that were equally inconvertible into dollars was also of limited value unless supplies were offered in return that limited the need to buy from America. In a world of inconvertible currencies it was only too easy to end up with a large export surplus to countries making payment in 'soft' currencies and a deficit in 'hard' currencies that could be met only by drawing on reserves. Exports in total might then exceed imports in total without disposing of the balance of payments problem because the reserves continued to drain away in settlement of the deficits with hard currency countries like the United States.

The dollar shortage did not come to the forefront immediately after the war, partly because most countries had substantial reserves and partly because the United States was pouring out dollars through UNRRA, (The United Nations Relief and Reconstruction Administration), foreign loans, and in other ways throughout 1946. It was only gradually that the imbalance in British trade was seen to be part of a wider international imbalance that was reflected in an excess of American exports over imports. This imbalance created the strain in settling accounts between the United States and other countries that lay at the root of 'the dollar shortage'.

From the British point of view the dollar shortage had a double significance. On the one hand, it meant that sterling was less acceptable than dollars in international dealings and restricted Britain's freedom of manoeuvre in financing transactions with other countries. On the other hand, it meant that it was no longer possible to rely on a triangular or multilateral settlement of accounts such as had enabled Britain before the war to apply surpluses in trade with other continents to meeting a deficit with North America, or indeed with the whole of the western hemisphere. It was necessary to take direct measures to reduce that deficit, by reducing imports or expanding exports, within the limits of what could be furnished in settlement. This was not easy when so much of what Britain imported came from North America and so little was exported to North America in return. In 1938 imports from the United States and Canada had been more than four times as large as exports to those two countries; in 1945 they were not far short of ten times as big and even in 1946 nearly six times. Indeed, exports to the United States in the early post-war years did not do much more than cover the bill for imports of American tobacco. Yet since the markets of North America were highly competitive − far more competitive in those years than the markets elsewhere in the world − it was peculiarly difficult to effect a large increase in exports to them except in traditional lines such as scotch whisky, of which there was only a limited supply.

On the import side, the difficulties were just as great. North America had been before the war and remained after the war a major source of raw materials and foodstuffs, supplying a little over one-fifth of British imports in 1938 and nearly one-third in 1946. The rise in the proportion was an indication of the difficulty of procuring supplies elsewhere. Buying as much as possible in non-dollar markets, the government could procure in 1946 only two-thirds of the pre-war volume of imports and any further compression of dollar purchases meant a corresponding reduction in rations or a more acute shortage of raw materials.

Negotiations for an American loan

Given the international situation as seen at the end of the war, with the prospect of a large and obstinate deficit stretching out over several years, the need for a substantial loan (or grant) seemed inescapable. Since no other country, except perhaps Canada, was in a position to lend, this meant approaching the United States for assistance.

The incoming Labour administration which took office on 26 July 1945 hoped at first for a grant; and shortly after the cessation of lend-lease in August it despatched a mission under Lord Keynes to conduct negotiations in Washington. The mission's instructions gave it no authority to propose a loan while the Americans made it clear that they were not prepared to offer an outright grant or interest-free loan. They insisted that Congress would not entertain such a possibility and would only accept the case for further assistance to the United Kingdom if it could be persuaded that this was to the advantage of the United States. For this purpose it would be necessary for the United Kingdom to support the American vision of a multilateral trading system with convertible currencies and trade that was free from discriminatory trade restrictions. In concrete terms this would mean acceptance of the Bretton Woods Agreement, the introduction of sterling convertibility within one year from the ratification of a loan agreement, and the abandonment of discrimination between imports that cost dollars and those that did not.

The negotiations were long and troubled. After a brilliant initial exposition of Britain's economic situation, Keynes wore himself out in coping with the misunderstandings of American negotiators in Washington and British ministers in London. Agreement was not reached until December 1945 and not approved by Congress until July 1946. It was not well received in the United Kingdom and had a rough passage in Parliament where the only convincing defence of it came from Keynes in the House of Lords. In the

United States, approval came only after a swing in American opinion as differences with the USSR began to multiply and the threat of Soviet expansionism raised the value of a reliable European ally.

The loan was for a smaller sum than the government's advisers had thought necessary − $3750 million rather than the $5000 million that had been contemplated − but it was made up to $5000 million by the Canadian government, at considerable risk to its own balance of payments. In addition, the United Kingdom was to pay $650 million in final settlement of lend-lease obligations and credit for this amount would be added to the American loan. The rate of interest on the loan was nominally 2 per cent, beginning after five years, and repayment, which was also to begin after five years, was to be completed in fifty years. Annual instalments of interest and capital worked out at $140 million and were equivalent actuarially to an interest charge of 1.6 per cent over the life of the loan.

While these terms fell short of ministerial hopes they were not only generous by commercial standards but allowed the United Kingdom to borrow on a scale that was several times larger than what might have been raised on commercial terms (e.g. from the Export−Import Bank). The additional dollar obligation, which seemed so formidable a burden in 1945−6, was subject to a complex waiver clause that suspended it when exports fell short of about 160 per cent of the pre-war volume. While it was large in relation to current dollar earnings in 1945−6, it has to be seen against a total value of British exports of nearly £1000 million in 1946, £2700 million in 1951 when payments began, and total foreign exchange earnings of £40,000 million in 1976, half-way through the life of the loan. The service of the loan speedily became a matter of little importance except in one or two acute balance of payments crises in the 1950s.

More important in the long run were the conditions attached to the loan. Under the Bretton Woods Agreement Britain would have been free to defer making the pound convertible until the end of a period of transition, generally expected to last five years. The loan agreement, however, obliged ministers, much against their will, to shorten the period of transition and adopt convertibility by mid 1947. As we shall see, this was an undertaking that could not be fulfilled and the effort to carry it out had the effect of discrediting convertibility as an aim.

The loan provided a breathing space but did not by itself produce any of the adjustments that were necessary in order to restore external balance. These depended on the economic recovery of Britain's trading partners, on a redeployment of domestic resources, and in the meantime on a limitation and rationing of imports to what the country could afford.

Balance of payments crises

The process of readjustment of the external balance was far from smooth. It was punctuated by a succession of exchange crises in 1947, 1949 and 1951–2 (see figure 2.1). Even before the first of these, the recovery of exports was interrupted by a fuel crisis in February 1947 which cut off electricity from a large section of British industry for three weeks and knocked at least £100 million

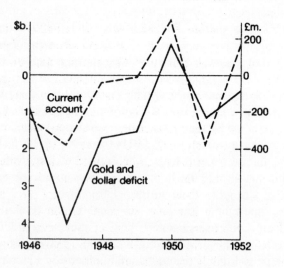

Figure 2.1 Gold and dollar deficit (RHS) and current account (LHS) of the balance of payments, 1946–1952
Source: Cairncross, *Years of Recovery,* p. 79

off exports during the year. While industry was recovering, the drain on the reserves accelerated, especially after the resumption of convertibility in mid July. In the last full week of convertibility before its suspension on 20 August, the loss of reserves reached $230 million and by the end of the year the total had reached $4100 million – more than the whole amount of the American loan. After an anxious winter and a long period of suspense, the drain was staunched by the first payments of Marshall Aid in 1948. The dollar deficit was cut to $1700 million and in 1949 to $1500 million. But these were still formidable amounts, even with $1500 million in Marshall Aid over the two years and it was necessary to draw on the limited gold and dollar reserves. The reserves, indeed, proved quite insufficient to withstand a fresh exchange crisis in the summer of 1949, brought on by a brief depression in the United States when it seemed as if the dollar and sterling worlds might be torn apart. A devaluation from $4.02 to $2.80 to the pound took place on 18 September after a long struggle. Most other countries devalued simultaneously against the dollar so that although the par value fell by 30 per cent, the trade-weighted devaluation of sterling was very much less – about 9 per cent.

The improvement in 1950 following devaluation was greatly assisted by the recovery of the American economy and its re-stocking with materials from the outer sterling area. For the first time there was a large-scale replenishment of reserves. At the end of 1950, this moved the United States to discontinue Marshall Aid which had brought over $2500 million in grants and loans to the support of the balance of payments over the previous three years.

Six months previously, at the end of June 1950, war had broken out in Korea, an event that almost coincided with two other major developments at that time: the announcement of the Schuman Plan for a European Coal and Steel Community on 9 May and the formation of the European Payments Union on 7 July. The Korean war soon overshadowed both of those events and led to a major effort of rearmament. By January 1951 the government was aiming to multiply the output of munitions by a factor of four, there were acute shortages of raw materials, primary commodities of all kinds had risen steeply in price and the terms of trade were in course of shifting against the United Kingdom by nearly 20 per cent. This created a major sterling crisis that lasted well into 1952. It was in the middle of this crisis that the Labour government lost power in October 1951 and the Conservatives began what proved to be a thirteen–year tenure of office.

The dollar deficits just quoted represent the deficit of the entire sterling area, not just of the United Kingdom. Other members of the sterling area could draw from the central pool of gold and dollars held by the Bank of England and make payment for the dollars out of their sterling balances except where such drawings were subject to an agreed limit. In pre-war years the outer sterling area had paid dollars into the pool in exchange for sterling (and this continued to be true after the war of the colonial territories). But in the early post-war years things worked the other way: the independent members of the sterling area – mainly Commonwealth countries – drew heavily on the dollar pool, adding to the United Kingdom's difficulties. In 1947, for example, they drew $1100 million (less gold sales by South Africa) out of a total drain of $4100 million; and it was not until 1950, when the United Kingdom itself was in surplus, that they were able to make a net contribution to the dollar pool.

The fluctuations in the current balance of payments were much less violent than those in dollar outgoings except at the end of the period. On current account the deficit rose from £230 million in 1946 to a peak £380 million in 1947, virtually disappeared in 1948–9, changed to a surplus of £300 million in 1950 and plunged again in 1951 into a deficit of £370 million. The dollar drain, on the other hand, rose much more alarmingly from $900 million in 1946 to $4130 million in 1947, then fell steeply to $1700 million in 1948. There was also a much bigger improvement in the dollar deficit in 1950 (from a drain of $1500 million in 1949 to a gain of $800 million) and the turnaround in 1951 although nearly matched by the swing in the current account, was equally dramatic.

The frequency of exchange crises in spite of exchange control was the almost inevitable consequence of lack of reserves (which never reached $3 billion until the end of 1950), heavy short-term indebtedness in the form of sterling balances (amounting to $16 billion at the time of devaluation in 1949) and violent swings in the terms of trade. These made sterling vulnerable to balance of payments deficits, which were usually reinforced by speculative pressure in the form of 'leads and lags', and could only be countered by strong and immediate action. Usually this meant cutting the import programme and trying to limit outgoings on capital account (not, however, very effectively, especially as there were no restrictions on capital flows to the rest of the sterling area).

The weakness of sterling could only be overcome in the long run by a sustained improvement in the balance of payments and it was a prime object of the government to accomplish this by administrative means. It did its best to encourage exports, first in general and later to dollar markets; and it held down imports well below the pre-war level. With an eye on the long-term difficulties of enlarging Britain's share of world trade in manufactures to the extent necessary to pay for imports on the pre-war scale, the government launched a major agricultural expansion scheme in 1948.

The priority that it attached to eliminating the external deficit is apparent from table 2.2 which shows the changes over the five years 1945–50 in the allocation of resources between the main categories of demand. While exports increased in volume by 77 per cent over those years (they had already more than recovered to the pre-war level by the end of 1946), and imports were held down to an increase of only 14.5 per cent, the rise in consumption was no more than 6 per cent. Roughly speaking half of the increase in gross domestic product went to improving the balance of payments. For a country that had been at war for six years and emerged exhausted but victorious this was no mean achievement.

The domestic situation

This brings us to a consideration of the domestic situation at the end of the war. Here, too, the true circumstances were not widely appreciated. The experience of the 1930s was still vividly recalled as well as the short boom and deep slump that had followed the first world war. Well into the post-war period ministers continued to express anxiety that that experience might recur and instructed their officials to bring to their attention any signs of deflation. In fact, however, there was never any serious danger of

Table 2.2 Changes in the allocation of resources, 1945–1950 (increase from year to year in £ billion at constant 1985 prices)

	1946	1947	1948	1949	1950	Changes between 1945 and 1950
Consumers' expenditure	(9.3)	3.3	−0.6	1.5	2.5	16.0
Public authorities' final consumption	(−26.9)	−9.8	−0.2	2.1	−0.1	−34.8
Gross domestic fixed capital formation	(6.3)	3.0	1.5	1.5	1.0	13.2
Value of physical increase in stocks and work in progress	(−4.2)	5.0	−2.1	−0.8	−1.8	4.5
Exports of goods and services	(6.3)	1.1	5.0	2.3	3.4	18.1
Total final expenditure	−0.9	2.6	3.6	6.3	5.5	16.9
Imports of goods and services	–	1.8	−0.4	1.8	0.2	3.4
Gross domestic product (at market prices)	−0.9	0.8	4.0	4.4	5.4	13.6
Gross domestic product (average at factor cost)	−1.0	1.5	3.8	4.6	4.7	13.6

Source: For 1949–50, *Economic Trends Annual Supplement* (1990 ed) table 3; for 1946, C. H. Feinstein (1972) table 5; for 1947–8, *National Income and Expenditure 1957*, table 11. I have adjusted from 1948 to 1985 prices by using a uniform multiplier of 12. As with the method of price adjustment used by the CSO (Central Statistical Office) prior to 1983, the figures do not add up.

unemployment except from a shortage of fuel and power or of the materials needed to keep the factories busy. At no time did unemployment reach the 3 per cent that Beveridge had suggested to a sceptical public as a norm, apart from a week or two in the fuel crisis of February and March 1947. From the beginning it was excess demand and inflation that was the principal threat.

Full employment

Employment policy, nonetheless, was what dominated the government's thinking in 1945. It had proved possible in war-time to reduce unemployment well below 100,000 and much thought had been given to maintaining full employment, although not to this degree, once peace returned. In May 1944, after prolonged debate at the official level, a White Paper on employment policy had been issued by the coalition government. This foresaw 'no problem of general unemployment immediately after the end of the war in Europe' although some increase was likely while demobilization was in progress.[4] A greater danger was that excess demand would bring on an inflationary boom as happened after 1918 and that there would then follow the kind of slump that had raised unemployment to over 20 per cent in 1920 and proved so difficult to climb out of thereafter. The danger of inflation made it desirable to retain war-time controls over prices and consumption, to encourage a high rate of saving, and to regulate the flow and direction of investment. Since full employment would change the balance of power in the labour market in favour of organized labour, there was also a risk of inflation from the side of costs unless there was 'moderation in wage matters'.

It was not, however, the passages in the White Paper on inflation that commanded attention but the commitment of the government for the first time to 'a high and stable level of employment' as a primary aim and responsibility. It was a commitment to which the government had many reservations. It recognized that the level of demand and employment depended on conditions elsewhere in the world over which the United Kingdom had no control. If workers did not move to places and occupations where there were jobs, increased public spending might merely drive up prices; and if wages and prices could not be kept 'reasonably stable' it would be 'fruitless' to try to preserve full employment by increasing the flow of government expenditure.[5]

What seemed at the time an even bigger reservation was the reluctance of the government to commit itself to full use of fiscal and monetary policy in the management of demand. Full employment was to be preserved by stabilizing the flow of total expenditure, or final demand, and this was to be done by operating on the main components of the total such as consumer spending and capital investment. But on the instruments to be used for this purpose the White Paper provided only a rough sketch and studiously avoided any commitment to unbalance the budget or raise interest rates. It contemplated little more than an effort to stabilize investment through a mixture of public works and jockeying larger enterprises into parallel action. Consumption was to be regulated through hire purchase restrictions and other expedients. It took some years before the government worked out the techniques of influencing demand in what remained throughout the post-war period an overloaded economy. At no time until 1952 was it faced with the problem of *raising* the level of employment.

Excess demand

The pressure of demand was acute throughout the post-war period. In the early stages of reconversion demobilization was rapid but failed to remove the shortage of labour. In the eighteen months after the end of the war, over 7 million workers were released from the armed forces or from making supplies to meet military requirements. The numbers in other civil employment increased by 5 million, or over 40 per cent, while most of the 2 million women workers who had taken paid jobs in war-time withdrew from the labour market. During this upheaval unemployment rose to 400,000; but after the fuel crisis in February–March 1947 when the figure rose to over 2 million and another 500,000 were stood off from work but continued to receive their pay, unemployment fell to below 300,000 in the second half of the year and fluctuated over the next three years between a minimum of a little under 300,000 and a maximum of just over 400,000.

During these three years, 1948–50, there would appear to have been some slight easing of pressure. But in 1951, with the onset of rearmament after the outbreak of war in Korea in June 1950, the pressure again became intense. At the seasonal low point in July unemployment touched 210,000 before beginning a fresh climb that carried the total for the first time to over 500,000 in the spring of 1952. This turn of events was largely due to the deflationary effect of soaring import prices. Rearmament in Britain increased the pressure on domestic resources but rearmament worldwide squeezed the incomes of consumers by raising commodity prices and turning the terms of trade against importing countries like the United Kingdom.

Inflation

The sustained pressure of demand had its inevitable impact on prices. Not that there was the violent inflationary surge of 1919–20. In 1946 consumer prices were up by only a modest 3 per cent above the 1945 level. But the rise persisted, with peaks in 1947 and 1951, when prices rose by 11.6 per cent and 12.5 per cent respectively, more gradual increases of around 3 per cent in 1949 and 1950 and intermediate rates of increase in 1948 and 1952 when inflation was subsiding from a peak in the previous year. By 1951 the cumulative increase was 35 per cent. This was a good deal less than the rise of 50 per cent in the six years of war and compared favourably with post-war experience in most other countries. It did not necessarily, however, do full justice to the inflationary pressure still remaining in the system in 1951.

The price structure

The persistence of such pressure is evident from the controls by which price rises·continued to be held in check. These controls are discussed below at pp. 65–72. It is also evident in the distortion of the price structure in comparison either with pre-war years or with the position in 1945. Export and import prices had roughly doubled in the course of the war and capital goods had risen in price by about 80 per cent, while other price indices – for consumer goods, the services of public authorities, final output, gross domestic product – were all up by about 50 per cent. These divergent trends continued after the war. By 1952 exports and imports had again risen most in price, exports by 85 per cent, imports by 118 per cent, while the indices for consumer prices, public authorities, final output and GDP were grouped around a 45 per cent rise and capital goods again occupied an intermediate position with an increase of about 65 per cent.

The rapid climb in international prices put pressure on domestic costs. The biggest single influence on the inflation of those years was the rise in import prices which doubled in war-time and more than doubled again by 1952. This influence is particularly apparent in the two peak years, 1947 and 1951, when import prices rose in the first by 22 per cent – three times as fast as consumer prices – and by 33 per cent in the second – a rise nearly equal to that in consumer prices over the entire post-war period to 1951.

Wage inflation

These increases not only raised costs and prices directly but affected wages in so far as the government was obliged to acquiesce in some rise in domestic prices and could not hold down all prices by subsidy. The food subsidies introduced during the war to stabilize the cost of living had risen to about £200 million in the last year of the war and, together with the subsidies to agriculture, had reached £400 million in 1948. Subsidies on this scale were equivalent to one-fifth of consumers' expenditure on food, about 4 per cent of GNP, and a heavy burden on the Exchequer. There can be no doubt that the food subsidies played an important part in keeping wage increases within modest limits and averting the danger of a wage–price spiral. But the rise in import prices was on such a scale that it was almost beyond the power of the government to offset them completely; and they already involved a damaging distortion of prices both directly and because of the high level of indirect taxation necessary in order to meet the cost. In the absence of additional subsidies, higher import prices had a large impact on the cost of living and eventually on wages.

Pressure on wages came also from two other directions. The rise in export prices, although falling short of the rise in import prices, far outran the rise in domestic costs. This left exporters with a profit that disposed them to bid for additional labour; and what the export industries paid in wages other industries had to match. This was an illustration of a more general influence at work, namely the shortage of labour resulting from excess demand. The shortage, under conditions of full, if not over-full, employment, put organized labour in a strong bargaining position, and, as had been foreseen from the beginning, this was only too likely to start off an accelerating rise in wages.

No such acceleration occurred. It is true that money wage-rates rose by no less than 33 per cent in the first six post-war years. But this was rather less than the rise in consumer prices.[6] Moreover, the response of money wages to conditions of excess demand was remarkably moderate. In 1947 when other prices were roaring up, the increase in wage rates was no more than 3.6 per cent and over the four years, 1947–50, the biggest increase in any one year was 5 per cent in 1948. The government used its influence with the trade unions, especially after the devaluation of 1949, to moderate the rise in wages; and it was only after the wage freeze of 1949–50 broke down and rearmament had begun in 1951 that the first double-digit increases occurred. In the first five post-war years the rise in wage rates averaged only double the rate in the last five pre-war years (4.4 per cent as against 2.2 per cent per annum) although unemployment had fallen from 2 million before the war to 350,000 or so after the war.

Labour shortages

The shortages of dollars and of manpower were accompanied by other more specific shortages. Within the manpower shortage, for example, some industries found it particularly difficult to attract sufficient manpower and were labelled 'undermanned'. These industries included agriculture, textiles and coalmining. Of these, agriculture had taken on more labour in war-time and employed a substantial number of prisoners of war. As these were repatriated, the shortage was intensified. It deepened still further when the government embarked in 1948 on a major expansion programme in order to relieve the balance of payments by cutting down imports of food. Curiously enough, employment in agriculture fell steadily from 1948 onwards while agricultural expansion nevertheless continued. The textile industries had lost about one-third of their labour in war-time and as major exporters were encouraged to re-expand. They did not, however, regain the pre-war level of employment before they, too, began to shed labour, beginning in 1952. Coalmining proved to be the most difficult case of the three. It had lost about 5 per cent of its man-power during the war and unlike almost every other industry continued to lose labour when demobilization was at its height. After the fuel crisis in 1947 there was some recovery and employment was almost back to the pre-war level by the end of 1948. But from then on, as with agriculture and textiles, employment was at first more or less flat for some years and then began to fall steeply in the 1950s.

Commodity shortages

In the commodity markets there were similar shortages. In the case of manufactured goods they might simply be unobtainable, as with motor cars, supplies of which to the home market were severely restricted by agreement with the manufacturers, so that second-hand cars sold for twice the price of new ones. Most of the staple foodstuffs were rationed, the size of the ration varying with the supply currently available. Clothing and sweets were also rationed and some other commodities were released for sale only against a licence of some kind.

The most serious shortages from the point of view of production were of raw materials. Coal, steel, timber and many other materials were in short supply and were allocated by official agencies. Some of these shortages resulted from a contraction in available supplies from abroad either because of war damage and dislocation or because they would have involved a higher outlay in dollars than the government could afford. Some reflected also a higher level of demand than in pre-war days, now that employment had expanded well above the pre-war level. In yet other cases the source of the shortage lay in domestic arrangements: the output of steel was limited by a shortage of fuel which in turn was aggravated by lack of labour and transport.

The rationale of controls

All of these shortages, whether general or specific, could have been handled in one of two ways: either through the price mechanism or by administrative action. In war-time when the priorities that mattered were those of the government and could not find adequate expression in market dealings, it was natural to co-ordinate activity in relation to government priorities by administrative action. But when production was for the benefit of private consumers was there any reason why their preferences should not find free expression in market prices which were always capable of balancing supply and demand and eliminating shortages?

Those who thought in those terms would have dismissed the dollar shortage as a blind to conceal overvaluation of the pound sterling (and other currencies): the dearer the dollar the less the shortage. Similarly, they would have dismissed the shortage of labour as excess demand, easily cured by tight money or a budget surplus. Devaluation and a good dose of deflation would have put things straight. As for specific shortages, higher prices would soon have done the trick by confining supplies to the highest bidders and offering a stronger incentive to suppliers.

Ministers in 1945 would have had little sympathy with those views. They were not prepared to entrust the direction of the economic system to the unplanned operation of the price mechanism. They wanted a planned economy and planning was impossible without control. They did not at first visualize the possibility of control through the budget and the management of demand although by the time he left office in 1950 Cripps had come round to that approach and regarded the budget as 'the most powerful instrument for influencing economic policy which is available to the government'.[7] Dalton, four years earlier, had taken satisfaction from the leverage over the economy afforded by the various controls inherited from the war; and most of his colleagues regarded them as natural to a planned economy. They would have objected strongly to the removal of controls if it meant a rise in prices, both from fear of open inflation and because higher prices were unfair to those who could not afford them and unfair also in the gains they yielded to sellers of scarce goods.

The ministerial line of argument was not very convincing. They might not like open inflation but they were quite prepared to accept suppressed inflation. They saw nothing wrong with over-loading the economy – nor, for that matter, did the Governor of the Bank of England or senior Treasury officials – and rather liked a little excess demand while protesting their horror of inflation. They had not suspended the price mechanism, raising the prices of controlled materials when costs increased and leaving large tracts of the economy uncontrolled. More than half of what con-sumers spent on food, for example, was not rationed at any time; and even at its most extensive in 1948 rationing never covered more than one-third of consumer spending.

Moreover the government provided no very coherent explanation of how the controls were intended to fit together or how long they were intended to last. There was much talk of planning but no published plan. The economy moved from one economic crisis to another in a way that seemed to make nonsense of the idea that it was planned.

The various 'bonfires' of controls that began in 1948 made it clear that the continued use of controls after 1945 was essentially a *transitional* strategy. It was not intended to maintain the controls indefinitely or to perpetuate the shortages with which they dealt. On the contrary, most of the controls would disappear as supply recovered to a more normal level without any change in price. Until recovery was well under way and supply and demand were nearer to balance, there was no point in distorting the price structure in an effort to procure instant balance. Higher prices might do little to hasten an expansion in supply that was already in progress; and the substitution of rationing by price for rationing by govern-ment might provoke unrest that with patience could be avoided.

There was also a danger that once the price structure was set in motion by violent changes in particular prices, the whole system of prices might lose its normal inertia and begin to rise. A change in price that restores equilibrium in one market may create disequi-librium in other markets. In the labour market in particular a rise in wages in one industry may set off parallel claims in other indus-tries that are difficult to resist so that the rise spreads throughout the system. In such a major upheaval as the transition from war to peace there was much to be said for holding price relationships as steady as possible even if this meant prolonging war-time controls.

We can apply the same reasoning to the dollar shortage. It might appear that such a shortage would disappear if only dollars were dear enough, i.e. if the pound were sufficiently devalued. But to devalue at a time when exports could not respond strongly because the necessary manpower was still locked up in the armed forces would have been counter-productive. It would have raised the sterling price of imports and so increased inflationary pressure, turned the terms of trade against the United Kingdom, and in all probability enlarged the deficit in the balance of payments because of the low elasticcity of supply and, even more, of demand.

It might well prove, however, that an eventual devaluation against the dollar would prove necessary and helpful. Once there had been time for the full deployment of domestic resources and for the normal sources of imports to resume production, there might still be a shortage of dollars, i.e. a disequilibrium in the United States' balance of payments. In such circumstances a devaluation of the pound (and other currencies) against the dollar would operate not only on the volume of exports and imports in total but more powerfully on the markets to which exports were directed and from which imports were procured. This in fact is what happened when devaluation did occur in 1949, four years after the end of the war. Most currencies moved with sterling so that what took place was as much a revaluation of the dollar as a devaluation of the pound. The dollar shortage did not disappear at once; but the new price relationships made possible a gradual transformation from shortage to surplus in the course of the next ten years.

Controls[8]

The controls of which the government made use in the post-war period came under six main headings.

Price control

First there was price control over all items purchased and sold by government and over about half consumer spending or, making allowance for items already under the influence of government or not susceptible to control, about 60 per cent. There was little relaxation until 1949–50 when some items such as non-rationed foodstuffs and ironmongery were removed. In July 1951 during the Korean war control was reimposed on various items and an effort was made to tighten the controls. But apart from rents, 'bus and railway fares, coal and a few other items, price control was effectively abandoned in 1952–3. Control was tightest over rationed goods and where, as with the utility schemes, it was possible to specify precisely the items controlled. It could not hope to contain all the pressures towards higher prices but does seem to have been successful in keeping prices more or less in line with costs.

Consumer rationing

Next, there was consumer rationing: either 'single line' rationing of specific items, points rationing of canned and processed food-stuffs, clothing and furniture, or limitations on the amount that could be spent, e.g. on holidays abroad or on housing repairs. The extent of consumer rationing varied. The proportion of consumer spending covered by the various schemes was never more than one-third and from 1949 never more than one-eighth. Bread and potatoes, which had not been rationed in war-time were put on ration after the war, the first for two years from July 1946, the second in the winter of 1947–8. But the main effect of this was probably to reduce the amount fed to animals. Food consumption in the aggregate had regained the pre-war level by 1947 and consumption per head was above the pre-war level by 1950, long before the end of rationing. Clothing was de-rationed in June 1948, furniture in March 1949 but fats, butter, cheese, bacon and meat were not de-rationed until the summer of 1954.

Control over investment

A third form of control was over investment. In principle, the government was in a position to control investment in the public sector but in practice did not find it at all easy to vary public investment over periods only a year or two ahead. Control of private sector investment was exercised through building licensing, allocations of steel and timber, and pressure on manufacturers to give preference to exports. The first of these was rendered ineffective in the first three post-war years by an enormous over-issue of licences. The shortage of building materials, however, operated in the opposite direction. Allocation of steel and timber gave the government power to influence the scale and pattern of investment and the division of output between home and export markets. It could divert building activity in favoured directions (e.g. house building), or to favoured areas (e.g. the development areas); limit the input of timber per house; require car manufacturers to export three-quarters of their output; and put pressure on engineering firms to meet specific requirements at home or abroad. From 1948 onwards the investment programme was the subject of careful planning even if the government was not always sure how far investment was diverging from programme.

Raw material allocations

Apart from their use in the control of investment, raw material allocations provided a fourth form of control over production. Nearly all raw materials except coal and steel were imported, either by the government itself or under licence from the government, and nearly all were at first subject to allocation. Of fifteen main raw materials 94 per cent by value were subject to allocation in 1946 and 47 per cent in 1950, but with the Korean war the proportion rose again to 64 per cent in 1952. Aluminium, wool and rubber ceased to be allocated in 1947, tin, cotton, and most hardwoods in 1949. The process of de-restriction was brought to a halt by rearmament, which made it necessary to renew some of the features of a war economy. In February 1952 the allocation of steel which had been discontinued in May 1950 (except for sheet and tinplate) was reintroduced along with control over many other materials. The renewal of control was short lived. The allocation of steel and some other materials ceased in 1953 and by 1954 the only allocation schemes remaining were for coal and tinplate.

Import restrictions

Among the most important forms of control, given the central importance of the balance of payments was that over imports. This had several different aspects. Apart from the need to keep imports within the limits of what could be afforded, there was also the need to switch as far as possible to non-dollar sources of supply, often at higher cost, and to engage in bilateral deals with individual countries. The Labour government was also anxious to continue the bulk purchase of imports on long-term contracts in the expectation of driving a better bargain than private traders. All this made for the retention of a large proportion of the import trade in government hands. In 1946 four-fifths both of food and of raw material imports were on government account. All imports of manufactures, although in private hands, required a government licence. Oil imports, which were also in private hands, were subject to quota limitations. Only some 4 per cent of imports were left uncontrolled.

Import restrictions remained largely unchanged during the first four years of peace apart from some shift back from direct government purchase to private trade under government control. In 1949, however, the members of the OEEC (Organization for European Economic Co-operation – the forerunner of OECD) agreed on a programme to 'liberalize' imports from each other, i.e. to free imports from control. The concessions made by the United Kingdom were extended to other non-dollar countries outside the Soviet bloc while imports from dollar countries continued to be restricted. This meant undisguised discrimination against dollar countries; but since imports from sterling area countries were already admitted more freely than from other areas, it was by no means the beginning of such discrimination.

Liberalization proceeded rapidly in 1950, when half the imports made by private traders and a quarter of total imports were unrestricted. In 1951 the process was at first carried further. But in the payments crisis that accompanied rearmament in 1951–2 it was halted for a time and reversed as import cuts totalling £600 million were made in November 1951, January 1952 and again in March 1952. About a quarter of the cuts made were designed to fall on goods that had previously been liberalized. Once the crisis

had passed, liberalization was resumed, the proportion of imports
free from control reaching 50 per cent in 1953.

Import control varied in severity with the state of the balance
of payments. Cuts were made in each successive balance of payments crisis, sometimes, as in 1949 and 1951, in association with
other sterling area countries, and always with a view to reducing
outgoings in dollars. At other times, when a more hopeful view
could be taken, imports were increased without any change in the
system of control.

Of the effectiveness of import controls there could never be
any doubt. In 1947, to take one example, cuts in dollar imports
produced a fall in their value of nearly 30 per cent in 1948 and
reduced the proportion of imports coming from the western hemisphere from 43 per cent to 30 per cent. In 1951–2 the best available guess is that of the fall in imports by £400 million in 1952,
£250 million can be attributed to cuts in the import programme.[9]
It is likely also that the low level of imports in post-war years
owed something to import control even if most of it was the result
of structural changes that reduced the importance of industries
like textiles that had high import requirements or increased the
output of industries like agriculture that provided substitutes
for imports.

Residual labour controls

Finally there were some residual labour controls. In war-time the
government had enjoyed, but rarely used, powers to direct labour.
It had put a 'ring fence' round certain industries to prevent workers
from leaving or being dismissed from essential work except with
the consent of the Ministry of Labour and had required recruitment
to certain employments to be made through the labour exchanges.
From December 1945 these powers were largely abandone and
over the next eighteen months further relaxations were made.
The powers retained by the government were by then confined
to coalmining and agriculture under Essential Work Orders and
to these industries and building and civil engineering under the
Control of Engagements Order. These powers were extended, but

to little effect, after the convertibility crisis of 1947, but abandoned completely at the beginning of 1950.

The government found it more fruitful to rely on other means of influencing recruitment to an industry. As in war-time it was possible to persuade applicants for work at the labour exchanges to take jobs conforming to a list of 'first preferences'. The government could also offer training facilities, deferment of call-up, better rations, more housing in designated areas, etc., and it could promote immigration, from Eire or from the refugee camps in Europe, to specified jobs.

Financial controls and demand management

The history of post-war economic management is essentially the story of how physical controls were gradually replaced by financial controls. Under the Labour governments this meant primarily increased reliance on budgetary policy as physical controls were relaxed or discontinued. In particular it meant an attempt to close what was seen as 'the inflationary gap' by running a large budget surplus. Control of investment and of imports on the one hand and a growing volume of public sector savings on the other were the pivots of economic management in the late 1940s.

The budget surplus that emerged for the first time in 1947–8 was of Dalton's making. He had begun with a budget deficit of £2200 million in 1945–6 but in his four budgets transformed this into a surplus of £636 million in 1947–8. Cripps's achievement over the three years following Dalton's resignation in November 1947 was to maintain a surplus of this dimension against strong criticism from his own party and ministerial colleagues. By the time he handed over to Gaitskell in October 1950 the central importance of what came to be called 'the budget judgment' was widely recognized.

The 'budget judgment' was essentially an exercise in demand management. It rested on a forecast of the prospective change in the pressure of demand based on an assessment of the likely increment in each of the main categories of demand on resources (consumer spending, fixed investment, stockbuilding, current expenditure of public authorities on goods and services and exports) and the simultaneous increment in the flow of supplies from current production (gross domestic product) and from imports. If the forecast pointed to excessive pressure, the increase in output leaving too narrow a margin of unused labour and capacity, the judgment would be that purchasing power should be withdrawn through the budget. Since inflationary pressure remained high throughout, the issue did not arise whether more purchasing power should be *released* even if a budget deficit resulted. The question was rather how far to go in running a budget surplus, against which ministers were liable to rebel, especially as they felt in their bones that a deep depression was just round the corner.

In the early post-war years Ministers preferred to base economic management decisions on a manpower budget. This was possible so long as they had a buffer stock of manpower in the armed forces, but not when demobilization was complete and they had no direct control over the supply and distribution of manpower. The alternative technique of national income forecasting which had begun to take shape in the war, came gradually to the fore. It remained crude and uncertain in its application, partly because of weaknesses in the statistical data, partly because the concept of excess demand was more ambiguous than it seemed. Nevertheless, it was gradually developed as an indispensable element in the management of demand which had become a central preoccupation of government by 1950.

Monetary policy was seen differently. Not much importance was attached to the influence of monetary conditions on investment or economic activity: the main object of the government was to reduce the burden of interest charges on the Exchequer. The government had far less need to borrow than in war-time, had the benefit of a large loan from the United States, and believed that, so far as interest rates did affect economic activity, *lower* rates would be appropriate after the period of transition had passed and given way to the danger of deflationary conditions.

These considerations led Dalton to embark on a campaign to lower interest rates. He cut the rate on Treasury Bills from 1 per cent to $\frac{1}{2}$ per cent in November 1945, and short-term rates remained unchanged thereafter until the incoming Conservative government increased the bank rate from 2 to $2\frac{1}{2}$ per cent in November 1951, the first increase since 1932. He then brought pressure on the market to reduce the long-term rate from the 3 per cent at which it had been held, quite deliberately, in wartime to $2\frac{1}{2}$ per cent. For a brief interval in the autumn of 1946 he was successful and the price of Consols reached a peak of 99 in October. But by that time the public had become net sellers of gilt-edged, the money supply, already much swollen, was increasing at a rate that alarmed the City, and a new issue of undated Treasury Stock at $2\frac{1}{2}$ per cent had had a disappointing reception. The bond market began to weaken in November and weakened further in the fuel and convertibility crises of 1947. By the spring of 1948 gilt-edged were 25 per cent below the peak reached eighteen months earlier and the Dalton 'experiment' had clearly failed.

Under Cripps no fresh attempt was made to manoeuvre a fall in long-term interest rates. £300 million in long-term debt was redeemed in March 1948 and some gilt-edged was taken in by the government broker to steady the market in 1949. But in the main, the government used its stronger budgetary position to redeem short-term debt and slow down the growth of the money supply. Over the two financial years 1948–9 and 1949–50 the growth was stopped. From then until the change of government the money supply increased slowly.

The main way in which the government sought to make use of monetary policy was through pressure on the banks to limit credit creation. This could not be done by using the pre-war system of ratio control. Nor would the Bank of England have taken to the idea of issuing a directive putting a ceiling on advances. Instead, the Chancellor wrote a number of letters to the Governor asking for his collaboration in holding inflationary policies in check by limiting advances for speculative purposes.

In general, monetary policy after Dalton was a by-product of fiscal policy and exercised little independent influence on economic activity.

Resource allocation

The various controls, physical and financial, were designed to promote certain adjustments in the economy: elimination of the external deficit, reduction in inflationary pressure, etc. What adjustments did take place? How fast did the economy grow and how was the growth allocated between different purposes? The changes from year to year in the allocation of resources between the main categories of demand are shown in table 2.2 (p. 58).

In the first two years output, as measured by GDP, grew very little. Civil employment at first grew rather slowly as women returned to household duties, the net increase over the first year of peace and demobilization being only 1 million. But in the next six months nearly another million entered employment and after one more year, at the end of 1947 civil employment had expanded by $2\frac{1}{2}$ million since June 1945. Productivity, however, suffered from the large-scale adjustments that had to be made over this period and from the shortages and bottlenecks that arose. Additionally, the severe winter of 1946—7 and the fuel crisis that arrested industrial production for weeks in many parts of the country, caused an appreciable loss of output.

It was only after some of the excess demand was chopped off in the autumn of 1947 that industry was able to advance on a more even front. The housing programme in particular had been allowed to get out of balance, with more houses started than could be finished. Drastic cuts were made in the entire investment programme with the unexpected result that investment nevertheless increased in 1948. By that time GDP was growing at a fast rate of about $3\frac{1}{2}$ per cent per annum and continued to grow at or above it over the next two years, dipping slightly in 1951 and ceasing to grow at all in 1952. Over the six years 1945—51 GDP increased by 15 per cent or about $2\frac{1}{2}$ per cent per annum and output per head at about 1 per cent lower, say $1\frac{1}{2}$ per cent annum.

The period started off with a big drop in government claims on resources with demobilization and a running down of munitions production. Some of the benefit of this was conveyed to the consumer by Dalton's first two budgets in October 1945 and April 1946 which reduced taxation by about £530 million. Consumers' expenditure rose by about £1000 million (at 1948 prices) and had probably returned to the pre-war level or a little above it by 1948 in spite of the hardships of rationing, licensing, and other restrictions. Fixed capital formation rose by almost as much as consumption from a far smaller base and it, too, had regained the pre-war level by 1948. The contraction in fixed investment in war-time had been on a par with the contraction in exports and so, too, was its recovery in 1945–7. After 1947, however, fixed investment was more tightly controlled and grew more slowly. Exports, on the other hand, after an initial leap in 1946 were held back by the fuel crisis in 1947 and then made rapid progress during Cripps's three years at the Exchequer before their growth petered out in 1951. Stockbuilding, the most erratic element in demand, reached its peak in 1947, contributing to the aggravation of inflationary pressure and the big increase in the external deficit in that year. In the next three years of rising exports, stockbuilding subsided, only to explode again in 1951 and contribute once more to a balance of payments crisis. Imports increased in each of the three crisis years 1947, 1949 and 1951 but were more or less unchanged in the even years 1946, 1948 and 1950, with a sharp dip in 1952 that reflected the import cuts made in the exchange crisis during the winter of 1951–2.

The economy depicted by table 2.2 is one in which the running is made by exports and investment with the rise in consumption after the first post-war year held within narrow limits. Indeed, consumption absorbed only a quarter of the extra resources that were made available by 1952 for exports and fixed investment. One of the first questions that the table raises is how it was possible to keep such a tight control over consumption.

The question is the more natural in view of the changes taking place in personal incomes and in savings. At the end of the war, weekly wage earnings were roughly 80 per cent higher than in 1938 while prices were only about 50 per cent higher. In war-time much of the increase in income remained unspent and was banked in savings accounts against the day when consumer goods would again be freely available. personal savings as a proportion of disposable income had risen from about 3.5 per cent in 1938 to over 16 per cent in 1944. But what if all this were now reversed and there was a rush to buy? If nothing were done the only check to consumption in those circumstances would be inflation. Personal savings did in fact fall steeply: at their lowest point in 1948 they were virtually zero. On the other hand, the budget had by that time moved into surplus and the surplus continued thereafter throughout the transition period. The withdrawal of purchasing power on an increasing scale from 1945 to 1950 allowed public saving to take the place of private. Consumer spending increased by only 1 per cent per annum after 1946 because real after-tax incomes rose even less.[10] This was the result of somewhat higher taxation and a large adverse swing in the terms of trade by about 16 per cent over the six years, a steep rise in import prices eating into consumer incomes, especially in 1946–8 and again in 1949–51.

The developments we have so far discussed were not foreshadowed in the original programme on which the government was elected. That programme was more concerned with the enlargement of the public sector through nationalization and the expansion of the social services – what is now thought of as the creation of the Welfare State.

Nationalization

Nationalization occupied much of the time of Parliament and the administration. First, the Bank of England was taken into public ownership early in 1946, then the coal, gas and electricity industries over the next three years, with rail and canal transport and long – distance haulage at the beginning of 1948 and civil aviation and telecommunications a year or so previously. Thus apart from the Bank of England, which was already a semi-public body, the programme was confined to fuel and power on the one hand and transport and communications on the other: that is, to the most capital-intensive sectors of the economy. The only manufacturing industry – and the only source of really violent political controversy – was the steel industry which did not pass into the public domain until February 1951.

The nationalization measures were very dear to the Labour party. They persevered with them even when it meant splitting a country they were trying to unite behind their economic policy and when it endangered American goodwill. The decision to proceed with nationalization of the steel industry was taken when the convertibility crisis was at its most acute and dollars were draining away at nearly $1 billion a month. Arrangements for the nationalization of the coal industry took up scarce managerial time all through the year before the coal crisis finally broke in February 1947. What did the measures accomplish?

They added nearly $2\frac{1}{2}$ million workers to the public sector and gave the government direct control over the basic industries of the country. But the government was not at all clear to what purpose such control should be put. The legislation seemed to envisage a group of public-spirited monopolies, free in most matters to run their own affairs on the model of commercial undertakings. There was no very apparent gain in efficiency, no revolution in industrial relations, no real reinforcement of the government's grip on the economy.

The main immediate consequence of the measures, as might have been expected, was on investment. A far higher proportion of the total investment programme was now within the public sector – it eventually reached 50 per cent in the 1960s – and large amounts of capital from the budget surpluses were needed to recondition some of the newly nationalized industries such as coal, railway transport and steel. The increased importance of public investment may have seemed welcome as a means of ironing out fluctuations in the total; but in practice it proved difficult to make quick changes in these mammoth projects. Whatever the merits of public ownership in the longer run, an extensive programme of nationalization did not fit very well into a policy of post-war reconstruction.

The coal industry, in this respect, may have been an exception. There was a desperate need for more coal both for domestic use and for export to European neighbours who were even more in need of fuel. Even small amounts were of the utmost value in bilateral trade agreements. But the output of deep-mined coal had fallen year by year throughout the war to a level 25 per cent below that of 1939. It was clear even in 1945 that a crisis was imminent if manpower was not increased and manpower continued to fall. Perhaps a new deal for coal, with public ownership, high invesment, shorter hours and freedom from call-up, would attract more labour and increase output.

Things did not prove quite so easy. Much of the reconstruction work itself required mining labour and the cut in hours involved some sacrifice in output. For a year or two, in 1947—8, there was a trickle of additional labour but in 1951 there were no more men in the mines than at the low point five years previously. The output of coal expanded slowly but left little for export, and rationing of domestic consumers continued. Anxiety over coal supplies was never far away and in the autumn of 1950 it looked for a time as if there might be a replay of the 1947 crisis. Yet if coal in those years was the weak spot in British industry things might have been worse in the absence of nationalization and the increased investment that this brought, small though it was for so large an industry.[11]

The Welfare State   * *important*

The other main extension of the public sector was in the provision of social services. These did not, of course, originate in the post-war years; public expenditure on health, education, pensions, etc. had grown from £35 million in 1900 (nearly all education and poor relief) to over £400 million in 1936. State contributory pension schemes went back before the first world war.

Some of the changes introduced after the war derived from the work of the war-time coalition government. This passed the 1944 Education Act which laid the basis for modern secondary education although it was not until 1947 that the Labour government raised the school-leaving age to fifteen. The National Health Service had similarly been accepted in principle by the coalition government but it was left to the Labour government to give substance to it. The main changes associated with the idea of the Welfare State were founded on the war-time report on *Social Insurance and Allied Services* by (as he then was) Sir William Beveridge. The central idea of his report was to unite a wide range of social services that were previously unconnected with each other into a comprehensive system of national benefits. These benefits would extend 'from the cradle to the grave' and cover maternity, sickness, unemployment, retirement, death and other contingencies. The cost of these benefits was to be met from national insurance contributions – indeed, these contributions also met a small part of the cost of the National Health Service. The extra burden on the taxpayer came partly from the added cost of education and health services but much more, under the Labour government, from the need to cover the cost of the food and agriculture subsidies. By 1950 this exceeded total expenditure on national insurance and was also larger than expenditure on the health services.

Between 1936 and 1950 gross expenditure on the social services in Great Britain increased from about £400 million to £1500 million, excluding expenditure on food and housing subsidies. But since prices had doubled in the meantime the increase in real terms was much less, probably about 80–90 per cent. The main source of this large increase was the National Health Service which rapidly outstripped initial estimates and in the last three years of the Labour government was costing an average of £460 million a year.[12] It was the weight of this burden on the Exchequer that drove successive Chancellors to propose the introduction of health charges, a proposal strongly and at first successfully resisted by Aneurin Bevan, the architect of a free National Health Service; and it was over the principle of a free Health Service (as well as the rearmament programme) that Bevan resigned in April 1951.

The food subsidies, which imposed an even larger burden, were allowed to increase under Dalton until they were well on the way to £500 million a year. In 1949 Cripps accepted the need to impose a ceiling on the total and from then onwards the subsidies were held at £465 million. No reduction was made, however, until after the Conservatives took office.

These expenditures have to be seen against a total for ordinary expenditure by the central government of about £3000 million in the late 1940s. Excluding debt charges and defence expenditure, the total for all civil purposes rose from £1650 million in 1946–7, before the expansion in the social services had got very far, to £2060 million in 1949–50 when most of the changes had already been made. This may give a more accurate picture of the additional financial burden on the Exchequer. But it excludes the cost of subsidies on the one hand and exaggerates the additional burden on national resources on the other.

International economic relations

We turn finally to Britain's economic relations with other countries in the period of transition.

The war had cut off many traditional markets and sources of supply and it was a long time before normal conditions of trade could be re-established. Nearly all European countries had difficulty in finding the means of paying for the imports they so badly needed and turned to the American hemisphere, and particularly the United States, for indispensable imports not obtainable elsewhere. This was true not only of foodstuffs and raw materials but also of the capital equipment they badly needed in order to provide productive capacity for a more fully employed labour force.

The resulting dollar shortage and inconvertibility of currencies drove countries to make bilateral trade and payments agreements with one another. The effort to balance accounts country by country distorted the pattern of trade flows, reduced the total volume of trade and hit with particular severity countries that had been accustomed to the blessings of multilateral trade and the settlement of deficits with one group of countries out of surpluses with others. Countries like Belgium, Sweden and Switzerland, with their pre-war economy largely intact, were in a relatively strong position since they could supply what other countries most required and they might even, like Belgium, try to obtain settlement in gold. Other European countries ran substantial deficits against loans, credits and what reserves of gold and dollars they could spare.

Britain's main suppliers and markets fell into three groups: North America, the sterling area and Western Europe. Other countries, in Latin America, Eastern Europe and elsewhere, although important for particular purposes played a subordinate role. The changes in Britain's trade with those groups between 1938 and 1946, and again between 1946 and 1950, are shown in table 2.3.

Table 2.3 tells its own story. It shows the increased reliance on imports from North America after the war and the subsequent drop as supplies from Western Europe and other parts of the world began to recover. The sterling area remained the main source throughout and was an even more important source in 1950 than in 1938. The post-war percentages, however, are of a much diminished volume of imports so that the movement of the percentages is not a good guide to changes by volume. For example, imports from North America were little if at all greater by volume in 1946 than in 1938 and supplies from the sterling area were quite appreciably lower. It is also not apparent from the

Table 2.3 The pattern of British trade, 1938, 1946 and 1950

	% of total imports by value from				% of total exports by value to			
	North America	Western Europe	Sterling Area	Rest of world	North America	Western Europe	Sterling Area	Rest of world
1938	21.7	24.0	31.2	23.1	9.3	23.4	44.9	22.4
1946	33.1	14.9	32.8	19.2	7.5	28.3	45.3	19.0
1950	15.0	25.1	38.0	25.9	11.0	28.3	47.8	12.9

Source: Annual Abstract of Statistics 1953, tables 211 and 212

percentages that the sterling area made the biggest contribution to the doubling in the value of imports between 1946 and 1950, accounting for 42.5 per cent of the increase while Western Europe accounted for 35.5 per cent.

The picture for exports shows the sterling area in an even more dominant position, taking a proportion of British exports higher than before the war and one approaching 50 per cent in 1950. By contrast, North America took a relatively small proportion that was raised from 7.5 to 11 per cent between 1946 and 1950 only with the greatest difficulty. Western Europe, in the absence of German competition, took a higher proportion of British exports than before the war and continued to do so in 1950 when the total volume of exports was about 75 per cent higher than in 1946. Even so, it was the sterling area that took the lion's share – roughly half – of the increase in British exports over those four years.

British recovery thus rested heavily on an expansion in trade with the sterling area, most members of which were also members of the Commonwealth, and to a lesser extent on the recovery and continued growth of trade with Western Europe. It was by such means that Britain hoped to put an end to her shortage of dollars. Apart from drawing in imports in substitution for imports from America there was also the possibility of earning some gold and dollars directly from South Africa, Malaya and some of the colonial territories.

There was however a price to be paid in the need to supply, as part of the general sterling area arrangements, capital for the development of sterling area countries. That large sums flowed abroad is obvious when one compares the cumulative drain of gold and dollars over the years 1945–52 with the cumulative deficit on current account. The gap between the first, amounting to $9.2 billion and the second, amounting to no more than £700 million – at most $3 billion – indicates either an error in the figures or an outflow of capital equal to the difference between the two. Over the seven years the net outflow of capital was probably about £1700 million of which £900 million went to the sterling area and most of the rest to Western Europe.[13] More was lent or invested abroad than had been borrowed in North America. The United Kingdom had run a large current account surplus with non-dollar countries but the surplus had brought in only a limited quantity of gold and dollars; most of it had been provided in one form or another as capital.

The pattern of British trade exercised an important influence on Britain's attitude to Europe. The United States had hoped when Marshall Aid was launched that the United Kingdom would take the lead in integrating Europe. There was no sign in the middle of 1947 that France would ever think of assuming that role: the French were then bitterly opposed to American efforts to put Germany back on her feet. The role proposed was not one that the British government found attractive. It was hard enough for Britain to pay her own way; and to tack on a group of countries in much deeper trouble would be an aggravation of the difficulty. Association with North America and the Commonwealth seemed a better bet and was not easily reconciled with leadership in the economic integration of Europe. When the French, under the influence of Jean Monnet, came round to a different way of thinking about Germany and Europe they were satisfied that the United Kingdom was unlikely to be a helpful partner. The Schuman Plan was devised in the full expectation that the United Kingdom would not be a participant.

In those years the United Kingdom occupied a position in Europe very different from that of today. As late as 1951 her industrial production was still as great as that of France and Germany combined and so, too, were her exports. By comparison, in the mid 1980s France's industrial production was double that of the United Kingdom and Germany's three times as large. Similarly, while France, Germany, Italy and the Netherlands struggled with large and persistent deficits throughout the post-war period, the United Kingdom had balanced her current account by 1948. She saw herself, quite mistakenly, as cast in the role of creditor almost indefinitely in her dealings with the continent and thought it more important to mount a joint programme for freer trade in Europe combined with a joint attack on the dollar problem than to follow the path of union with Europe.

In 1949–50 under the auspices of the OEEC in Paris, the British government collaborated in a programme of trade liberalization which gave a new boost to intra-European trade (although from 1949 onwards the recovery of Germany was much the most powerful factor and the largest single contribution to the elimination of the dollar shortage). The Americans brought pressure for schemes to settle intra-European payments on a multilateral rather than a bilateral basis and although the early schemes were not altogether satisfactory, a fresh initiative at the end of 1949 led to the creation in July 1950 of the European Payments Union.

The scheme was not altogether to the liking of the Bank of England and was at first opposed both by Britain and Belgium. The Belgians hankered after settlement in gold and dollars of any surpluses or deficits while the British would have liked to see a complete absence of gold and dollars from such settlements. The Bank of England also feared for the use of sterling and the future of the sterling area. It had helped to devise a system of bilateral agreements under which each side offered limited credit to the other and settlement beyond these limits was made in sterling. These arrangements would be superseded under the European Payments Union and there was a question how far other countries might use their holdings of sterling to make a settlement through the union. In the end it was agreed to bring all payments in currently earned sterling, whether with the United Kingdom or the rest of the sterling area, within the scheme. A country in deficit (within the limits of its quota) would settle part of the deficit in gold and receive credit from the EPU on the other part. On this basis, the British were satisfied and it was the Belgians whose acceptance was most difficult to obtain. In spite of many upsets the scheme was a great success until it disappeared with the introduction of convertibility at the end of 1958.

Conclusion

The adjustments necessary at the end of the war had been largely completed by the close of 1951. The position was obscured by the distortions introduced by an enormous rearmament programme. But in the light of after events it is clear that the dollar problem was on the way to a solution; the economy, although temporarily in heavy deficit, would swing back into balance as soon as the terms of trade returned to a more normal relationship, and the transfer of resources to sustain high levels of exports and investment had been made on an adequate scale. The consumer boom that began soon after 1951 was itself a testimony to the extent of the adjustment in the use of resources that had already been accomplished.

There were other adjustments that had not been made. Inflation had not been mastered; the danger that wages would rise faster than productivity and that the rise might accelerate in a fully employed labour market had not been dispelled. The trade unions had collaborated in restraining the growth of money wages; but they had not been taught to accept this as the price of full employment and were doubtful whether wage restraint could ever be effective except intermittently. More important, neither the unions nor the public had developed attitudes favourable to change and innovation: whether in labour practices in face of changing technology or in attitudes to Europe in face of changes in Britain's position in the world.

The Labour government accomplished most of what it set out to do under difficult conditions that seemed to keep changing for the worse. But its performance was highly variable. Things were at their worst in 1947 with one crisis after another. There were times under Dalton when the government seemed to be heading for the abyss, content to let the balance of payments exhaust the reserves and inflation produce an empty economy. Endless parliamentary time and much political capital was expended in moving a number of industries from the private sector to the public sector without much of a notion how to run the public sector. Precious time was wasted before devaluing in 1949. But from the autumn of 1947, thanks largely to a series of firm budgets, the government pursued a resolute policy that was highly successful until in its final year rearmament was pressed too hard. Post-war policy worked no miracle; but at least it avoided the very real threat of utter disaster and set the stage for the long boom that followed.

Notes

1   This chapter is largely based on my *Years of Recovery* (Methuen, 1985). The reader seeking elaboration of the points made is referred to that volume which also contains a detailed account

of some of the more important episodes. I have not felt it necessary to provide references to all the relevant passages or repeat
all the sources indicated there.

2 *Statistical Digest of the War* (HMSO and Longmans, 1951). In
all, grants by other governments to the United Kingdom totalled
£7500 million (of which £6700 million was lend-lease aid from
the United States) but against this has to be set reciprocal aid
granted by the United Kingdom to other countries, amounting
to £2100 million. Reciprocal aid to the United States from the
United Kingdom was almost as large in relation to British GNP
as lend-lease aid to the British Empire was in relation to American
GNP (R. G. D. Allen, 'Mutual aid' in Journal of the Royal
Statistical Society 1946).

3 H. C. Deb., 5th ser., vol. 413, col. 956.

4 *Employment Policy* (Cmd 6527, 1944), Foreword.

5 Ibid., para. 49.

6 Earnings rose about 10 per cent faster than wage rates so that
pay, in real terms, was somewhat higher by 1951.

7 H. C. Deb., 5th ser., vol. 474, col. 39, 18 April 1950.

8 For a full treatment of direct controls see Dow (1964), ch. 6.

9 W. M. Corden,. 'The control of imports: a case study'; *The
Manchester School*, September 1958. Of the £250 million, half
may have represented a fall in government-held stocks.

10 The White Papers on *National Income and Expenditure* show
an increase in personal disposable income of 45 per cent
compared with a rise in retail prices of 43 per cent. In the first
four years, 1946–50, real incomes rose by perhaps 6 per cent
but fell over the next two years, 1950–2.

11 Total investment (including opencast coal, pithead baths, etc.)
was estimated at £16½ million in 1947 and never rose above
£30 million per annum before 1952.

12 National Health Insurance before the war cost the state only
about £40 million per annum.

13 It was officially estimated in April 1947 that grants and
credits to Western Europe since the war had reached a
total of £710 million of which £140 million represented
economic assistance to Germany and £100 million a loan
to France. The rest included £155 million for relief and re-
habilitation (not exclusively to Europe) and the value of surplus
military stores and equipment. Churchill in 1949 claimed
that the total had risen to over £900 million (Cairncross,
1985, p. 229n.).

Further reading

Barnett, Correlli 1986. *The Audit of War*, London: Macmillan.

Cairncross, A. 1985. *Years of Recovery*, London: Methuen.

Cairncross, A. and Watts, N. 1989. *The Economic Section 1939–1961: a Study in Economic Advising*, London: Routledge.

Clarke, R. W. B. (ed. Cairncross) 1982. *Anglo-American Collaboration in War and Peace*, Oxford: University Press.

Dell, Edmund 1995. *The Schuman Plan and the British Abdication of Leadership in Europe*, Oxford: Clarendon Press.

Devons, Ely 1961. 'Economic planning in war and peace', in *Essays in Economics*, London: Allen & Unwin.

Devons, Ely 1970. 'Planning by economic survey', in A. Cairncross (ed.), *Papers on Planning and Economic Management*, Manchester: Manchester University Press.

Dow, J. C. R. 1964. *The Management of the British Economy 1945–60*, Cambridge: Cambridge University Press.

Durbin, E. F. M. 1949. *Problems of Economic Planning*, London: Routledge.

Gardner, R. N. 1980. *Sterling Dollar Diplomacy in Current Perspective* (new expanded edition), Oxford: Oxford University Press.

Henderson, H. D. 1947. *The Uses and Abuses of Economic Planning*, Cambridge: Cambridge University Press.

Hennessy, P. 1992. *Never Again: Britain 1945–51*, London: Jonathan Cape.

Hogan M. J. 1987. *The Marshall Plan*, Cambridge: Cambridge University Press.

Howson, Susan 1993. *British Monetary Policy 1945–51*, Oxford: Oxford University Press.

Jones, R. B. 1987. *Wages and Employment Policy 1936–1955*, London: Allen & Unwin.

Kaplan, J. and Schleiminger, G. 1989. *The European Payments Union*, Oxford: Clarendon Press.

Kindleberger, C. P. 1987. *Marshall Plan Days*, Boston: Allen & Unwin.

Meade, James 1948. *Planning and the Price Mechanism*. London: Allen & Unwin.

Meade, James (ed. Howson) 1990. *The Cabinet Office Diary 1944–46*, London: Unwin Hyman.

Mercer, H., Rollings, N. and Tomlinson, J. (eds.) 1992. *Labour Governments and Private Industry: the experience of 1945–51*, Edinburgh: Edinburgh University Press.

Milward, A. S. 1984. *The Reconstruction of Western Europe 1945–51*, London: Methuen.

Morgan, K. O. 1984. *Labour in Power 1945–51*, Oxford: Oxford University Press.

Pressnell, L. S. 1986. *External Economic Policy since the War: Vol. 1 The Post-War Financial Settlement*, London: HMSO.

Robbins, L. C. 1947. *The Economic Problem in Peace and War*, London: Macmillan.

Roberthall, Lord (ed. Cairncross) 1989. *The Robert Hall Diaries*, vol. 1 1947–53, London: Unwin Hyman.

Robinson, E. A. G. 1986. 'The economic problems of the transition from war to peace', *Cambridge Journal of Economics*, June.

Rogow, A. A. and Shore, P. 1955. *The Labour Government and British Industry*, Oxford: Oxford University Press.

Tew, J. B. H. 1952; 10th edn 1970. *International Monetary Co-operation*, London: Hutchinson University Library.

Tomlinson, J. 1987. *Employment Policy: the crucial years 1939–55*, Oxford: Oxford University Press.

Worswick, G. D. N. and Ady, P. H. (eds) 1952. *The British Economy 1945–50*, Oxford: Oxford University Press.

3 The 1950s

The course of events

By 1950 the main adjustments to post-war conditions had been made. The armed forces had been run down to a sustainable, if relatively high, level. Production was running well above that of the pre-war period and unemployment was extremely low. There was a surplus in the balance of payments and the reserves were at last on the increase. Prices and wages were relatively stable. On the other hand, many direct controls over the economy remained and consumption was being held severely in check.

Within a few months the picture changed abruptly. New initiatives were taken in Europe: in May the launching of the Schuman Plan, in which Britain took no part, and in July of the European Payments Union, in which Britain collaborated with her European neighbours. Both of these were important departures of policy; but of far more immediate importance was the outbreak of war in Korea in June and the tremendous effort of rearmament that was put in hand shortly afterwards. By the autumn the United States was planning to double its pre-Korea level of defence expenditure and by January the United Kingdom was contemplating an even larger expansion. Spending on this enormous scale drove up the price of primary commodities – in some cases fourfold – and created physical shortages that threatened to hold up production and limit exports.

The disruption produced by rearmament deflected effort in Britain from exports and investment and threw the balance of payments into heavy deficit. The resulting crisis precipitated an agitation for immediate convertibility in 1952 but the crisis passed without action being taken. Over the next six years convertibility continued to be discussed until it was ultimately introduced at the end of 1958.

Meanwhile the boom associated with rearmament in 1951 had been succeeded by an inventory recession in 1952; and since this followed the revival of bank rate and other monetary weapons by the incoming Conservative government, there was a tendency to attribute the change to the raising of interest rates. When recovery in 1953 had flowered into a boom in 1955 the experience of 1952 encouraged renewed reliance on monetary policy to offset the effects of a reduction in income tax; but on this occasion credit restriction seemed to have little effect. Even after an autumn budget imposing fresh taxation, inflationary pressure continued into 1956 and an effort was made to tackle inflation more directly through agreements with industry to hold down prices and an attempt to secure acceptance of the need for more moderate wage settlements.

Later in the year came Suez and fresh foreign exchange difficulties which were overcome only after an abandonment of the whole enterprise. The effects of Suez on the domestic economy, however, were relatively slight and in 1957 the economy continued to expand at a slow pace. Ministers remained preoccupied by inflation but had no success in checking wage-increases. In September the Chancellor (Thorneycroft) decided to tackle inflation at what he took to be its root — namely the stock of money, or alternatively, public spending and bank credit. He announced his determination to halt inflation whatever the increase in unemployment. But when the Cabinet was unwilling to cut the last £50 million to bring down public spending to the level he had set, he resigned. A few months later, in 1958, ministers were in a panic as unemployment rose above 2 per cent and they insisted on reflationary measures. Amory, the new Chancellor, tried hard to avoid over-expansion. But, bit by bit, the pressure built up again and the 1950s ended in almost as over-heated a condition as they had begun.

Although the period was attended almost throughout by balance of payments anxieties, there was a current account surplus in all but three years: 1951, 1955 and 1960. There was a serious crisis in the winter of 1951−2 but nothing of comparable gravity thereafter. In September 1957, when bank rate was raised to 7 per cent, external pressures were not the primary difficulty since the current surplus was larger than it had been since 1950 and was still increasing. Once capital movements are taken into account the record becomes less satisfactory. In four out of six years from 1951 to 1956 the reserves fell; and although imports roughly doubled in value between 1950 and 1960 so that the need for reserves was much greater, the reserves were rather lower at the end of 1960 than they had been at the end of 1950.

Before we turn to look in more detail at the main developments we can take a bird's-eye view of the year-to-year changes in the main aggregates in table 3.1. The growth in production, which averaged 2.7 per cent per annum over the decade, shows a marked slowing down in 1951–2, no doubt because of the many shortages and other difficulties in those years. In 1953–5 production expanded rapidly. Thereafter growth again slowed down in the prolonged credit squeeze that began in 1955. In 1958 there was, for the first time, an actual fall in production but in the last two years of the decade there was a strong recovery with particularly rapid growth in 1960.

The most volatile element in demand was stockbuilding which showed peaks in 1951, 1955 and 1960 and troughs in 1952 and 1958. Consumer spending fell in 1951 as the cost of living rose and remained flat in 1952 but took the lion's share of additional output thereafter. Public expenditure on goods and services expanded with rearmament in 1951–2 as consumers economized and then contracted for five successive years, reviving in 1959–60 under the government's effort to reflate the economy. Exports maintained a relatively modest pace of expansion barely sufficient to keep pace with imports, and even then only with the help of a gradual improvement in the terms of trade.

Taking the decade as a whole, economic performance was disappointing in comparison with the early post-war years, when major adjustments were successfully carried out; or with the 1960s, when growth was perceptibly faster and exports much higher; or with foreign competitors who gained more ground on the United Kingdom in the 1950s than in any other post-war decade. Where the 1950s score is in the low level of unemployment, which averaged not much over 300,000, and in the comparative stability of prices:

Table 3.1 Changes in the allocation of resources, 1950–1960 (increase from year to year in £ billion at constant 1985 prices)

	1951	1952	1953	1954	1955	1956	1957	1958	1959	1960	Changes between 1950 and 1960
Consumers' expenditure	-1.3	–	4.1	4.1	4.4	1.0	2.3	2.7	4.9	4.6	26.8
Public authorities' final consumption	2.9	4.2	1.2	-0.2	-1.2	-0.5	-0.8	-1.2	0.8	0.9	6.0
Gross domestic fixed capital formation	0.1	0.2	2.1	1.8	1.3	1.1	1.4	0.2	2.0	2.6	12.8
Value of physical increase in stocks and work in progress	4.3	-2.6	0.3	-0.3	1.5	-0.4	–	-0.8	0.6	2.5	5.0
Exports of goods and services	-0.3	-0.5	1.1	1.5	1.8	1.3	0.8	-0.5	0.9	1.9	8.1
Total final expenditure	5.3	-0.6	9.1	7.5	8.9	3.0	4.3	0.8	9.5	13.0	60.9
Imports of goods and services	1.8	-2.0	2.0	1.0	2.8	0.1	0.8	0.3	2.1	4.0	12.7
Gross domestic product (at market prices)	3.4	1.7	7.0	6.6	5.9	2.9	3.5	0.5	7.4	8.9	47.8
Gross domestic product (average at factor cost)	2.5	1.1	5.3	6.0	5.4	2.1	2.6	-0.3	6.4	9.2	40.3

Source: Economic Trends Annual Supplement (1990 edn) table 3

...ars retail prices rose by under 50 per cent and it was still
...e for an entire year like 1959 to show no rise at all.

Policy aims and instruments

The main aims of policy under a Conservative government in the
1950s were much what they had been under the Labour government: full employment, stable prices, more even development in
different parts of the country and provision for social security
on the Beveridge model. There were, however, differences of
emphasis. The Conservatives attached more importance to market freedom, were much more willing to use monetary weapons,
gave higher priority to stability of prices, were more equivocal
about full employment, and disliked anything that smacked of
planning. They continued to issue the *Economic Survey* but stipu-
lated that it should contain no forecasts. They revived the use of
bank rate almost as soon as they came to power, spoke of freeing
the pound, introduced hire purchase restrictions, showed a marked
preference for financial over physical controls and were much
more inclined than the Labour government to follow the advice
of the Bank of England.

Not that they showed any particular reluctance to introduce
controls when they thought it necessary. They continued food
rationing until 1954 and price control until 1952−3; they continued
for a time the various raw material controls introduced by their
predecessors in face of acute shortages and themselves resumed
steel allocation between February 1952 and May 1953; they did
not abandon building licensing until 1955; above all, they made
extensive use in 1951−2 of import controls, inheriting one batch
from the plans prepared by the Labour government and introducing
two batches of their own in January and March 1952. But once
the crisis occasioned by rearmament in 1951−2 was past and the
controls were gradually removed, they were resolved not to revive
them. Hire purchase restrictions were the only example of powers
freshly taken after abandonment; and they were not part of the
group of physical controls inherited from war-time. Exchange
control was almost the only example of a war-time control surviving
into the 1960s.

The Conservatives accepted in principle the use of monetary and fiscal policy in managing the economy but they were reluctant Keynesians and practised demand management only so long as it did not conflict with what they took to be sound principles. Thus they were never prepared to budget for a deficit. The tax changes made in the budgets of the 1950s were never very large, except perhaps in 1959; apart from 1959 the maximum ever pressed on the Chancellor, up or down, was £150 million. Demand management relied on gentle nudges rather than body blows.

Put another way: there was never all that need for demand management. Unemployment, for example, fluctuated between 1 per cent and 2 per cent and only in two years, 1958 and 1959 did it average over 400,000. Even then the government had a hand in the higher level of unemployment which was largely the aftermath of Thorneycroft's efforts to deflate the economy in 1957 by reducing public expenditure and public investment. In other years the known commitment of the government to a 'high and stable level of employment' no doubt helped to sustain employment by influencing prevailing attitudes. But until 1959 the government faced no serious slack in the economy that was not of its own making. This is not to suggest that fiscal policy did nothing to promote economic stability. The nudges were sufficient; and they were supplemented by other instruments of policy — hire purchase restrictions, monetary policy, public investment. In spite of stop-go and balance of payments crises, the economy rarely needed much management.

By the end of the 1950s management meant first of all the preparation of macro-economic forecasts three times a year; consideration of the forecasts by the Budget Committee; a judgment (usually by the chief Treasury economist) of the change required in the pressure of demand; and its translation by the Budget Committee into tax proposals to put to the Chancellor. Forecasting became increasingly sophisticated over time and the statistical framework became firmer as quarterly data became available and figures were seasonally adjusted. But there was always a large element of hunch in the budget judgment and uncertainty as to the effect on the economy of specific acts of intervention.

The influence of monetary policy was harder to judge since it had been little used for twenty years. The Labour government had shown a bias in favour of low interest rates and a reluctance to raise them carried over from war-time. The Conservatives were more willing to use interest rates in a restrictive direction and kept hoping that tight money would leave more scope for tax reduction.

Monetary policy took different forms at different times. Dalton had thought of it in terms of exerting leverage on interest rates, particularly in the bond market, and had done so by switching official holdings into longer-term debt and issuing more Treasury bills in substitution for an equivalent amount of longer-term debt. Cripps had relied on 'requests' to the banks to be selective in their lending and the use of budget surpluses to mop up short-term debt held by the banks and so reduce the money supply. Butler started off in 1951 by raising bank rate (which Gaitskell had refused to do) and funding some of the banks' liquid assets. In 1952 bank rate was raised to 4 per cent in March; and the inventory recession that followed was widely (but almost certainly mistakenly) associated with the rise in interest rates. In 1955, when Butler cut the income tax at the height of a boom, he professed to rely on 'the resources of a flexible monetary policy' to prevent over-heating.

The Bank of England began in 1955 by reducing the banks' liquidity; but this was replenished by the sale of bank investments. Bank lending, which was what the Treasury wanted to see reduced, continued unabated. Some of this lending was to the boards of nationalized industries which had been obliged to defer bond issues because of the depressed state of the stock market; and the banks objected to meeting their needs when other customers in the private sector had to go without. In late July the banks agreed to a request from the Chancellor for 'a positive and significant reduction' in advances. Even then there was little sign at the end of the year of any check to activity and the credit squeeze continued for a full three years, ending only in July 1958.

This experience gave rise to prolonged discussion of how the monetary system worked. It was clear that the banks did not simply build on a fixed monetary base as in pre-war textbooks: on the contrary, the Bank of England supplied them with the cash appropriate to their liabilities. Nor did they even maintain a fixed ratio of credit to their liquid assets: they could add to their liquid assets by selling investments or even by borrowing. The bond market, weakened by inflation, had difficulty in absorbing repeated conversion issues and fresh issues by the nationalized industries. Funding was not on a scale sufficient to avoid government recourse to the banks and so to keep the banks short of liquid assets.

How the banks were to be controlled became the subject of three separate enquiries in the years after 1955. First came an enquiry in 1956 by the Treasury and the Bank of England which considered the possible use of an advances ratio and rejected it. It also rejected a prescribed liquidity ratio except in 'dire necessity'. Governments that could not meet their financial needs out of taxation or long-term borrowing inevitably lost control of the stock of money. The report thus put the onus on the government rather than the central bank, calling for a big enough exchequer surplus to afford freedom in deciding on debt management operations.

Early in 1957 the Bank of England proposed a public enquiry into the working of the monetary system. A committee under Lord Radcliffe was appointed and heard extensive evidence before reporting in August 1959. Long before then, in September 1957, the Chancellor (Thorneycroft) set up a working party consisting of Lord Robbins, Sir Robert Hall (Economic Adviser to HMG) and Sir Humphrey Mynors (Deputy Governor) to study how bank credit should be controlled. This followed an attempt by the Chancellor to direct the banks to make a 5 per cent cut in advances which had come to nothing because the Bank of England refused to issue the necessary directive, and under the 1946 Act the Chancellor had neither the power to issue a directive himself nor to dismiss the Governor as he contemplated. The working party, Mynors objecting strongly, recommended (1) a prescribed liquidity ratio, which was not adopted, and (2) the introduction of an illiquid alternative to bank-held Treasury bills, which took shape as the scheme for Special Deposits first used in 1960.

Apart from the initial tightening in 1951−2 and the credit squeeze of 1955−8 monetary policy played little part in the 1950s. Until 1958 bank rate was never changed more than twice in one year, falling from 4 per cent in March 1952 to 3 per cent by May 1954, rising again to $5\frac{1}{2}$ per cent by February 1956, reaching 7 per cent in September 1957 and staying there for six months before falling again in five steps to 4 per cent in November 1958 where it remained until it began rising again in 1960. The government allowed long rates to drift upwards without any very clear policy: the yield on $2\frac{1}{2}$ per cent Consols rose from $3\frac{1}{2}$ per cent in 1950 to just under $5\frac{1}{2}$ per cent in 1960, with most of the rise in the second half of the decade. The money stock expanded slowly – much more slowly than GDP: from 57 per cent of GDP in 1950 bank deposits fell to 33 per cent in 1960. These movements in interest rates and bank deposits have to be seen against a rise of 40 per cent in the price of consumer goods and services in ten years (50 per cent in retail prices) and growing inflationary expectations.[1]

Perhaps the most powerful financial weapon used by the authorities was hire purchase control. Restrictions were first introduced in January 1952, taking the form of statutory regulations specifying the minimum 'down-payment' and the maximum period of repayment. In July 1954 the regulations were withdrawn and had to be re-enacted less than a year later when the first restrictive moves were made in February 1955. They were tightened in July and again in February 1956 and not removed until October 1958 although the terms for car purchase were relaxed in December 1956. Hire purchase finance companies were also subject to restrictions from 1945 until February 1959 in raising capital by public issues or from the banks but they could accept deposits made by the public and raise money in other ways.[2] The effect of the financial restrictions was probably to delay the spread of hire purchase; while the statutory terms, when imposed, limited spending on durable consumer goods, especially cars and furniture, and when removed produced a surge in demand. The order of magnitude of the effect on demand was probably of the order of £100–200 million.[3]

The Radcliffe Report, when it appeared, seemed to many readers to underrate the importance of monetary instruments. It emphasized the limited role of bank credit in the finance of economic activity and the need to take into account both other kinds of liquid asset than bank money and the operations of financial institutions other than banks. It regarded money itself as the most important of liquid assets but attributed no unique significance to the stock of money. Control, it suggested, might have to extend in emergency beyond the banks to other financial institutions. It should operate on interest rates; and there should be a more deliberate 'change of gear' from time to time at the longer end of the market instead of changes confined exclusively to the shorter end. In a concluding chapter it suggested that monetary policy should be considered by a joint committee of the Bank and the Treasury. While this was not pursued in the form in which it was expressed, it did lead to closer co-operation between the two bodies and to representation of the Bank on key Treasury committees.

The report was more significant for the controversy that followed than for any action on its recommendations. Monetary policy acquired a new prominence and within a few years new and radical ideas very different from those in the report were spreading rapidly.

Rearmament

A month after the invasion of South Korea in June 1950 all NATO countries were asked by the United States to say what additional military expenditure they proposed to undertake on their own and what larger programme would be physically possible with American help. The British government, conscious of the dangers of the situation, was anxious to offer support to the Americans and, as by far the strongest military power among the Western European members of NATO, to give a lead to its continental neighbours in mounting an immediate effort of rearmament. The Cabinet was advised that it would be possible to add £1100 million to the programme for the three financial years 1951−4 which earlier in the year had stood at £2300 million. Rearmament on that scale, however, carried obvious dangers to the balance of the economy, and especially to the balance of payments. The government was unwilling to commit itself to so large a programme without an assurance of American financial assistance. Such assurances had been received informally and the Cabinet assumed that at least the balance of payments effects of rearmament would be underwritten. They decided to bear half the additional cost (i.e. £550 million) leaving £550 million to come in balance of payments support over the three year period.

The Cabinet's assumption proved to be unwarranted. As the winter went on, the rearmament programme continued to expand, reaching a total in excess of £5000 million by January, while the prospect of balance of payments aid faded gradually away. Meanwhile rearmament in America and elsewhere was driving up commodity prices and adding greatly to Britain's import bill while at the same time Marshall Aid to Britain was being brought to an end in December because Congress could see no justification for continuing to make payments to a country whose dollar reserves were increasing − a view that paid no regard to the fact that the rise was largely the result of deposits by countries in the sterling area and might be followed by withdrawals in subsequent years when commodity prices were less high.

In spite of their fears for the balance of payments, the Cabinet not only maintained the new defence programme but raised it, first to £3600 million at the end of August and then, after Attlee's visit to Washington in December, when Truman appeared to be threatening the use of the atomic bomb against China, to £4700 million in January. By this time the programme had expanded above the original £780 million per annum to a peak of £1780 million in 1953−4 and in the three financial years from 1951 amounted to an extra £2300 million instead of the original offer of £550 million from British resources. American aid was no longer in prospect in bilateral terms but was to be shared out among all NATO members and was likely to consist almost entirely of military equipment.

A programme on this scale in an economy with a national income of not much over £10,000 million meant a considerable upheaval. The economy was already under strain, with unemployment about 250,000 and falling, serious shortages of raw materials including coal and steel, and sharply rising import prices. The pressure was at its greatest in the metal and engineering industries which accounted for 40 per cent of total British exports and about half of fixed capital investment. It was proposed to double the output of this sector of industry in 1951−2 and double it again in the next two years. Such a pace of expansion could not fail to have damaging repercussions on exports and fixed investment. It was estimated that at least a third of the motor-car industry would have to switch to defence work. The building work to be done would require a work force half as large as the housing programme. Expenditure on clothing and textiles by the military would expand sevenfold.

In facing such a tremendous task, the United Kingdom had at least the consolation of starting with a surplus in its balance of payments. The reserves continued to mount until the middle of 1951 when they stood at nearly three times the level to which they had fallen on 18 September 1949 when the pound was devalued. But in the next nine months they fell by over £2000 million, giving rise to a crisis in February 1952 as severe as that preceding devaluation. The balance of payments swung from a surplus of £300 million in 1950 to a deficit of £370 million in 1951 largely under the influence of a shift in the terms of trade. By June 1951 import prices had risen by 60 per cent in eighteen months while export prices were up by only 26 per cent. The swing from surplus to deficit cast a heavy burden on the consumer who had to pay the higher import prices out of an income that moved with export prices. In addition, as the boom in world industrial production gathered momentum in 1950, with a rise of 13 per cent over the previous year, physical shortages of raw materials multiplied, creating bottlenecks and limiting production. At the same time the rise in the cost of living drove the TUC to call off the wage freeze to which they had agreed after devaluation; and as the cost of living increased with the rise in import prices the danger of a wage–price spiral intensified.

All this made the shape of the 1951 budget a matter of great complexity. There was no point in raising taxes if this released resources where they were not needed; and, as we have seen, rearmament pressed hard only on a rather limited group of industries. The swing in the balance of payments was also likely to make available substantial additional resources. On the other hand, the consumer would be grappling with the rising cost of living and in his capacity as taxpayer would not welcome further imposts.

Gaitskell decided to limit the increase in taxation to £150 million, and to take credit for a release of £400 million in resources through the swing in the balance of payments, the last £100 million being offset through the accumulation of a strategic stockpile of materials. He also took credit for a 4 per cent rise in industrial productivity in spite of the accumulating shortages and bottlenecks. Included in his measures was a proposal to levy a charge on false teeth and spectacles so as to raise £13 million (£23 million in a full year) – a proposal reflecting the concern of the Treasury at the continuing rise in the cost of the National Health Service. This proposal was resisted by the Minister of Labour, Aneurin Bevan, the architect of the National Health Service, who insisted on the inviolability of a free National Health Service and resigned shortly after the Budget, arguing that to depart from that principle for a mere £13 million was 'the economics of Bedlam' and that in any event shortages of one kind or another would effectively prevent the fulfilment of the defence programme for which the budget provided.

Bevan's resignation was followed by that of Harold Wilson, President of the Board of Trade, and a junior minister, John Freeman. These resignations seriously weakened the Labour government, which had already lost Cripps through ill health and Bevin through death, and contributed to its downfall six months later.

That the defence programme would prove unattainable had always been on the cards. Not only were there design and production difficulties and shortages of materials and machine tools. It became necessary also to make cuts so as to allow exports to expand more rapidly. In 1951–2 over three-quarters of the shortfall of about £120 million was in metal products and in 1952–3 the revised programme fell £200 million short of what had originally been projected.

Rearmament seems to have reached its peak in 1952 at a level well below – at least £500 million below – the level planned in January 1951 but two-thirds or more above the pre-Korea level. Production for defence expanded in a larger proportion. A picture of the changes in metal goods over the three years 1950–2 is given in table 3.2, and shows that defence production more than doubled but that this was accomplished with an expansion of less than 7 per cent in the total production of metal goods without any curtailment in the various other uses except for a slight fall in investment. Passenger cars and metal consumer goods for the home market expanded a little and so, too, did exports and miscellaneous industrial goods.

Rearmament in Britain probably did less harm to the economy than the rise in import prices and shortages of raw materials re-

Table 3.2 Supplies and uses of metal goods, 1950–1953
(£ million at 1951 factory prices)

	1950	1951	1952	1953
Supplies				
Production	3125	3350	3335	3425
Imports	65	80	110	95
	3190	3430	3445	3520
Uses				
Defence	185	275	410	460
Exports	1000	1050	1010	975
Investment	965	985	940	960
Other industrial goods, repair work, etc.	735	790	745	710
Passenger cars for home market	65	65	95	150
Consumer goods for home market	240	265	245	265

Source: *Economic Survey 1953* and *1954*

sulting from rearmament elsewhere. It was these factors that caused inflation, made it necessary to renew or extend physical controls and gave rise to a major balance of payments crisis. A rise in import prices of over 50 per cent between 1949 and 1951 was the main factor behind a 13 per cent increase in retail prices and a 72 per cent increase in the import bill (although the 1949 devaluation contributed to both). Controls were revived to handle the situation. Many of these took the form of allocations of scarce materials: sulphur, zinc and copper were made available in relation to consumption in a base period. The use of other materials – aluminium, nickel and timber – was restricted. Some firms supplying the home market (e.g. with radios) were obliged to change over to defence orders or release labour for work elsewhere. Price controls were re-imposed. Hire purchase restrictions were used for the first time. But the main control was quantitative restriction of imports, the balance of payments deficit being the most urgent and important threat to be countered. Import cuts totalling £600 million were made in three successive batches: in November 1951, January 1952 and March 1952. These did not have much effect until well into 1952 when they were reinforced by a minor recession. It has been estimated that of the fall of £400 million in imports in 1952, £250 million can be attributed to the cuts.

Some writers have attributed a more decisive role to rearmament and have blamed it for a fatal check to the momentum of British recovery. On this view it marked the beginning of Britain's industrial decline, interrupting the export drive and the expansion in industrial investment. The check to the export drive is not in question since the volume of manufactured exports ceased to increase in 1951 and did not regain the 1950–1 level until 1955. It is true also that the progress of rearmament in 1951 coincided with a marked slowing down in industrial production. But the slowing down in 1952 affected all the leading industrial countries including Germany and Japan and was not confined to the United Kingdom. The check to exports was mainly in textiles, not engineering products, and within the engineering industries the impact of rearmament was highly concentrated on limited sectors, such as aircraft and shipbuilding, which could hardly claim to have suffered a loss of competitive power because of rearmament. The difficulties in finding markets experienced by British industry after 1952 can more plausibly be ascribed to the ending of the post-war seller's market and the re-entry of Germany and Japan into world markets. Yet even in 1955, ten years after the war, British exports were almost as large in volume as the combined exports of Germany and Japan.

Domestic policy after 1952

Economic recovery from the shallow depression in 1952 was rapid. But in 1953 there were still fears of a deep depression sooner or later in the United States and doubts as to what if anything would take over as the driving force in the economy in succession to rearmament and the housing boom. Macmillan had succeeded in getting over 300,000 houses built in 1953 (involving an investment two-thirds higher at current prices than in 1951) but no appreciable further increase in housebuilding was expected thereafter. At the end of 1953 the United States was entering a recession and nobody quite knew how deep it would go. Industrial investment, moreover, seemed to be lagging behind just when it was of the greatest importance that it should be expanded in the interests of providing additional capacity and maintaining competitiveness. All these circumstances pointed to a need for some fresh stimulus to the economy, and in particular to industrial investment, in order to maintain demand. The Treasury estimated that there was capacity in the economy for an extra £1000 million in output but that at most only £400 million was likely to be added in 1953.

The Chancellor was unwilling to make any reductions in taxation, especially as the Inland Revenue were warning him of a likely budget deficit ('above the line') of over £50 million and a possible £300 million deficit in 1955–6. He and some of his advisers appeared to interpret this as implying that the country was on the verge of ruin. It turned out, however, that the Inland Revenue were using forecasts that assumed a serious depression in the United States that never happened. At the end of the financial year, there was a budget surplus of £433 million instead of the surplus of £10 million that had been budgeted. Output increased by £600 million rather than £400 million. And manufacturing investment, although lagging badly, was just about to increase by 50 per cent over the next four years.

Before the 1954 Budget the Chancellor was persuaded, against strong opposition from the Inland Revenue, to introduce a new provision designed to encourage investment by allowing firms to add to the depreciation of their assets an 'investment allowance' or tax credit which would allow them to debit against their profits for tax purposes more than the original cost of the assets they acquired. The investment allowance had a chequered life. It was withdrawn in 1956 when demand was excessive and reinstated in 1959. In the 1960s it was again withdrawn and replaced for a time by an investment grant.

It was about this time that the idea of economic growth began to take hold. The Treasury undertook a review of the policies appropriate to promoting growth and the problems that would arise as the national income increased. The Chancellor, at the Conservative Party conference in 1953 held out a vision of a doubling of incomes in twenty-five years. Not that the idea was a novel one. As soon as there was reasonable stability of employment, attention was bound to focus on growth, all the more because regular statistics of national income and annual estimates of the change in productivity showed it to be in progress. There had even been, in the days of Stafford Cripps, a campaign to raise productivity and promote economic growth involving government-sponsored visits of selected teams to the United States to see for themselves how higher productivity could be achieved. Not much came of these visits, or of the Chancellor's appeals for a joint effort by employers and employed to increase output. Labour productivity rose, year by year, at a rate that showed little variation from 2 per cent per annum.

Nor did much come from the discussion of growth over the next ten years, whether by economists, officials or politicians. The economists talked too exclusively in terms of 'warranted rates of growth' (as if there were some equilibrium rate that could be reached by macro-economic planning) or of the incremental capital-output ratio (as if growth responded predictably to changes in the input of capital, regardless of other factors). Little thought was given to the factors governing the rate of technical progress and conditioning the commercial introduction of improved products and processes. Officials tended to concentrate either on encouraging investment or on the obstacles to growth that were so difficult to remove. Politicians were inclined to exaggerate the contribution of government to fast rates of growth; and, in looking abroad for explanations of other countries' success, tended to fasten on those countries such as France where they saw in a published plan (rarely fulfilled in detail and postulating no acceleration in the average rate of growth achieved in the past) the presumed source of current performance.

Concern with growth and fascination with economic planning developed over the 1950s but had not got far in 1953. It was only after years of faster growth on the continent and the gradual overtaking of British levels of performance that the country woke up to its comparative failure and looked to government for remedies.

Production expanded rapidly from 1953 to 1955 (see figure 3.1). The labour market grew increasingly tight – as tight as it had been in 1951, with unemployment falling to 1 per cent by July 1955 – and as the pressure mounted the danger of inflation rose with it. The rise in consumer prices, which had slowed down

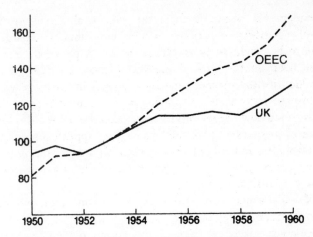

Figure 3.1 Industrial production in the UK and OEEC (Continent only), 1950–1960
Source: National Institute *Economic Review*, March 1961; OEEC *General Statistics*, 1962

from $9\frac{1}{2}$ per cent in 1951 to 2 per cent in 1953 and 1954, quickened to $3\frac{1}{2}$ per cent in 1955 and over $4\frac{1}{2}$ per cent in 1956 (see figure 3.2). For this speeding up, import prices were not to blame: they lagged well behind. But wage rates had begun to accelerate. After moderate increases in 1953 and 1954 the pace quickened to $4\frac{1}{2}$ per cent in 1955 and 8 per cent in 1956. These were high but not unprecedented rates. What made the difference in 1956–7 was that the inflation seemed to be wage-driven and that it was accelerating.

Behind the inflation lay excess demand, for which no single factor was to blame, but which had been fed by expanding bank credit and exacerbated by a cut in income tax in the 1955 budget. Since 1955 was an election year it was not altogether surprising that little had been done to check the boom until after the election in May. Bank rate had been raised twice at the beginning of the year, but no higher than $4\frac{1}{2}$ per cent, and hire purchase restrictions had been introduced in February. Thereafter government action was expansionary until the beginning of the credit squeeze in July and a year later unemployment was still no higher than 1.2 per cent.

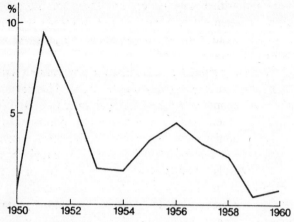

Figure 3.2   Increase in consumer prices in the UK, 1950–1960
Source: C. H. Feinstein. (1972)

In 1956, when Macmillan was Chancellor, a sustained attempt
was made to talk industry into holding prices stable and to persuade employers and unions into accepting moderate settlements.
Neither effort succeeded. The trade union leaders knew that it
was hopeless to stand against their members in campaigning for
moderate settlements when the shortage of labour was so acute.
If one union won a large increase from an employer desperate to
retain his workforce, others would find it difficult to hold back.
The employers also found it difficult to maintain a united front.
Employers in the private sector felt let down by the public sector
and vice versa. A price 'plateau' was held to for a time but was
never more than a short-term expedient. It would have required
a sustained political campaign aimed at changing public attitudes
and driving home the virtual impossibility of preserving full employment in the absence of stable wages and prices before public
opinion could be brought to bear with any real hope of success.
The government made a beginning, issuing a White Paper on
Economic Implications of Full Employment that had been under
preparation for years. They held meetings with different groups

of employers and with union leaders but there was no coherent strategy or clear statement of policy. In the end wage settlements became more moderate for the usual reason: the pressure in the labour market fell away.

In 1957 the feeling gained ground that the government had lost control of inflation and had given up the fight. This may seem strange when the economy was in fact beginning to cool off; but it was an attitude evident in the autumn when the pound weakened in spite of a substantial current surplus. In the third quarter of the year the reserves fell by over £500 million, largely because of capital withdrawals. These were occasioned by uncertainty over international currency relationships, aggravated by what amounted to a devaluation of the French franc and expectations of a revaluation of the dentsche mark (which, however, proved to be without foundation). Against this background the Chancellor, now Thorneycroft, decided on firm action. He was disturbed by the constant insistence of departments on the need for higher expenditure and induced the Prime Minister to issue a directive to ministers requiring them to keep their current civil expenditure in 1958–9 within the limits of the previous year's figure. He also asked his colleagues to refrain from increases in public investment while the position was reviewed.

What Thorneycroft, backed by the Prime Minister, was aiming for was a reduction in the pressure for higher wages without having to face a succession of costly strikes. He had in mind a rise in unemployment to 2–3 per cent and thought that this could be brought about if the money supply were held steady. But although Thorneycroft kept talking about money what he tried to do in practice was to limit *demand*, whether in the form of current public expenditure, public investment or bank-financed private sector expenditure. It would have been a more accurate expression of his ideas if he had spoken of limiting money GNP.

What he asked Cabinet to agree to, a standstill on government current expenditure having already been approved, was a limitation of public investment to £1500 million in the next two financial years, whatever the movement in prices, and a cut of 5 per cent in bank advances below the level in 1957–8. He would have liked also to reintroduce building controls and to tighten hire purchase restrictions but dropped both of these proposals when other ministers opposed them. At the last moment, when speculative pressure developed against the pound after the devaluation of the franc on 10 August, he added to the measures to be announced on 19 September an increase in bank rate to 7 per cent (the highest level since 1921). This, however, was coincidental. The measures represented a clear change of priorities: a willingness to sacrifice employment for the sake of price stability.

It was not a well considered strategy. Deflationary measures might reduce wage claims eventually but they were not very likely to have much effect over the winter. On the other hand, unemployment would be sure to increase and there was no guarantee that it would stop increasing when it reached 2−3 per cent; or that that would be enough to put a stop to inflation, or that the government would stand up to the political consequences of the measures when they had so often failed to stand up to far smaller cuts in expenditure.

Before these uncertainties could be resolved Thorneycroft had resigned. As the year ended, the Treasury sought to bring down the estimates, swollen by the entry into the national insurance scheme of a large block of pensioners, by £150 million. They expected to squeeze out £40 million and the Chancellor insisted on the remainder being shared equally between welfare and defence services. The Cabinet succeeded in putting together half the total required but could make no progress with the other half. Thorneycroft, together with the two junior Treasury ministers, Nigel Birch and Enoch Powell, having taken a stand on a point of principle, resigned.

Soon after Amory took over the Chancellorship, there were signs that industrial production was turning down. The new Chancellor, however, was anxious to avoid anything suggesting a sudden change of policy and allowed bank rate to remain at 7 per cent throughout the winter. It was reduced to 6 per cent in March and then in stages to 4 per cent in November where it remained until January 1960. Meanwhile industrial production fell throughout the first year after the September measures and unemployment kept increasing.

The 1958 budget made only modest reductions in taxation amounting in all to about £50 million in the current financial year. Until the main wage settlements were out of the way, the government was unwilling to take expansionary action and continued to give price stability precedence over full employment. The Prime Minister, it is true, had wanted to see income tax reduced in the Budget but was persuaded to wait by the Chancellor who was more in fear of inflationary wage settlements that would call for further deflationary action.

The first expansionary moves were taken in June and July with an amendment to the Finance Bill raising initial allowances, a small increase in public investment, and the removal of the ceiling on bank advances. The Chancellor was advised that the recession was likely to be short lived, since it was largely the product of a decline in the rate of stockbuilding, and was averse to spending commitments that might still be pre-empting capacity after the economy had already recovered. He was willing, however, to take quick acting measures that would stimulate consumption and began by relaxing hire purchase restrictions in September.

By the beginning of October Ministers who had been invited a year before to approve measures calculated to produce $2-3$ per cent unemployment were in something bordering on panic when unemployment did in fact approach 2 per cent. The Chancellor took note of the anxieties of his colleagues who feared that unemployment might reach 750,000 in the spring and reminded them that eight separate expansionary moves had already been taken. It was in fact clear by October that unemployment, seasonally corrected, was levelling off and production had also touched bottom. The Prime Minister, however, was more 'in fear of the slump coming' than of another boom and called for prompt measures to expand demand. Hire purchase restrictions were completely withdrawn; and in spite of the Chancellor's warnings against longer-term commitments further increases in public investment were approved in November and February.

Although unemployment was already beginning to decline in the first quarter of 1959 further expansionary measures were taken in the budget. Apart from the increases in public expenditure already sanctioned, tax concessions amounting to £360 million in a full year were made and post-war credits of £71 million were released. An overall budget deficit of £730 million was projected − a larger deficit and more powerful stimulus to the economy than any since the war.

The outcome was a rapid expansion of production and increase in pressure. Between October 1958 and October 1959 industrial production rose by over 10 per cent while unemployment fell by 100,000. There may have been some expectation that the shedding of labour in 1958 would represent a 'shake-out of labour', leaving a correspondingly large margin of capacity. But it soon proved that the margin was a limited one. After a further rise in production in the two concluding months of 1959, there was little or no perceptible increase in 1960 although unemployment fell by another 50,000. It continued to fall during the first half of 1961 until it reached the level (1.3 per cent) from which it had begun to climb in September 1957. Meanwhile the current account of the balance of payments deteriorated year by year from a satisfactory surplus of £350 million in 1958 (the best performance since well before the war) to a deficit of £237 million in 1960. Restrictive measures had again to be taken. Bank rate was put up in January 1960 and again in June; and the new expedient of special deposits was brought into use first in April along with hire purchase restrictions and then in June. These did not prevent an increase in pressure on resources as measured by the rate of unemployment although production remained sluggish. But confidence in sterling fell away in 1961, especially after the revaluation of the dentsche mark in March and the currency speculation that followed, and a fresh balance of payments crisis developed in the early summer.

Incomes policy

 The Conservative party was never able to obtain the agreement of the trade unions, as Cripps and Bevin had done, to a period of wage restraint. They were willing to appeal for moderation but without much expectation of success. By about 1953 the wage round, in which wage settlements occurred in one industry after another on an annual footing and largely in the summer months, had become something of a national institution.[4] At the same time the pace of wage inflation quickened and it came to be seen as a long-term problem, distinct to some extent from the problem of excess demand.

In 1956, as we have seen, Ministers embarked on a campaign for greater moderation, without being at all precise as to how they wanted negotiators to act, and held a series of meetings with the unions and with employers in the private sector and the nationalized industries. The meetings were chaired by the Prime Minister, Eden, but failed to have the impact intended, at least as far as the unions were concerned. Later in the year, Macmillan, Chancellor in 1956, hoped to be allowed to address the TUC at its September conference but had to content himself with a press conference a few days earlier. He pointed out that since 1953 wages and output per man had risen *pari passu* in Germany and America while in Britain wages had risen twice as fast as output per head. In the years since 1951 wages in Britain had gone up by 40 per cent and retail prices by considerably less – 24 per cent.[5]

At the conference the general secretary of the TUC (Tewson) responded by pointing out, quite reasonably, that the job of the TUC was merely to co-ordinate the policies of autonomous unions and that it had no power to impose a policy on its members which they did not approve. After a less measured speech by Frank Cousins, the newly elected general secretary of the Transport and General Workers Union, Congress carried, 'with a great roar of approval', a resolution that flatly rejected the Chancellor's appeal for restraint.[6]

This and other incidents led the government to conclude that the need for wage restraint was little understood and that it should be driven well home so as to make sure of public support before any fresh appeal was made to the unions. There had been little insistence since the 1945 White Paper on the link between full employment and 'moderation in wage matters'. Nor had there been much emphasis on the line taken by Cripps that if prices were to be kept stable money wages should rise no faster than productivity.

A Court of Inquiry in May 1956 had appealed, in the light of the difficulties faced by independent experts asked to make arbitration awards, for 'some authoritative and impartial body' that could provide general guidance on the making of such awards. This idea was adopted and a Council for Prices Productivity and Incomes (COPPI) was appointed in July 1957 by the Chancellor. It was originally intended that it should include representatives of employers and employed but as appointed it consisted of three independent members of whom one, Sir Dennis Robertson, was an economist, and another, the chairman, was a lawyer.

It was not a success. The committee's first report, issued in February 1958, was written largely under the influence of Sir Dennis Robertson, and antagonized the trade unions. It regarded the deflationary measures of September 1957 as 'justified and indeed overdue' and argued that 'a free and flexible economic system [cannot] work efficiently without a perceptible . . . margin of unemployment'. Inflation should be not only slowed down but stopped; and indeed the level of prices ought perhaps to decline gradually as productivity increased. On the key issue of wage restraint, it was unwilling to suggest a so-called 'guiding light', i.e. a percentage by which average money wages might be increased without damage to the national interest, but hoped that the increase in 1958 would be 'substantially below the average of the last few years'. An increase of $4\frac{1}{2}$ per cent, equalling the rise in retail prices in 1957, would exceed the rate of growth of productivity, produce an upward pressure on prices and weaken the competitive position of British exports. But the report abstained from giving a specific figure.

From the perspective of the 1990s the argument of the report expressed defensible aspirations and many of its propositions were to be reiterated in later years. But it went too far to have any hope of persuading the unions. Three further reports were issued at increasing intervals, but the council was boycotted by the unions and was wound up in 1961. By that time the entire membership had changed and the council had ceased to command the public attention with which it began. The appearance of the fourth and final report coincided with Selwyn Lloyd's statement on 25 July 1961 which opened an entirely new chapter in incomes policy.

Foreign economic policy

The balance of trade

Foreign trade had been dominated after the war by import controls on the one hand and the export drive on the other.

The import controls took the form initially of government buying or import licensing or, increasingly, of quotas limiting the quantity that could be imported and specifying the source. The export drive involved preferential supply of scarce materials for use in exports, limitation of production for the home market, backed in some cases by high taxation of domestic sales, and agreements with enterprises in particular trades as to the priority to be given to exports. When balance was restored in the current account in 1948 these controls continued because of the need to conserve dollars. Trade and payments agreements were made with other countries that allowed a surplus or deficit in bilateral trade within credit limits in both directions, settlement in gold or dollars being confined to swings in the balance beyond these limits. The balances that came into existence in this way in one currency could only be converted into balances in another country by administrative agreement unless there was provision, as within the sterling area, for free convertibility within agreed limits. Trade controls, in other words, were supplemented by exchange controls which multiplied international means of payment and atomized international trade.

By 1950 a beginning had been made with the freeing of trade from purely bilateral exchanges and with transferability from one currency to another. A major development was the formation of the European Payments Union which allowed all surpluses and deficits between member countries (including surpluses and deficits with the sterling area) to be set off against one another, leaving only the net balance to be settled with the union. The net balance was cumulative, so that at any time it represented the outcome of all surpluses and deficits since July 1950. Settlement, which was organized by the Bank for International Settlements in Basle, was on a monthly basis and was partly in gold and partly in credit from the Union. For debtors the proportion paid in gold increased gradually from zero up to 100 per cent when the debt exceeded the agreed limit of the country's quota. For creditors the proportion jumped from 0 to 50 per cent once the cumulative surplus reached 20 per cent of the creditor's quota. The object of these arrangements was to put increasing pressure on debtors to correct a persistent deficit and at the same time oblige creditors to make some credit available to their trading partners.

Earlier there had been a drive within the OEEC to raise the proportion of each country's trade that was liberalized, i.e. freed from quota restrictions; and until the rearmament crisis substantial progress had been made. There was a major setback in 1951–2 because of worldwide rearmament and it was only gradually that the move towards liberalization was resumed.

It must not be supposed that trade restrictions were quickly abandoned once rearmament had passed its peak. Some quota restrictions on dollar imports remained until nearly the end of 1959 – indeed, they outlived convertibility for a time. In 1955 even imports from other members of the OEEC were not completely free of quota, the percentage liberalized being held at 85 per cent for balance of payments reasons. Imports from the USSR, the Soviet bloc and China, as well as Japan, remained subject to licensing arrangements that included items such as tin, textiles and meat throughout the decade. Imports of bacon, ham and pork did not revert to private trade until 1956. There was a quota on imports of synthetic rubber until at least 1957. Coal imports were strictly controlled. The tourist allowance continued into the 1960s although by then it had reached £250 per annum.

Both the quota restrictions and the limited convertibility of European currencies in the EPU automatically involved discrimination against the United States. This discrimination was uncomplainingly accepted by the United States throughout the life of the EPU although it had a considerable impact on the dollar balance of payments of the OEEC countries and hence also of the USA. But once full convertibility was established, the United States, by that time in substantial deficit, felt a natural impatience at the discrimination which it continued to experience.

After 1952 the dollar shortage began to ease and the British balance of payments improved. The terms of trade, which had been the source of much of the trouble in 1951–2, moved back to the more favourable position of 1950 and the level of imports regained the 1951 level. The balance of payments, already in surplus in 1952 when the economy was under less pressure, remained in current surplus in 1953–4 and the reserves began to increase at a fairly satisfactory rate (see figure 3.3).

All this disposed the government to relax or abandon physical

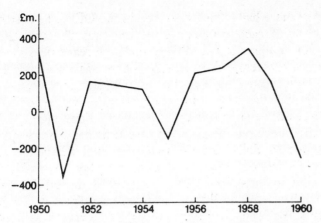

Figure 3.3 Balance of payments on current account, 1950–1960
Source: Economic Trends Annual Supplement 1990

controls over imports and exports. After 1952 there was no further attempt to make extensive use of quotas as a means of overcoming balance of payments difficulties. There were times, as in October 1964, when a new government contemplated introducing quota restrictions as an alternative to a 15 per cent surcharge on manufactured imports; and, as in 1976, when protection was urged as a remedy for unemployment and a balance of payments deficit. What restrictions were used at other times were essentially protectionist and not prompted by a balance of payments crisis. The Tories were determined after 1952 to avoid the wholesale use of quotas if only because it would have invited retaliation and was not in keeping with the movement of opinion in the OEEC.

But if quotas were ruled out, how was the balance of payments to be kept stable? There was no wish to vary the exchange rate, especially after a major devaluation, and the government had few ways of operating quickly on competitive power. When a deficit arose there were two main possibilities: attracting capital from abroad by raising interest rates and reducing the pressure of demand in the domestic market. Borrowing was likely to be a short-term device, since an accumulation of debt – particularly short-term debt – tended to make holders of sterling nervous of ultimate devaluation. But it was capable of meeting a temporary imbalance over a year or two and bank rate was in practice used from time to time for this purpose. The alternative of reducing demand pressure amounted to a deliberate sacrifice of potential output in unemployment and impoverishment so as to cut expenditure on imports and free resources for possible use in exports. But if the source of the deficit was rising labour costs there might be no other way of restoring competitive power through more moderate wage-settlements unless these could be achieved through some form of incomes policy.

The use of the second device was almost inescapable in an economy where unemployment could sink as low as 1 per cent and up to one-third of economic activity was tied to markets abroad. In 1955–7 and again in 1960–1 when inflationary pressure produced a balance of payments deficit and an acceleration in money wages it was necessary to check demand in what was derided as 'stop-go'. What was not recognized was that similar, and often larger, fluctuations were taking place in other European countries where the pressure was also intense but the underlying rate of growth was faster so that when production slowed down it did not, as in Britain, cease to increase.

The checks to expansion in Britain tended to be the more severe because of the low level of exchange reserves. These never exceeded 4 billion dollars in the 1950s and were, for most of the time, between 2 and 3 billion, whereas liquid liabilities, the sterling balances held by other countries, never fell much below 4 billion. It required only a limited withdrawal of these balances to make serious inroads into the reserves and alarm other holders. Measured against the level of imports, the reserves were equally inadequate. Reserves averaging about 2.5 million dollars and showing no distinct upward trend were not much more than enough to pay for three months imports in the first half of the decade and less than enough in the second half.

This comparison, however, understates the position: for the United Kingdom's reserves were the gold and dollar reserves of the entire sterling area, and the outer sterling area could on occasion – as in the second half of 1951 – run a large deficit with non-members of the area and draw on the gold and dollar pool in London. The normal position was that the United Kingdom, while in deficit with non-sterling countries, was in substantial surplus with the outer sterling area, which in turn was in surplus with non-sterling countries. The United Kingdom's surplus with sterling area countries could be settled either in gold and dollars by countries with a dollar surplus like Malaysia, or by drawing on sterling balances, or (since these balances constituted a large part of the reserves of the outer sterling area and were drawn upon rather reluctantly) out of capital lent or invested by the United Kingdom. This capital outflow, like all capital flows within the sterling area, was not subject to exchange control although borrowing in the London market required official sanction. In a year like 1953 over £100 million was raised in this way apart from grants to the colonies and in 1954 over £200 million.[7] Part of this total represented inter-government loans or credits extended through the Export Credits Guarantee Department but there was also substantial private investment, for example by the oil companies on refinery construction in Aden, Australia and India.[8]

The dependence of the outer sterling area on these capital flows meant that it might be difficult to enlarge Britain's current account surplus with the members of the area without additional investment; and if the object of enlarging the surplus was to permit a much-needed addition to the reserves there could be no guarantee that, if achieved, a larger surplus with the sterling area would have that effect. Since the sterling area accounted for about half Britain's trade, it might seem as if the only way of adding to the reserves was through a larger surplus on the other half. This would, however, be going too far since British exports to the sterling area might displace imports costing dollars; and reduced purchases by Britain from the sterling area might free commodities for sale in dollar markets.

These complications did not deter the Treasury from advancing a balance of payments target of £350 million in 1953 and increasing it to £450 million in 1958.[9] The targets may have expressed a recognition of need both for more reserves and for more freedom of manoeuvre and higher external investment. But the targets were never met except possibly in 1958; and it would not appear that those who argued in the Treasury for a consistently lower pressure of demand ever had much success except with Thorneycroft. Even Amory who was set on avoiding a recrudescence of the boom of the mid 1950s was unsuccessful. The higher target set in 1958 had no perceptible influence in the 1960s.

The volume of trade expanded relatively slowly. Between 1950 and 1960 exports increased by only 21 per cent when the rate of increase per annum between 1946 and 1950 had been 15 per cent. The sterling area continued to provide the most important markets: but over the ten years the proportion of exports sold there declined from 47 per cent to 39 per cent while sales to Western Europe rose from 26 per cent to 29 per cent and to the United States from 11 to 16 per cent. These were trends that were to become more marked in the 1960s.

At the same time the United Kingdom's share of a rapidly expanding volume of world trade was declining rapidly. In 1948 over 29 per cent of world trade in manufactures was supplied by British exports; in 1950 25.4 per cent; in 1960 16.3 per cent. The long decline in Britain's position as the world's leading exporter was already far advanced.

Robot and convertibility

After the devaluation of 1949 there was at first some doubt whether the devaluation would succeed. In the course of 1950, however, the balance of payments improved, thanks in part to the recovery of America from the brief recession of 1949. As commodity prices rose with rearmament, the primary producers of the outer sterling area paid their inflated export earnings into the central reserves. This gave rise to proposals for a revaluation of sterling as a protection against imported inflation, or alternatively to let the pound float, but after debate within the Treasury in the spring of 1951 the Chancellor decided to take no action. Two factors in this decision were an expected deterioration in the balance of payments later in the year and the recognition that revaluation would bring pressure for a relaxation of the restrictions on dollar imports.

The deterioration was not long in coming. The balance in gold and dollars which had been in surplus in the first half of the year plunged into heavy deficit in the second half and looked like continuing in deficit in 1952. The United Kingdom was also in deficit with the other members of the European Payments Union and was likely to have to meet the whole of any deficit from March 1952 in gold and dollars. There seemed every prospect of an exchange crisis in the spring.

Meanwhile a Conservative government had been elected in November. One of its first acts was to raise bank rate from 2 to $2\frac{1}{2}$ per cent, the first increase since 1932 apart from a flutter in September 1939. The Bank of England had pressed Gaitskell for a rise in bank rate on several occasions without success but the new government was determined to make full use of monetary weapons. It also introduced import restrictions planned by the outgoing Labour administration, began to talk of 'freeing the pound' and discussed without accepting, as an ultimate aim, 'total convertibility [of sterling] based, not on fixed rates of exchange, but on flexible and variable exchanges'.

The theme of convertibility recurred throughout the 1950s but it was not until the end of 1958 that the United Kingdom, in common with other members of the EPU, were able to introduce it. For all their talk of convertibility, Conservative ministers had no wish to abandon dollar discrimination but other members of the sterling area were less anxious to retain it. At a Conference of Commonwealth Finance Ministers in January 1952, each member was invited to live 'within its means' even if this meant — as it did in the case of Australia — making large cuts in imports from the United Kingdom that would do little to improve the balance of payments of the sterling area as a whole. Concerted action was to be taken to eliminate the deficit with the non-sterling world by the second half of 1951, mainly through the use of further import restrictions.

Since the United Kingdom accounted for nearly £600 million out of the sterling area's deficit of £750 million in the second half of 1951 it was clearly required to take the lead in the effort to restore balance. In addition to repeated import cuts and a tightening of credit, the government introduced hire purchase restrictions, cut fixed investment and the defence estimates and prepared for a severe budget. More far-reaching proposals were also advanced. The Treasury and the Bank of England prepared a scheme, code-named Robot, for announcement in the budget speech on 4 March, to fund or block sterling balances, allow full convertibility for externally held sterling, and let the pound float against other currencies. It was also proposed to abandon discrimination between non-sterling sources throughout the sterling area and to introduce exchange control on capital movements to sterling area countries (a measure ultimately taken in 1972).

The supporters of the scheme despaired of maintaining the existing parity for lack of adequate reserves and thought it better to float at once than run the risk of having to devalue twice. They also counted on the goodwill of the United States and Canada as protagonists of convertibility and the support of sterling area countries like South Africa and Ceylon which chafed at the burden of inconvertibility. Convertibility, however, would not extend to individual residents of the sterling area but would be confined to the monetary authorities of sterling area countries in transactions with non-residents either in unblocked sterling balances or new sterling earned abroad.

An argument to which the Bank of England attached great importance was that 'cheap (inconvertible) sterling' was being used on a large scale by competitors of Britain to purchase raw materials and pay for services abroad while British manufacturers had to procure similar materials and services at the official rate. There was also extensive transhipment of goods acquired for use in sterling markets to markets willing to pay in dollars. The turnover in cheap sterling in the New York market – which was by no means the only one – was estimated at between £¼ million and £1 million per week and the total loss to the reserves might be as high as £80 million per annum. But if there was a leakage of dollars through the control, would the disappearance of import restrictions and dollar discrimination bring any less outflow if it were necessary to balance accounts in a world of convertible currencies?

There were serious objections to the proposals, not least the limited time in which to decide on all aspects of them. To let the pound float was in flat contravention of the articles of the IMF which was also bound to oppose the further proposal to reopen the London gold market and allow sales at a premium. There was an incompatibility also with the partial convertibility of the EPU which was likely to be destroyed by the move. Since countries earning a surplus in sterling would become free to convert it into dollars there was a strong incentive to discriminate against the United Kingdom on the same basis as against the United States. Above all, the pound was likely to drop steeply with the suspension of dollar discrimination, prices would become more unstable and unemployment would increase.

After long debate, extending over two days, the Prime Minister ruled against proceeding with the plan and the Chancellor was left to introduce a package of more traditional measures focusing on import restrictions and including both a further rise in bank rate to 4 per cent and a substantial cut in food subsidies. Contrary to the predictions of the sponsors of the plan, it did prove possible to maintain a fixed rate of exchange and when the Budget proved to contain neither a devaluation of sterling nor a floating pound, confidence in sterling began to revive. By the last week in March the reserves had begun to increase and over the next six months they remained steady. The change in trend seems to have owed little to government measures and to have been largely a by-product of the inventory recession then in train. The accumulation of stocks which had been so prominent a feature of 1951 virtually ceased, import prices fell and the terms of trade improved. None of these changes, which helped to put an end to the crisis, were foreseen in February when disaster seemed so close.

The Robot proposal was not abandoned after the debate in Cabinet on February 28 and 29. Officials continued to urge convertibility on the Chancellor and the battle went on at the official level throughout March and April. The Governor kept pressing for 'a definite line of policy' and at the end of June predicted a renewed exchange crisis in August unless Robot was adopted at once. The scheme was considered again by ministers on 30 June. On this occasion the Chancellor was almost the sole supporter and the matter was not even put to Cabinet.

From then on until 1955 the original plan gave way to a modified scheme for the introduction of convertibility subject to a number of conditions and usually referred to as 'the collective approach'. It was no longer proposed to block sterling balances. Instead, a large support fund of $5000 million was to be raised, in order to supplement the reserves and the United States would be asked to provide it. At the same time 'good creditor policies' on the part of the United States were to be a precondition of convertibility.

As before, convertibility would be limited to non-residents and the pound would be allowed to float. The move to convertibility would be made in conjunction with the main European countries who would, of course, have to be consulted.

These proposals were given a lukewarm reception when put to a conference of Commonwealth officials in October 1952. There were many other plans in the air — for an Atlantic Payments Union including the United States, for a Sterling Union from which gold and dollar settlements would be banned, and for carrying on with no attempt at a 'decisive advance'. The sterling area countries had no enthusiasm for non-resident convertibility; and it soon proved that the Americans and continental Europe were equally unimpressed, disliking continuing discrimination in the one case and a floating pound in the other.

In the spring of 1953, after discussing the plan with Commonwealth Prime Ministers, Eden and Butler visited the United States to seek their support for an early move and for a US loan and IMF standby to provide the necessary finance. The Americans thought the move premature and could see no possibility of Congressional approval for a loan. The Europeans who had been kept in the dark while the discussions were in progress showed equally little enthusiasm when all was revealed. They had no wish to wind up the EPU, nor to abandon discrimination, nor to accept floating currencies.

Over the next two years no dramatic changes occurred, but the Bank of England took steps to unify all non-dollar, non-resident sterling within a single transferable account area so as to allow a regular market to develop in overseas countries in transferable sterling. The Bank envisaged fluctuations in the rate for transferable sterling a little below the official rate, with occasional intervention to narrow the spread between the two rates. Later an approach would be made to the IMF and the USA to seek approval for a widening of the spread in the official rate and an eventual coalescence of the official and transferable rates. This amounted to a proposal for de facto convertibility by another route, without fulfilment of the conditions governing 'the Collective Approach'.

The rates for transferable sterling were unified in March 1954 and in January 1955 the Governor sought approval for official intervention and a widening of the spread in both the official and transferable rates to $2.70 to $2.90. Since this involved no legal obligation to merge dollar and non-dollar accounts, the Governor claimed that it was not tantamount to convertibility: it was a move, he said, from 70 per cent to 80 per cent convertibility. The Treasury thought otherwise but failed to persuade the Chancellor. The Bank was given authority to intervene in the market for transferable sterling but not to widen the spread in the official rate. The result was that from 24 February 1955 sterling was convertible at a small discount and at a fixed, not a floating, rate.

The Bank continued to press for a widening of the spread and a unification of the official and transferable rates before the renewal of the EPU at mid-year. In this they were unsuccessful. The Chancellor had already promised, in addressing the OEEC, of which he was chairman, 'no early action on convertibility'. It had also been agreed that the EPU (which the Bank wanted to see wound up) should continue for another year unless countries accounting for half the total quotas made their currencies convertible. In the meantime a scheme for multilateral settlements after the termination of EPU was to be worked out; and for this purpose it would be necessary to state in Paris the limits within which sterling would be free to vary. Butler, after consulting officials, decided that there was no chance that a scheme for wider spreads would win international acceptance and thought it wiser to stick to the Collective Approach, moving forward gradually and tightening up the domestic economy which was then in high boom.

As the Governor foresaw, this led in the end to convertibility at a fixed rate which no one at that time wanted. The Chancellor, he thought, would be obliged to make a statement that no change was contemplated in exchange rate policy for some considerable time; and this is exactly what happened. Talk of a wider spread had got around, the balance of payments had weakened and there were rumours of an impending devaluation. In banking circles the impression spread that the Bank had secured agreement to what it had long proposed: convertibility with a floating pound. The Chancellor on 26 July repudiated any intention of floating or widening the spread. The exchange parity of $2.80 would be maintained before and after convertibility. Nevertheless, rumours of a devaluation persisted and the Governor himself maintained that within the next six months there would have to be either a convertibility operation or a devaluation. Neither occurred: but the Chancellor had to issue an even more emphatic denial at the IMF meeting in Istanbul in September.

Although the Governor argued year after year for unification of the official and transferable rates, and proposals for a floating rate or a wider spread were periodically revived, no further change took place until December 1958 when France and Germany both pressed for an early move for their own reasons, officials were already of the same view and ministers needed little persuasion. With convertibility there could be no justification for continuing discrimination against dollar imports but it was some time before the last traces of discrimination disappeared.

Relations with Europe

In 1950 Britain had joined the European Payments Union but declined to join the European Coal and Steel Community. Membership of the EPU continued until its dissolution but there were times, as in 1952, when policies were contemplated that were inconsistent with membership and might have broken up the Union. Joining the ECSC would have meant a surrender of sovereignty which Britain was not prepared to make although it hoped for close association with the Community and would have been willing to accept a scheme for the integration of the coal and steel industries of Western Europe subject to the retention of a power of veto by a Council of Ministers and the inclusion in the terms of reference of an injunction to pursue expansionary policies and not behave like a producers' cartel.

The Schuman Plan in which the ECSC originated represented a volte-face in French policy. Unable to prevent the recovery of Germany, with participation in the Marshall Plan and the institution in 1949 of a federal German government, the French decided to seek security in a partnership with the Germans in the rebuilding of the European economy. It was a partnership that could be shared with Germany's other neighbours, all lesser powers, but might have been disrupted by the adhesion of Britain with its involvement with the Commonwealth and other continents and continuing pretensions as a world power. As the Marshall Plan drew to an end there was a strong movement in favour of closer European integration which could be led successfully only by France. The OEEC, to which the British had devoted much effort, continued to function and at the end of the decade was reconstituted to include the United States and Canada. But the OEEC was primarily a consultative body and could not meet the aspirations of those who wanted a more permanent, political grouping based on the development of a common market.

The early 1950s in Europe were taken up with negotiations for a European Defence Community which to many seemed a more hopeful route to European integration. But with Britain holding aloof, nothing came of it. Instead, the six members of the ECSC moved on to proposals for a common market without specifying at first whether this would involve a customs union or a free trade area and without raising the issue of sovereignty. Their foreign secretaries met at Messina in June 1955 but no British minister attended and when inter-governmental negotiations began in Brussels the United Kingdom was again represented by an official who could make no commitments. There seems to have been no expectation in Whitehall that anything would come of the negotiations. When it became clear in 1956 that on the contrary they were likely to reach a successful conclusion, Britain put forward a proposal intended to prevent a final division between the six, united in a customs union, and the rest of OEEC.

The proposal (Plan G) was for a free trade area, to embrace the Six as a single unit and the other members of OEEC as individual countries. There was to be free trade in industrial products but for agriculture separate (unspecified) arrangements would be necessary; against other countries outside the area each country could maintain its own tariffs. In confining the free trade proposal to manufactures the British were seeking to maintain freedom of entry for Commonwealth foodstuffs whilst avoiding the need to surmount tariff walls in Europe against their manufactures.

The plan was considered in the OEEC by a working party under a Belgian chairman which reported in February 1957, a month before the signature of the Treaty of Rome which brought into existence the European Economic Community. Negotiations continued throughout the year and in October the Council of Ministers of the OEEC declared 'its determination to secure the establishment of a European Free Trade Area' that would 'in practice take effect in parallel with the Treaty of Rome'. A special committee of ministers, chaired by Reginald Maudling, was set up but after prolonged negotiations the French announced their rejection of the plan in November 1958, six weeks before the first tariff reductions within the European Economic Community came into effect.

Although the exclusion of agriculture was not the main reason for the failure of the negotiations since no member of the OEEC except Denmark wanted free trade in foodstuffs, it was clear that Britain could not have become party to arrangements acceptable to the other members without a major change in the treatment of Commonwealth producers. Some countries felt that Britain was trying to torpedo the Common Market or, if not to torpedo it, at least to dilute it by depriving it of its political raison d'être. Britain seemed to be asking for the best of both worlds as a member simultaneously of a Commonwealth preferential system and a European preferential system. The French in particular were afraid of having to face competition simultaneously from British and German producers without the protection to which they were accustomed. They wanted a share for Europe in the preferential arrangements of the Commonwealth; and they wanted to delay free trade on an industry by industry basis until competition in industries under pressure had been 'harmonized'. There were also difficulties over differences in external tariffs that would allow countries with low tariffs or none on raw materials to undersell their competitors within the Community.

With the breakdown of the negotiations, Britain and three Scandinavian countries, with the addition of Austria, Portugal and Switzerland, formed their own free trade association in 1959. These countries had worked closely together in 1958 in the later stages of the negotiations for a free trade area and the convention which they signed in November 1959 followed closely the lines of the original British proposal to the OEEC. Tariff cuts on their trade with other members were to begin with a 20 per cent cut on 1 July 1960 and to be followed by the removal of all tariffs on manufactured goods over a period of ten years. This was much the same time as the complete removal of tariffs in the EEC was likely to take.

Britain's refusal to take part in the negotiations for a European Coal and Steel Community was understandable and in keeping with popular sentiment. British interests lay far more heavily outside Europe than within it and the emphasis in British policy had been on international, not continental, arrangements. The ties with the Commonwealth and with the United States were much closer, and the trade much more extensive, than the bonds and trade between continental countries and the world outside Europe. The United Kingdom had made it a prime aim of policy after the war to keep the United States firmly attached to Europe in the interests of security and did not warm, as many Europeans did, to a Community from which the United States was excluded. The emphasis of British policy was throughout on an economic association but it did not regard this as a stepping-stone to political association and expected efforts to achieve some form of political union as likely to founder. It was unwilling to embark on negotiations for ends that were not limited, clear and achievable and feared that by taking the first steps in negotiations they regarded as visionary they would be forced to assume unwelcome commitments.

But if the enthusiasts for a United Europe were visionary, the United Kingdom was short sighted. Its international standing and weight declined steadily all through the 1950s while the continental countries gained rapidly in economic potential, confidence and bargaining power. Long before the Treaty of Rome trade between the countries of the Six was expanding at a remarkable rate, with the economic recovery of Germany providing the driving force. Economic integration was already well advanced before it became the object of political agreement. The United Kingdom found that its markets in the Commonwealth were slow in growing while it was handicapped in access to the most rapidly growing markets anywhere.

An earlier opportunity of a closer link with Europe was in the efforts to establish a European Defence Community. Churchill had called for a European Army in 1950; and had the British been prepared to contribute by stationing troops on the continent as part of a NATO force, as they did once the plan for a defence community collapsed, the continental countries might have persevered. When the Messina Conference revived the idea of an

Economic Community in 1955, Britain had one more chance to join in the negotiations, this time with no fixed conditions. By that time, the trends were unmistakable, the workings of the institution proposed more clearly discernible, and the balance of advantage more in favour of participation. But the reaction was one of apathy and disbelief. Whether negotiations at that stage would have enjoyed more success than the free trade area negotiations is, however, highly uncertain. The continentals would perhaps have been more accommodating and willing to follow a British lead; but it is difficult to see how Britain could have retained Commonwealth free entry and tariff autonomy as well as its own system of agricultural protection. There was no sign even in 1960 that it was willing to abandon any of them.

Relations with international institutions

The United Kingdom took an active part throughout the 1950s in the affairs of the OEEC. At meetings of the Council of Ministers, a British Minister was usually in the chair and at the official level British representatives took a prominent part. The most important activity of the OEEC was the European Payments Union in which Germany, after a balance of payments crisis in 1950–1, was in more or less consistent surplus. The Germans were repeatedly pressed to take steps to reduce their surplus, especially in 1957, but since they were already fully employed and expanding rapidly there was not a great deal they could do except lower tariffs, pursue liberal trading policies and make funds available to deficit countries and international bodies like the IMF. Various ad hoc arrangements were also made: to increase Germany's contribution to the cost of stationing British troops in Germany; to make deposits with the Bank of England for the prepayment of post-war German debts; and to make additional deposits for arms purchases. It was not until 1961 that they revalued what had been from the beginning an undervalued currency, and then only by 5 per cent. They were more willing to see other countries devalue; in the mid 1950s Erhard publicly proposed that the pound be allowed to float.

After the winding up of the EPU, the Americans proposed a reconstitution of the OEEC to include themselves and Canada and this took place in 1960 when the title was changed to Organization for Economic Cooperation and Development (OECD). New working parties were formed to hold regular consultations on the economic situation (Working Party 3), economic growth and labour relations (Working Parties 2 and 4). The first of these had been foreshadowed by an international expert group, chaired by Sir Robert Hall, which went back to 1953 and allowed a frank interchange between senior governmental advisers meeting in Paris at regular intervals such as was completely new in international affairs. A somewhat similar interchange between the Governors of European central banks in Basle also developed in the 1950s.

Another activity set on foot at the end of the 1950s was the discussion of aid to developing countries in the Development Advisory Group which came into existence in 1960 and a year later became the Aid Committee of the OECD. Aid had of course been given in one form or another by the United Kingdom for many years but this was the first time, thanks to an American initiative, that arrangements were made for a co-ordinated international effort.

Relations with the International Bank and IMF had been of limited importance in the early 1950s. The Robot scheme in 1952 would have meant flouting the IMF and at the same time seeking a large standby from it but the scheme was dropped. The United Kingdom did, however, seek help from the IMF after Suez when there were heavy withdrawals of sterling, particularly in November 1956. The portfolio of American securities held by the Treasury from war-time levies was pledged as security for a loan of $561 million and the total was brought up to $1300 million by a standby for the next twelve months. The loan was repaid in 1958–60 shortly before an even larger amount was borrowed.

Meanwhile the Treasury (and the Prime Minister) came to fear a growing shortage of international liquidity which would eventually exert deflationary pressure on world activity. This view was urged on the Americans in 1958 without much success but the Americans later came round to the same view. It was difficult to maintain that the swings in trade balances could not be financed from available reserves: the problem was much more the fluctuations in confidence in the stability of the currencies in which a large proportion of reserves were held. For that purpose the remedy appeared to be to enlarge the resources at the disposal of the IMF and contract the role of the reserve currencies.

Accordingly, agreement was reached to double the quotas originally set for the IMF and to add 50 per cent to World Bank quotas to provide it, too, with additional resources. The activities of the World Bank were further enlarged by the institution of the International Finance Corporation (IFC) in 1956 to assist the growth of 'productive private enterprise' in developing countries and by the creation of the International Development Association (IDA) in 1959 to make 'soft' loans to those countries for social and economic projects that were desirable but might not pay their way.

Notes

1 C. H. Feinstein, *National Income, Expenditure and Output of the U.K. 1855–1965* tables 61 and 65.
2 Dow, *Management of the British Economy*, pp. 246–7.
3 Ibid., p. 248.
4 Dow, *Management of the British Economy*, p. 402 n. In the five-year period 1945–50 the annual number of wage-earners given an award of higher pay averaged 6–7 million; in 1951–5 the average was 11 million; and in 1956–60 10.4 million.
5 *Annual Register*, 1956, p. 46.
6 *Annual Register*, 1956, p. 47.
7 *Economic Survey 1956*, pp. 33–4.
8 *Economic Survey 1954*, p. 17
9 The 1953 target was in the *Economic Survey 1953*; the 1958 target was in Treasury evidence to the Radcliffe Committee (*Report*, para. 734)

Further reading

Brittan, S. 1964. *The Treasury under the Tories*, Harmondsworth: Penguin Books.
Brittan, S. 1971. *Steering the Economy*, Harmondsworth: Penguin Books.
Cairncross, A. and Watts, N. 1989. *The Economic Section 1939–1961: a study in economic advising*, London: Methuen.

Dacey, W. Manning 1967. *The British Banking Mechanism* (5th edn), London: Hutchinson.

Dow, J. C. R. 1964. *The Management of the British Economy 1945–60.* Cambridge: Cambridge University Press.

Fforde, J. S. 1992. *The Bank of England and Public Policy 1941–58.* Cambridge: Cambridge University Press.

Kenen, P. 1960. *British Monetary Policy and the Balance of Payments 1951–59,* Cambridge, Mass.: Harvard University Press.

Paish, F. W. 1962. *Studies in an Inflationary Economy. The United Kingdom 1948 to 1961,* London: Macmillan.

Rees, G. L. 1963. *Britain and the Post-War Payments System,* Cardiff: University of Wales Press.

Roberthall, Lord (ed. Cairncross) 1991. *The Robert Hall Diaries,* Vol. II 1954–61, London: Unwin Hyman.

Seldon, A. 1981. *Churchill's Indian Summer: the Conservative government 1951–55,* London: Hodder & Stoughton.

Shonfield, A. 1959. *British Economic Policy since the War,* Harmondsworth: Penguin Books.

Worswick, G. D. N. and Ady, P. (eds) 1962. *The British Economy in the 1950s,* Oxford: Oxford University Press.

Official reports

Economic Implications of Full Employment, 1956, Cmd 9725, London: HMSO.

Economic Survey, 1953 (Cmd 8800), 1954 (Cmd 9108), 1955 (Cmd 9412), 1956 (Cmd 9728), London: HMSO.

Radcliffe Committee 1959. *Report,* London: HMSO.

Radcliffe Committee 1960. *Memoranda,* London: HMSO.

4 The 1960s

The course of events

The 1950s started with rearmament adding to the pressure on an economy that had little slack. The 1960s started with a balance of payments crisis in a rather sluggish economy. A short-lived boom in 1959 petered out early in 1960. Economic activity picked up again in the second half of the year and continued to expand until the middle of 1961 when deflationary measures arrested further growth. The occasion for these measures was a sharp drop in the reserves after a revaluation of the deutsche mark in March gave rise to currency uncertainties. Unemployment, which had been falling slowly since the beginning of 1959 and was down to 1.33 per cent in June 1961 rose sharply after the measures to a peak of nearly 4 per cent in the severe weather of the first quarter of 1963.

An expansionary budget in 1963 set off a fresh recovery which was still in progress when the Labour party took office in October 1964. The balance of payments, however, after registering small surpluses when the pressure was reduced in 1962–3, moved into heavy deficit in 1964 and for its first three years the incoming Labour government was struggling to balance its international accounts without changing the parity. In November 1967 it finally gave up and the pound was devalued from 2.80 to 2.40 dollars to the pound.

The devaluation did not bring any immediate relief. The balance of payments, which had temporarily improved in 1965–6 and slid back into deficit in 1967, remained in deficit throughout 1968 and there was heavy speculative pressure on the pound. But by the end of the year this had ceased and for the next three years, 1969–71, the balance of payments was in increasing and substantial surplus.

On the domestic front, efforts had been made to introduce planning machinery, in conjunction with representatives of employers and employed, in order to achieve more stable, and at the same time more rapid, growth. In 1962 a National Economic Development Council was created with an appropriate staff and a 4 per cent target for economic growth was announced by the Chancellor (Selwyn Lloyd). When the Labour Party took over, they set about the preparation of a national plan under a new department of government, the Department of Economic Affairs, and a plan was published in 1965. This, however, proved to be incompatible with the deflationary measures taken by the government and the plan was dropped.

Efforts were also made to slow down the rise in wages, first in a 'pause' called for in July 1961 by the then Chancellor and later through a compact with the unions negotiated by George Brown in 1964. The pause was short lived and the compact did not prevent an acceleration in wages over Labour's first year, hourly earnings rising by 10 per cent from October 1964 to October 1965. A National Board for Prices and Incomes was created in 1965 to administer the government's incomes policy; and after the deflationary measures of July 1966 a standstill was imposed for six months, followed by a period of 'severe restraint'. These measures slowed down inflation for a little but it received a fresh impulse from devaluation in 1967.

Over the decade 1960–70 retail prices rose by 40 per cent; this compared with nearly 50 per cent in the previous decade. At the same time production rose faster: by 34 per cent compared with 30 per cent. Neither decade's performance compared favourably with that of continental countries like Germany and France. But in retrospect these decades came to be viewed as a golden age.

The changes in the main aggregates are shown in table 4.1. The increase in GDP was a good deal higher than in the previous decade and the fluctuations that occurred were less dramatic, the outstanding exception being the dip in 1962. Two boom years, 1964 and 1968, stand out, the first following a recovery from the slowdown in 1962 and the second the rapid growth of exports after the devaluation of 1967.

Table 4.1 Changes in the allocation of resources, 1960–70 (increase from year to year in £ billion at constant 1985 prices)

	1961	1962	1963	1964	1965	1966	1967	1968	1969	1970	Changes between 1960 and 1970
Consumers' expenditure	2.7	2.8	5.9	4.1	2.1	2.5	3.5	4.1	0.8	4.4	33.3
Public authorities' final consumption	1.6	1.4	0.8	0.8	1.3	1.4	3.0	0.2	-1.0	0.9	10.4
Gross domestic fixed capital formation	3.0	0.2	0.5	5.8	2.1	1.1	3.8	3.0	-0.3	1.3	20.5
Value of physical increase in stocks and work in progress	-1.9	-1.7	1.0	3.4	-1.5	-1.1	-0.3	0.9	0.2	-0.7	-1.8
Exports of goods and services	1.1	0.6	1.8	1.3	1.7	2.2	0.2	5.5	4.9	2.9	22.1
Total final expenditure	6.3	3.0	10.4	15.5	5.5	6.0	9.3	14.0	5.1	9.0	84.7
Imports of goods and services	-0.7	0.8	1.6	4.2	0.4	1.1	3.1	3.7	1.7	2.6	18.5
Gross domestic product (at market prices)	6.7	2.1	7.7	9.9	5.1	4.4	5.7	9.5	3.6	5.0	59.6
Gross domestic product (average at factor cost)	4.7	1.6	7.1	10.4	5.8	3.9	4.6	9.3	5.5	4.6	58.6

Source: Economic Trends Annual Supplement (1990 edn) table 3

The growth in exports over the decade at a rate that absorbed 37 per cent of the increase in output is perhaps the most striking change between the two decades, the corresponding proportion in the 1950s being no more than 17 per cent. The contrast is mainly attributable to the setback in exports during the years of rearmament in 1951−2 on the one hand and the stimulus of devaluation on the other: three-fifths of the increase in exports took place in the last three years of the 1960s and accounted for nearly three-quarters of the increase in output over those years. The growth in imports, although more rapid than in the 1950s, lagged behind the growth in exports whereas in the 1950s it had been imports that grew faster than exports.

A second important improvement was in investment which expanded about 50 per cent faster than in the previous decade but with wider fluctuations from year to year. A large part of the increase was in public investment, especially in the years up to 1967 when fixed investment in the public sector for the first and only time exceeded fixed investment in the private sector. After 1967 while private investment continued to grow, public investment fell slightly. Investment in manufacturing industry fell off after 1961 to a low point in 1963 and then expanded almost without interruption to a peak in 1970, 50 per cent higher than in 1963 and 23 per cent higher than at the previous peak in 1961.

Stocks, both absolutely and as a proportion of output, were on a downward trend over the decade, but as usual there were sharp fluctuations in stockbuilding, much the most volatile of the aggregates. It was positive in the boom of 1963−4 and again in the recovery in 1968, to both of which it contributed powerfully, but in all other years except 1969 it was consistently negative.

Expenditure by public authorities on goods and services was another item that expanded faster in the 1960s. It increased most in 1967 when public investment was also at peak i.e. in the year when the struggle to avoid devaluation was finally abandoned. It increased least in 1968−9 after Roy Jenkins's post-devaluation budgets.

Consumer spending benefited from the more rapid growth in national income and increased fairly steadily except in 1969 when the post-devaluation budgets effected a marked slowdown in spending. Over the decade consumers absorbed 56 per cent of the increase in gross national income – the same proportion as in the previous decade.

The last years of the Conservative government, 1960–1964

It was clear early in 1960 that an awkward situation was building up. Output in 1959 had grown much faster than expected: between the last quarter of 1958 and the last quarter of 1959 by $6\frac{1}{2}$ per cent. The balance of payments had weakened from half-year to half-year since the beginning of 1958, was in deficit by the end of 1959, and showed every sign of moving into deeper deficit in 1960. Bank advances had grown by a third in 1959 and were still increasing rapidly.

The Treasury and the Bank of England were both concerned at these developments – the Chancellor more than his officials – and thought that some check should be applied to the expansion in demand before it got out of hand. Bank rate was raised from 4 to 5 per cent in January and preparations were made to raise taxes in the Budget.

The Prime Minister took a different view from the Chancellor. Having just won the election with an enlarged majority on a promise to preserve prosperity, he thought a deflationary budget 'either very foolish or very dishonest'. He was prepared, however, to accept the Treasury's proposals for other kinds of restrictive action; and, after the budget, hire purchase restrictions were reimposed and special deposits at 1 per cent were introduced (with a further 1 per cent in June).[1] Bank rate was again brought into play in June with an increase to 6 per cent. The budget itself followed Macmillan's prescription and was neutral in its impact on demand.

The boom petered out in the first half of 1960 as exports ceased to expand. World trade was growing more slowly and the fall in the British share of it was accelerating so that at the end of 1960 exports were no higher than at the beginning. There was also a switch in purchases from domestically produced to imported goods – especially manufactures, which grew in volume by a third – either because they were more competitive or because most of the restrictions on imports that lingered through the 1950s had been removed. To the failure of exports to grow and the displacement of demand towards imports was added a reduction in consumer spending on cars and other durable goods because of hire purchase restrictions and a rise in consumer prices after a year and a half of stability. All of these checked the growth of demand. Employment, however, continued to mount while the balance of payments moved into deeper deficit.

In July 1960 Amory was succeeded at the Treasury by Selwyn Lloyd. In the second half of the year a renewed expansion began but at a slower pace, assisted by a high and rising rate of stockbuilding. In October and again in December Bank Rate was cut by ½ per cent and in January 1961, after prolonged debate within the government, hire purchase restrictions were relaxed.

In the first half of 1961 the growth in production accelerated and the balance of payments on current account improved a little. Fixed investment was expanding strongly and exports were also rising while imports had ceased to grow. Consumer demand had also been stimulated at the beginning of the year by a large rise in money incomes, seven million wage-earners receiving increases in pay in the three months ending in February with little immediate effect on the price level.[2] The growth in consumer demand, particularly for cars, was reinforced by the relaxation of hire purchase restrictions. The pressure in the labour market increased as unemployment continued to decline. By July hourly wage rates had risen by 11 per cent over the previous eighteen months and working hours had also been reduced.

The principal source of concern, however, continued to be the balance of payments. The deficit on current account of £228 million in 1960 had been covered by an inflow of short-term funds transferred to London because of attractive rates of interest and doubts about the dollar. In March 1961 a revaluation of the deutsche mark and the Dutch guilder revived currency speculation, especially when there was every chance that revaluation by a mere 5 per cent would be followed by a second revaluation. The inflow of funds into sterling was reversed as speculators decided that the deutsche mark was a better bet. Macmillan noted that £67 million was lost from the reserves in a single day in March compared with a loss of only £26 million in the worst post-Suez day.[3] Thanks to assistance from European central banks under arrangements with the Bank for International Settlements, it was possible to cover large withdrawals of funds totalling about £600 million by mid-July. The situation was made worse by the publication at the beginning of April of revised balance of payments estimates for 1960 which doubled the size of the previous estimate of the current account deficit.[4]

The budget, when introduced in April, was more or less neutral like the budget of 1960. But it contained two important provisions. One was designed to exempt from surtax earned income under £5000 (instead of, as before, £2000); the loss of revenue was roughly offset by an increase in profits tax. The other was intended to allow the use of tax changes between budgets in order to stabilize demand. One of the tax 'regulators', as they were called, empowered the government to raise or lower indirect taxation across the board by up to 10 per cent at any time. The second, which was abandoned at birth, gave the Chancellor power to impose a payroll tax of up to four shillings per week on all employees through increased national insurance contributions. In a full year the first regulator could vary taxation in either direction by up to £200 million while the second, used to its full extent, would also have brought in £200 million.

The first tax regulator proved a useful addition to the government's limited range of instruments and the power to use it was renewed annually in successive Finance Acts. The greater flexibility that it allowed was more limited than it seemed, as became evident in 1967 when it was felt impossible to increase indirect taxation within a month or so of Christmas and almost as difficult after Christmas when the budget was only a few months away. In 1961 it was brought into use almost as soon as the Finance Act was passed.

Deflationary measures, July 1961

Pressure on sterling had continued after March with bad trade figures in May and rumours of a Swiss franc revaluation in June. The Bank of England feared a continuing drain on the reserves and the Treasury, looking ahead to 1962, expected demand pressure to go on rising. Well before deflationary measures were taken on 25 July, the steady fall in unemployment and the forecasts for the next twelve months pointed towards a need to check the growth in demand quite apart from any concern over the balance of payments. Investment was still rising strongly and other elements in demand, apart from stockbuilding, were either flat or expanding. It seemed likely that the remaining margin of spare capacity would soon disappear if no action were taken.

The government delayed restrictive measures until the passing of the Finance Bill on 25 July. The measures then announced included the use of the tax regulator to its full extent, a limitation of the increase in supply expenditure in 1962–3 to $2\frac{1}{2}$ per cent, and checks on government expenditure overseas and private foreign investment outside the sterling area. Bank rate was raised from 5 to 7 per cent and a further call was made for special deposits. Exchange control was also tightened by calling on firms operating abroad to remit a higher proportion of their profits to the United Kingdom and by new restrictions on private investment outside the sterling area. The Chancellor asked for a 'pause' in wage increases and imposed one in the public sector, inviting the private sector to follow suit. Finally, he sought and obtained from the IMF a credit of $2 billion.

Altogether these measures represented a more decisive 'stop' than any since 1957. They came at a time when there was much public discussion of planning on the French model as a recipe for faster growth, so the criticism which they aroused was more than usually severe. Two reports, one just before and one just after the announcement of the measures, added force to the criticism by stressing the need to take a longer-term view. The Plowden Report on *Control of Public Expenditure* (Cmnd 1432) condemned short-term economy campaigns and advocated the planning of public expenditure on a long-term basis. The final Report of the Council on Prices, Productivity and Incomes also concentrated on long-term growth and the need for an incomes policy to sustain it.

Planning

It was in this climate of opinion that the Chancellor included in his statement on 25 July a proposal for joint planning arrangements with representatives of employers and workers. After a delay of two months while the matter was debated in Cabinet, a formal invitation to join a National Economic Development Council (NEDC) was issued. It was readily accepted by employers' associations but only after much hesitation by the TUC. Beginning in March 1962 the Council held regular meetings, served by a staff of officials independent of the government machine and forming the National Economic Development Office (NEDO).

There were two strands of thought behind the establishment of the NEDC. One was concern for faster growth in the knowledge that nearly all the continental countries were outstripping the United Kingdom in their rate of growth and might soon outstrip it in their standard of living. The other was a reaction against 'stop-go', i.e. the periodic interruptions to expansion occasioned by deflationary government measures; this was thought to be an important element in Britain's relatively slow growth. The experience of France was thought to demonstrate that planning made for faster growth. The steady pursuit of long-term objectives which planning involved was contrasted with the frequent 'stops' that occurred in the absence of planning. It was also thought that, so far as the 'stops' resulted from balance of payments difficulties traceable to rising wage costs, discussions with the trade unions in the context of more rapid growth might bring wages within the framework of planning and help to eliminate the 'stops'.

It is always desirable to ensure that policy is properly co-ordinated and has adequate regard to long-term objectives. To that extent, the case for some form of planning is unanswerable. But how the plans of individual enterprises are best linked with the plans of governments is another matter altogether; so, too, is the problem of ensuring moderation in the innumerable wage bargains on which the value of a currency ultimately depends. In the 1960s the debate on planning paid little regard to some elementary facts.

First of all, only some continental countries engaged in planning. Those that did, such as France, grew no faster than the others, notably Germany. Even in France the contribution of planning to more rapid growth was by no means beyond dispute, especially when the growth in productivity had been at the same high level before planning began. There was also a common impression that planning in France proceeded independently of the government although in fact the plan was initially drafted by the French Treasury and the chief planner, M Massé, sat in the French Cabinet. As for stop-go, fluctuations in activity could be shown to be just as large in other countries the only difference being that, since the trend in Britain rose much less steeply than elsewhere, growth was completely arrested in the 'stop' phase instead of being merely somewhat slowed down. The fundamental issue was whether planning would affect the trend in productivity and this was hardly ever discussed.

There was a further misunderstanding. There could be no doubt that productivity growth was affected by the planning engaged in by individual firms and that the horizon of their planning was affected by the stability of market conditions. The further ahead they could see, the more likely they were to make the radical changes on which growth depended. But it was not true that growth could be made more rapid merely by making business men believe that it would be more rapid. This was a widely held view that regarded an increase in investment as the mainspring of growth and market expansion as the determinant of investment. But investment is only one factor in growth and its weight in comparison with other factors depends on the character of the investment undertaken, not just on its volume. What a burst of investment produces is a boom, not steady growth, unless the other elements in growth are brought into play. As a glance at the figures would have shown, manufacturing investment had risen rapidly in the 1950s − in 1961 it was about 80 per cent higher than in 1953 − without producing any perceptible improvement in the rate of growth.

Incomes Policy

The July measures not only gave birth to a new planning body, the NEDC, but also a more sustained effort to establish an incomes policy. In the year following the measures, it was this that chiefly preoccupied the government, along with simultaneous negotiations (discussed below) over entry into the EEC − the Prime Minister having announced the intention to apply for membership at the end of July.

Over the winter of 1961−2, the Treasury wrestled with the principles that should govern wage increases in an inflation-free economy and issued in February 1962 a White Paper setting them out.[5] This suggested that the average increase should match the growth in productivity which in the past had averaged $2-2\frac{1}{2}$ per cent. The White Paper thus gave official backing for the first time to what had been known in the 1950s as 'the guiding light'.

It need hardly be said that this interest in how wages *ought* to behave was due to the conviction that actual wage behaviour in Britain 'constituted both an important and independent inflationary force'. Treasury officials had accepted for many years the distinction between demand and cost inflation and the idea of a 'pay pause', to which the Prime Minister attached particular importance, was consistent with this distinction. An OEEC report, prepared by an international committee of distinguished economists chaired by Richard Kahn and published in 1961, gave timely expression to the distinction and attracted great interest in Britain.[6]

From the start, the pay pause met with resistance, most obviously in the public sector where the government had just as much difficulty as private employers in holding back wage increases. In November, in a much publicized failure to hold the line, the Electricity Council awarded an increase in excess of the prescribed limit and the government, unable to face a strike interrupting supplies of electric power, was obliged to acquiesce. In the private sector, too, wage claims were pressed well in excess of the norm. When the pay pause came to an end in March 1962 there had been a mixture of successes and failures but little overall change.

The government continued its efforts to arrive at a workable incomes policy and asked for wage restraint. Discussions on a long-term policy took place with the Prime Minister who came to feel that too much of the burden of preparing one fell on him and too little on the Chancellor. In July he made extensive ministerial changes including the replacement of Selwyn Lloyd by Reginald Maudling as Chancellor. A fortnight later, the government announced its intention to set up a National Incomes Commission to pronounce on wage settlements referred to it. This was to form part of a permanent incomes policy along with the norm of $2\frac{1}{2}$ per cent wage increases and the various criteria governing departures from the norm that were set out in the White Paper.

The NIC had the support of employers but not of the unions who complained that they had not been consulted and were opposed in principle to interference in collective bargaining by bodies which had not been invited by the parties to participate in it. The Commission took legal form, with a lawyer in the chair, invited

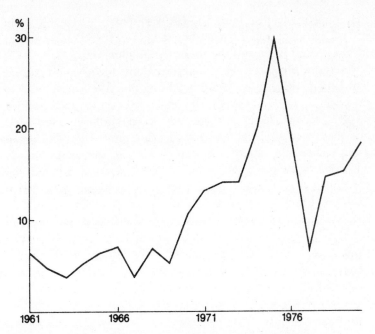

Figure 4.1   Increase in hourly wage rates, 1961–1981
Source: National Institute *Economic Review*

submissions and heard oral evidence. It could review only cases referred to it and had no powers of compulsion, the only sanction behind its rulings being that of public opinion. In the two years of its existence before it was wound up by the Labour government in 1964 it heard four cases only, three of them on wage agreements already made and one (on academic salaries) where it recommended increases in pay well above the norm.

As a means of mobilizing opinion against inflationary wage settlements the Commission was a dismal failure. This was partly because such settlements after October 1962 when the Commission started work had virtually ceased. In the year after its establishment hourly wage rates rose by an average of 2.3 per cent compared with an average of 6.4 per cent in the year to October 1961 (see figure 4.1). The cumbersome procedure followed and the boycott by the unions detracted further from its influence. Some suggested that it might have had more success with a more acceptable norm of $3-3\frac{1}{2}$ per cent, and the suggestion was accepted by the Chancellor in his 1963 Budget, but the unions were unmoved.

Interest in incomes policy faded away as unemployment increased and labour's bargaining power fell. The year 1962 turned out to be a very different one from what had been forecast in the spring when it seemed likely that the depression would be short lived and that there would be an early recovery under the influence of a big increase in exports. In accordance with these expectations no action was taken in the 1962 budget to expand demand, the net effect of all the tax changes occasioned by the termination of the regulator tax surcharge of 10 per cent being to leave prospective tax revenue slightly higher. The Chancellor submitted to the NEDC a target of 4 per cent growth (after being dissuaded from suggesting 5 per cent) and the implications of this target (which survived to form part of the National Plan in 1965) were examined by the NEDC for the period 1961-4.

Reflation, 1962-1963

For a time it seemed as if recovery had begun. But exports did not show the expected buoyancy and fell slightly in the second half of the year. Manufacturing activity fell away in the final quarter, and fell further in the very severe weather at the beginning of 1963. Production at the end of 1962 was only 3 per cent higher than two years previously when measured as GDP and had barely risen at all when limited to industrial production. In February 1963 when the weather was at its worst, unemployment reached 3.9 per cent (including temporarily stopped), the highest figure since the war up to that time.

The earliest relaxations of policy were on the monetary side. Bank rate was reduced gradually from 7 per cent till it reached $4\frac{1}{2}$ per cent in April 1962 with no further change for nearly two years except a cut of $\frac{1}{2}$ per cent in January 1963. Special deposits were also reduced, first in June 1962, again in October and finally in December. Minimum hire purchase deposits were reduced on all goods except cars in June. The new Chancellor, coming into office in July 1962, was anxious to avoid giving the impression of a change in policy and refrained from expansionary measures until October. He began by releasing £42 million in post-war credits as a boost to consumption, authorized an increase in public investment plans for 1963 by £175 million and abolished qualitative restraints on bank lending. These moves were followed in November by increased investment and depreciation allowances for industry and a very large cut (from 45 to 25 per cent) in the purchase tax on cars. All this added up to a considerable stimulus. The increase in investment, however, was likely to be delayed to 1964 (rather than 1963) when a stimulus might be the last thing needed; and the purchase tax reduction was on a very narrow front, adding to labour demand in areas where it was least required.

The main boost to the economy, however, came in the April budget. The long delay in recovery and the high unemployment in the first quarter encouraged large concessions.

Income tax allowances were substantially increased, Schedule A (on housing) was abolished and the firms in development areas were given 'free' depreciation (i.e. businesses were free to write off plant at whatever rate they chose). Other concessions to the development areas included grants to firms setting up or expanding in those areas and loans to developing countries to purchase heavy equipment there. In all, the tax concessions amounted to £270 million in 1963—4 and £460 million in a full year.

The effect of this powerful fiscal stimulus was much what it had been in 1959 — a rapid expansion in production followed after a time by a period of relatively slow growth as capacity limits were approached. In the fifteen months between the last quarter of 1962 and the first quarter of 1964, GDP increased by nearly 6 per cent (after seasonal adjustment) while in the next fifteen months to the middle of 1965 the increase was by 3.8 per cent. More strikingly, the increase in industrial production in the first period was nearly 11 per cent and in the second $3\frac{1}{2}$ per cent. More significantly still, the index of industrial production stood still for the first nine months of 1964 (i.e. up to the October election), leaving the Chancellor convinced that the rise in production had halted. A year or two later the figures had changed out of all recognition and showed a steeply rising curve, only to change back to their original flatness somewhat later.[7] The apparent stagnation of production, as indicated by the most up-to-date measure of economic activity, transfixed the government. Maudling, who had intended to take action to check the boom, held his hand.

He did, however, make a fresh attempt to reach agreement with the trade unions on an incomes policy. In this he had no success. For one thing the by-elections had begun to go against the government; and with a general election and possible change of government in the offing, the TUC wished to reserve their collaboration for a government of their own colour.

The Maudling 'experiment'

Meanwhile the balance of payments outlook was darkening steadily. The current account, even in the slowdown, had never looked very healthy: the estimates in 1964 were of surpluses of around £100 million in 1962 and 1963. There could be no doubt that in 1964 these would be succeeded by a deficit. But until fairly late in the day this was not found particularly disturbing. The National Institute, for example, expected in November 1963 'a temporary burst of stockbuilding' leading to a small current deficit which would be largely or entirely offset by additions to the sterling balances held by overseas sterling area countries. Support could be provided if necessary by the IMF; and 'the continued weakness of the dollar' made a flight of short-term capital unlikely.[8]

A similar line of thought had been expressed by the Institute in 1961 and had encouraged Selwyn Lloyd to think that he had the necessary foreign exchange to support expansion without a balance of payments crisis. Maudling had much the same idea: he wanted to maintain expansion long enough to break through to higher growth and put an end to the stop-go cycle. In the last resort, if he ran into balance of payment difficulties without the foreign exchange to overcome them, he was (privately) prepared to let the pound float.

In the 1964 Budget the Chancellor increased taxation by £100 million. This may have seemed quite a bold proposal in January when a neutral budget was widely expected but it was soon evident that it was insufficient. The National Institute suggested in February £200 million as a first instalment with another £200 million to follow in 1965 and pointed out later that if budgetary action was not taken to moderate demand there was also a shortage of other instruments available for that purpose.[9] The additional £100 million in taxation was levied on drink and tobacco and this made it difficult to make use of the regulator and hit these items a second time.[10]

The boom in investment, including stockbuilding, grew stronger as the year advanced and the margin of spare capacity narrowed rapidly; unemployment had fallen to 2 per cent by the end of 1963 and by the middle of 1964 was down to 1.5 per cent. The increased pressure told on the balance of payments which was already marginally in deficit on current account in the second half of 1963 and in substantial deficit on long-term capital account. By the first quarter of 1964 the joint deficit on current and long-term capital account — then the measure favoured officially — was £163 million; and in the following quarter this rose to £216 million. These figures (which have since been amended) were not available until much later. Forecasts of the balance of payments on current and long-term capital account (and including the balancing item) were at first much lower. In February 1964 the National Institute put the deficit for the next eighteen months at £375 million and in May put the deficit in 1964 at £300 million. By August the forecast had risen to £500 million.[11] The Treasury forecasts (which were not published) also showed a rise in the deficit every time they were revised during 1964. By the time the election was held in October they indicated a deficit in 1964 on current and long-term capital account of £800 million. When an official estimate was published in 1965 it showed a current account deficit of £374 million and a long-term capital account deficit of £371 million.

The government, in the expectation of a continuing boom, had put off the election until the last possible moment so as to profit from the popular reaction to growing prosperity. By October, however, the size of the prospective deficit was beginning to be widely realized so that the government had to go to the electorate just when a crisis was seen to lie ahead.

It is arguable that more than half the deficit (including any stockbuilding in excess of trend requirements) represented an accumulation of assets against which it was reasonable to borrow abroad. The remaining portion, however, could be interpreted as evidence of the country's inability to balance its international accounts when running at or near full employment. As the Conservative government left office, they left behind a large questionmark against the British economy's competitiveness and the possibility that nothing less than devaluation would restore external balance and permit a continuation of growth at full potential.

The Labour government, 1964–1970

The Labour government took office with ambitious plans for the restructuring of industry and faster long-term growth. Instead, they were soon involved in a day-to-day struggle to support the pound.

Before they took office they made much of the need to put an end to 'stop-go' by planning expansion. This meant establishing an incomes policy with the co-operation of the trade unions, improving industrial efficiency by investment allowances for export industries and various kinds of industrial equipment, founding or expanding hi-tech industries with state help, and promoting research and development and industrial training. There were also to be two new ministries, one a Ministry of Technology and the other what became the Department of Economic Affairs. The performance of British industry was to be transformed by a large dose of government policy.

The first exchange crisis, November 1964

The immediate problem, however, was what to do about the balance of payments deficit (see figure 4.2). An obvious possibility was devaluation, but there were both political and economic arguments against it. Politically, it would have been a shock to international opinion, particularly American opinion, since it would have weakened confidence in the dollar and the international monetary system based on the dollar. There was also a danger that by devaluing a second time Labour would acquire the reputation of a party given to devaluing even when the prime responsibility could have

Figure 4.2 Gold and dollar deficit, 1960–1970
Source: Economic Trends Annual Supplement 1981

been pinned on the outgoing government. On the economic side, it could be argued that the current account deficit was largely due to excessive pressure of demand and would subside or disappear if the pressure were reduced a little. Some reduction in pressure would have to occur even if the decision were made to devalue since it would be very difficult at such high pressure to effect a transfer of resources to take the place of imports and provide additional exports. There was also a doubt whether, given the right domestic policies and booming world markets, the balance of payments might not right itself as British industry improved its competitiveness. Would it not be best to apply a little deflation first to see how things worked out before plunging into a devaluation that might yet prove unnecessary?

A decision not to devalue was taken almost as soon as the Labour government was formed. It was a decision reached by the three key ministers, the Prime Minister (Wilson), the Chancellor (Callaghan) and the Secretary of State for Economic Affairs (George Brown), without reference to the Cabinet and no Cabinet discussion of devaluation occurred until July 1966. The alternatives considered when the decision was made were the use of import quotas or a surcharge of 15 per cent on imports. No consideration was given to any accompanying measures to relieve the pressure on resources and no fixed time was set for the quotas or surcharge. Quotas were permitted under international agreement and could have been used to reduce imports of manufactures which had increased by about one-third in 1962–4. A surcharge on imports contravened international undertakings in GATT and EFTA but was arguably a less damaging way of making the necessary adjustments to the trade balance.

It was decided to impose a surcharge, coupled with export rebates, rather than quotas. It was also made clear that the surcharge was a short-term expedient and would be withdrawn once the balance of payments improved. This was reiterated when the surcharge came under strong attack in EFTA and in the spring of 1965 it was reduced to 10 per cent. But the more insistence was placed on the short-term character of the surcharge, the more the need for other, long-term measures stood out: all the more because of the publicity given to the estimate of a deficit of £800 million in the balance of payments. The government no doubt hoped to find in incomes policy and industrial policy the means to improve competitiveness. But under boom conditions there was little prospect of holding wages and the impact of industrial policy was unlikely to amount to much within the next year or two. There seemed to be a clear choice between deflation and devaluation. The government, however, declined to choose either and announced that they did not consider the pressure on resources excessive.[12]

At first there was no increase in pressure on the pound. An autumn budget was introduced early in November which, taken in conjunction with the import surcharge, seemed likely to add slightly to the demand for domestic output. In line with manifesto promises, pensions and national assistance benefits were to be increased from March 1965 and the necessary revenue to pay for the increases was to come from higher income tax in 1965–6, higher national insurance contributions, and an addition to the tax on petrol. While the prospective revenue was appreciably in excess of the prospective additional payments, the budget was judged to be broadly neutral in its impact on demand. Two new taxes were to be introduced in April: a capital gains tax and a corporation tax (the latter in place of the existing system of company taxation).

The budget created alarm in the City. It neither checked demand, as many had expected, nor gave any details (for example, as to rates of tax) of how the new taxes would operate. Speculation against the pound increased and the drain on the reserves gathered speed. A speech by the Prime Minister on 16 November appeared to presage resolute use of monetary policy 'to keep sterling strong and see it riding high'. But on the following Thursday, after objections by George Brown, the expected rise in bank rate did not occur. On the same day EFTA was promised that the surcharge would be reduced in a matter of months.[13] Market reactions produced an immediate rise of 2 per cent in bank rate on Monday 23 November. When the speculative pressure continued, the Prime Minister asked Lord Cromer, Governor of the Bank of England, to seek financial assistance from other central banks. Thanks mainly to the good offices of the Federal Reserve Bank of New York and the Bundesbank in Frankfurt, the Bank succeeded in raising $3000 million at very short notice. This put an end for the time being to any pressure on the government to deflate. The markets became calmer and the exchange rate rose a little but the drain on the reserves continued.

By the end of November use had been made of swaps with other central banks arranged in 1963 and amounting in all to $1000 million. This was repaid at the beginning of December from the standby of $1000 million from the IMF negotiated in the autumn by the Conservative government. The banking credits arranged in November were for three months only and $605 million had been drawn by the end of the year. The credits were renewed for a further three months in February but had to be repaid in May. This was done out of a further drawing from the IMF of £500 million. By the middle of 1965 the government had contracted debts to the IMF and foreign monetary authorities (mainly the Federal Reserve System) of over £1000 million. In addition the Bank of England had sought to relieve the strain on the spot rate of exchange by entering into contracts in support of the forward rate that were tantamount to further borrowing.

It has been argued that any errors in the conduct of policy over those early months of the Labour goverment counted for little in the light of the prolonged speculative pressure over the next three years.[14] It is true that the really serious error was to refrain then from more decisive deflationary action. But the initial impression left by the actions taken − the harping on the size of the deficit, the delay in raising bank rate, the bald announcement of new taxes at unspecified rates, the hesitations over the surcharge − was of an indecisive government unfamiliar with its responsibilities and one in which it was difficult to have confidence. That impression lingered and underlay the continuing drain on the reserves in 1965−6.

The National Plan

Meanwhile the Department of Economic Affairs had been formed and was engaged in negotiating an incomes policy and preparing a national plan. On incomes policy representatives of employers and the trade unions agreed to sign a joint statement of intent in mid-December and a National Board for Prices and Incomes was established in March under Aubrey Jones. The TUC agreed to a $3-3\frac{1}{2}$ per cent norm for wage increases and had the agreement endorsed by a conference of affiliated unions in April. The actual increase, however, was very different. In the year to October 1965 average hourly wages rose by 7.3 per cent and average hourly earnings by 10.1 per cent. Productivity improved less than in either of the two preceding years. Wage costs per unit of output increased sharply and left little prospect of the improvement in competitiveness on which the government was counting. Britain's share of world trade in manufactures continued to fall.

The National Plan did not appear until September 1965. A target had been set by the government of a 25 per cent increase in output between 1964 and 1970. This may seem a reasonable target in the light of a 24 per cent increase in the previous six years but that was inflated by the recovery from a depression in 1958 to a boom in 1964. The target assumed an average 3.8 per cent rate of growth compared with an average rate of only 2.9 per cent from 1950 to 1964 and a rate actually achieved between 1964 and 1970 of only 2.6 per cent.

In a country suffering from a large external deficit, planning might have been expected to take the form of contingency planning weighing the chances of devaluation. But devaluation had been dismissed by ministers as 'unmentionable'. There was in fact a contradiction at the heart of the Plan since it could not assume devaluation overtly and yet could not reconcile a 25 per cent expansion in output with external balance at the existing parity except by assuming a major improvement in competitive power such as only devaluation was likely to bring. In addition, the Chancellor had announced in February 1965 that public expenditure was to be allowed to increase in real terms by 4¼ per cent per annum in the next six financial years, and on this basis large increases in public expenditure were sanctioned in 1965−6. One effect of this was to produce a 28 per cent increase in public investment (in real terms) between 1964 and 1967. Such a commitment of resources to the public sector, unaccompanied by any similar commitment by the private sector, which was merely offered targets, added to the strain on the balance of payments and made the achievement of industry's targets more rather than less difficult. If anything went wrong, as was only too likely, the necessary adjustments would fall on the private sector since the public sector, once committed, had difficulty in adjusting quickly. When the Plan was abandoned it was sometimes argued that it had done no great harm since it changed little. But this is not true of public investment (especially the electricity programme): the enlargement of this through the government's preoccupation with planning dislocated later investment programmes and added to the government's borrowing requirement in 1967 when it was already very high.

From the end of 1964 the balance of payments improved quite markedly, partly because of a falling-off in stockbuilding. Indeed from the beginning of 1965 until the last quarter of 1967 the current account was slightly in surplus. For most of the time, however, the pressure on sterling continued: over the period just referred to, the drain from the reserves amounted to over £900 million, much of which had to be borrowed abroad. On top of this was the support of the forward rate by the Bank of England involving net forward sales of dollars of about £2000 million against which delivery would have to be made.[15]

Over the winter of 1964—5 the economy had continued to expand at a rate that may have been as high as 6 per cent. The April Budget had been designed to check this expansion through higher taxes on drink and tobacco and increased motor vehicle duties. Military expenditure abroad was to be cut by £50—100 million. The increase in revenue in a full year was put at a little over £200 million and this conformed to the view expressed earlier in the OECD that nothing less than this would justify renewal of the $3000 million credits. In April the import surcharge was reduced to 10 per cent. At about the same time monetary policy was tightened by a 1 per cent call for special deposits and the imposition of a ceiling on bank advances. Bank rate had been held at 7 per cent throughout the winter but on 3 June it was cut by a full percentage point to 6 per cent. This was done partly for political reasons to improve the government's image, partly for economic reasons (e.g. to help housebuilding) and partly for tactical reasons (urged by those who set more store on renewing the power to make a sharp increase in bank rate than on keeping it at a high level). It had been intended to accompany the move by a tightening of hire purchase restrictions but this was whittled down to a small increase in down payments on cars and electrical goods.[16]

The second exchange crisis, July 1965

The budget had failed to impress continental opinion and there was a widespread expectation that the pound would soon be devalued. The trade figures for April and May showed deficits comparable with those in 1964. Switching out of sterling began in May and increased in June. Ministers seemed oblivious to the situation that was building up and were busy discussing the National Plan. In July speculative pressure increased and the losses of foreign exchange reached a high level in the week ending 24 July.

Devaluation was again considered and rejected. On this occasion, George Brown had been converted while the Prime Minister and the Chancellor remained opposed to devaluation. After a long wrangle on 26 July a package of measures was hastily prepared and announced next day. The measures included cuts in public investment estimated at £200 million in a full year, building licensing of offices and shops costing over £100,000, fresh hire purchase restrictions and tighter exchange control. Nobody quite knew what effect these measures would have. The postponement of building starts for example, when the building industry was over-loaded might simply accelerate the completion of existing projects as happened in 1947. As the National Institute put it: 'cuts of an unknown size are being made in an unknown sum, to take effect at an unknown time'.[17]

The measures seem at first to have intensified the run on sterling. Such hasty action smacked of panic. The public was unprepared, after earlier assurances, for action of this kind and concluded from their sudden introduction that the situation must be indeed serious. Market reactions were also unfavourable, particularly after a large fall in the reserves was announced at the beginning of August. A fresh effort was made, under US leadership, and with the participation of Canada and eight European countries (but not France), to organize support for the pound. Agreement was announced on 10 September before the annual meeting of the World Bank and IMF. By that time market sentiment had begun to change and speculative pressure was already dying down.

In mustering support for sterling the US Secretary of the Treasury insisted on a more effective incomes policy. It was decided to introduce legislation making the National Board for Prices and Incomes a statutory body, creating an 'early warning' system for increases in prices and wages and giving the government power to defer such increases while enquiries were made. The Bill incorporating these provisions had not passed through all its stages before the general election in March 1966.[18] It there-fore lapsed and had to be reintroduced (with some important modifications) in July 1966.

The TUC General Council, and later the TUC annual Congress, were persuaded to back the new government's policy, provided the government agreed not to activate its statutory powers unless the voluntary system failed to work. They would not accept, how-ever, any vetting of wage claims except by a committee of their own appointment and were only with difficulty induced to agree to voluntary notification. The vetting committee could comment on claims and discuss them with representatives of the union making them; but it had no power to enforce any recommendation and could delay a claim by no more than a few weeks. The committee considered all major claims from October 1965 until January 1970. The NBPI, although far more in the public eye, dealt only with a limited number of selected cases.

The third exchange crisis, July 1966

Over the winter of 1965–6 the foreign exchange situation improved. The dollar spot rate rose above par in September and remained there until February. The three month forward premium on dollars fell from 2.5 per cent in August to 0.8 per cent in January 1966 and 0.5 per cent in May. The forward commitments of the Bank of England started to fall in September, continued to fall until in January they were less than in January 1965 and fell heavily in February. The reserves increased and a small amount of debt was repaid.

The economy remained buoyant. Unemployment fell to an even lower level than in 1965. The Prime Minister kept pointing to a long list of deflationary measures in proof that the economy could not be overheated but with unemployment at 1.2 per cent this carried little conviction. Before the election in March, further restrictions were imposed on hire purchase transactions and a new ceiling was imposed on bank advances. The budget when presented in May was also intended to check the growth in demand. It introduced a new tax on services, the Selective Employment Tax, and aimed to raise an additional £400 million in revenue, mainly from SET. It also provided for the ending of the import surcharge in November 1966 and as a partial offset included a scheme for voluntary restraint in investment in the developed countries of the overseas sterling area.

The new SET tax did not begin to operate until September and its likely effects on demand were difficult to assess. It involved large and highly complex flows of funds into and out of the Exchequer in the course of collection and refunding; and although presented as a tax on services to go with indirect taxation of commodities, it was widely regarded as the fruit of the theoretical ideas of Professor Kaldor, then a Treasury adviser. In a much discussed lecture delivered in 1966 Professor Kaldor had argued that the slow growth of the British economy was largely attributable to a shortage of manpower in manufacturing and could be accelerated if a tax on service occupations forced them to release labour and relieve the shortage. It was also part of Professor Kaldor's thesis that an expansion in manufacturing made for greater efficiency and lower costs while this was not true of services: indeed, the imperfections of competition in services were such that the loss of labour would have relatively little effect on output. The controversy over these views deflected attention from the straightforward case for a tax on services.

A fortnight after the May budget a seamen's strike began and continued until the end of June. This set off a fresh run on sterling which was at first contained by drawing on the reserves and on new credit facilities arranged in June. Foreign opinion paid more regard to the continuing tightness in the labour market than to the improvement in the balance of payments that had occurred. Some official observers at OECD took the occasion to attack the government for 'wasting a year,' declaring that there was no further room for error. Ministers, however, had little awareness of the state of opinion abroad.

After the publication of the reserve figures on 4 July, the run on sterling recommenced. The trade figures, when they appeared, showed a large gap in June between exports and imports in consequence of the strike. The resignation of Frank Cousins, a prominent trade unionist, as Minister of Technology threw doubt on the future of the government's incomes policy. Interest rates were rising abroad: the rate on euro-dollars had reached 6.5 per cent.

The government at first issued press guidance that there would be no mini budget and this set off rumours of impending devaluation. On 14 July bank rate was raised to 7 per cent and a call was made for increased special deposits. Further unspecified measures were to follow later. The run on sterling, however, continued.

The decision to deflate

In mid July Ministers again discussed devaluation and for the first time the matter was raised in Cabinet. The Chancellor, convinced of the need to deflate, had brought forward to Cabinet on 12 July a package of measures that had been prepared in the Treasury with the object of improving the balance of payments by £250 million. These measures were calculated to reduce domestic demand by £500 million and overseas spending by £150 million and to raise unemployment to 2 per cent or more by the end of 1967. They included the use of the regulator to its full extent; a surcharge of 10 per cent on 1965−6 surtax payments; cuts in public investment; still tighter hire purchase restrictions; a reduction in travel allowances to £50 a year; and additional building controls. These deflationary measures were to be combined with an immediate voluntary freeze on wages and prices. The proposals divided the Cabinet, which was unwilling to accept them without some discussion of the economic background and alternative courses of action.

This opposition disturbed the Chancellor and disposed him to conclude that there might now be no alternative to devaluation. George Brown was by this time strongly in favour of devaluation as the only way of maintaining expansion and wanted to combine it with an application to enter the EEC and a limited amount of deflation. The Chancellor agreed to join forces with him in pressing devaluation on the Prime Minister but was induced to change round again when the Prime Minister undertook to secure acceptance of the proposed measures by the Cabinet and to announce them in person to the House of Commons. The disagreements over devaluation were conveyed to the Cabinet by the Prime Minister who then made a temporizing statement in Parliament promising details later of measures to provide 'the restraint that is necessary' and left for Moscow on 16 July.

In his absence ministers opposed to deflation tried to rally support for devaluation but were outvoted when Cabinet met on 19 July. Some ministers, including Jenkins, Crosland and Crossman argued for a floating pound but this proposal too was defeated. The Chancellor's measures were announced next day on 20 July.

The July package was similar to one that Ministers had been asked to consider in November 1964 and would not so much as look at. In total it was impressive and had a powerful effect on domestic demand. Consumers' expenditure in real terms remained at or below the level of the second quarter of 1966 for a full year. The freeze arrested almost completely the rise in wages and prices throughout the second half of 1966, and, less completely, in the first half of 1967. The balance of payments swung into surplus for the first time since 1963 and in the two winter quarters £500 million was repaid to foreign monetary authorities. From August until April the spot rate of exchange improved until it was nearly at par. By the spring of 1967 most of the outstanding debt to central banks – but not to the IMF – had been repaid.[19]

In detail the package was less impressive. There is no evidence in the historical record of the promised saving of £100 million on military expenditure abroad. Whatever cuts were made in public expenditure, it increased rapidly in 1967: public investment was up on 1966 by nearly £500 million at current prices and public expenditure on consumable goods and services was up by £700 million. These were both much larger increases than in the previous year and were very much at odds with the picture of drastic cuts presented in July 1966. Nevertheless the measures then taken did produce the expected rise in unemployment to over 2 per cent, with a peak of 2.4 per cent in September 1967.

The wages and prices freeze

The deflationary measures did not prevent devaluation in 1967. Their first effect, however, was on the DEA. George Brown resigned, was persuaded to withdraw his resignation, and moved shortly afterwards to the Foreign Office. The National Plan was abandoned and the department's influence on economic policy was greatly reduced. It remained in charge of incomes policy which now took the form of a freeze. This was accepted with reluctance by the TUC, which had no confidence in its effectiveness and reminded ministers of the objections that could be made to it. The policy remained a voluntary one until challenged by the Association of Supervisory Staffs, Executives and Technicians in October when the government activated the powers it had taken in July in the Prices and Incomes Act. This apart, there were very few standstill orders and no strikes against the freeze. As the freeze ended in January it was succeeded by a six months' period of 'severe restraint' with a nil norm and limited exceptions in conformity with criteria set out in a White Paper.[20] This allowed some increases to the lowest paid workers and for productivity agreements strictly interpreted on the basis of guidelines to be provided by the NBPI.

In the first half of 1967, during the period of 'severe restraint', the rise in wages and prices continued to be modest but in the second half of the year, as the various suspended wage agreements took effect, there was a sharp increase. Hourly wage rates in October 1967 were 5.3 per cent higher than a year previously. Even so, it is impossible to assign to any failure of incomes policy in 1966–7 responsibility for the pressure on sterling in 1967 or for the ultimate devaluation in November.

Relaxation, 1967

The government had for a time contemplated higher taxation in the April budget as an offset to the rise in public expenditure. But with the rise in unemployment to 2 per cent by April it was decided to introduce a neutral budget. This may be a fair description of the tax changes; but taken in conjunction with the rapid growth in public expenditure the impact of the budget would seem to have been expansionary. The public sector financial balance – a much wider concept than the budget – was expected to show a deficit nearly £850 million higher in 1967–8 than the deficit forecast for 1966–7 and £600 million higher than the recorded deficit in 1965–6. The actual out-turn in 1967–8 was a deficit higher than in 1966–7 by £660 million and higher than in 1965–6 by over £1100 million.[21] The larger deficit to some extent reflected a less buoyant revenue as the economy slowed down. But it also implied a much more relaxed financial and monetary policy.[22]

Relaxation had begun well before the Budget. Investment grants on investment undertaken in 1967 and 1968 were raised in December 1966 by 5 per cent. Bank rate was reduced from

7 to $5\frac{1}{2}$ per cent in three successive steps between January and May. Ceilings on clearing bank lending were removed in the Budget itself. Then came a series of events in May and June that began to build up pressure on the exchanges, a pressure that continued to grow until devaluation in November.

The change in sentiment began with the announcement on 2 May of Britain's intention to apply formally for membership of the EEC. Since the balance of payments cost of joining the EEC was known to be substantial there was a natural suspicion that an application might at some point be followed by a devaluation of the pound. In June came the Six Day Arab–Israeli war, an oil embargo and the closure of the Suez Canal. The reduction in interest rates was also reducing the incentive to hold sterling, weakening the gilt edged market and adding to market liquidity as the Bank of England became a net buyer of gilt edged. Hire purchase restrictions on cars were relaxed the day after the Suez Canal was closed and relaxed further at the end of August. By the second half of 1967 retail sales were running 3 per cent above the level in the first half.

Devaluation, November 1967

Devaluation was increasingly the subject of public discussion. As early as the Budget debate ten back bench speakers either contemplated or openly advocated devaluation. The drain on the reserves, beginning in May, reached crisis proportions in the third quarter when over £500 million was drawn. The government was warned that it was unlikely to be offered further support in Europe. In mid September dock strikes began in the leading ports and continued in London until late in November. These inevitably affected the trade figures and produced considerable uneasiness in the exchange markets.

The central fact, however, was that world trade in manufactures was no longer booming and had shown no increase since the beginning of the year. British exports, continuing to take a falling share of what was in 1967 a static total, fell throughout the year. The fall was accentuated in October and November by the dock strikes but there was no falling-off in imports and the balance of payments, after moving back into deficit in the second quarter, showed a record deficit of £250 million (after seasonal adjustment) in the final quarter of 1967. Equally important, there seemed no prospect of an early move back into surplus. It was necessary to reflect on the likely situation in the spring of 1968 with a continuing deficit and no possibility of further deflationary action. If devaluation offered the only escape in such circumstances there was no point in delaying it.

The Prime Minister and the Chancellor continued to hope that sterling would be rescued in one way or another, e.g. by a pre-election boom in the United States in 1968. They deferred a decision while the rumours on the continent multiplied and the expectation of devaluation grew ever stronger. When it finally came, the Bank of England was faced with a bill for £356 million to meet the losses it had incurred on forward transactions in an effort to sustain the parity. Had the decision been taken in September, or even October, much of this loss would have been avoided.

At some stage in the 1960s, almost regardless of government policy, devaluation was perhaps inevitable. In the eighteen years since the devaluation of 1949, the competitive power of British industry had failed to keep pace with that of other industrial countries and a proneness to inflation had developed that was difficult to control. What was not inevitable was that the devaluation would restore competitive power and external balance. Devaluation in a fully employed economy with no accompanying measures is a very different affair from devaluation with a substantial margin of spare capacity and measures to restrain domestic demand.

The sequel to devaluation

Not that the 1967 devaluation was an instant success. On the contrary, 1968 was one long year of crisis and the outcome remained in doubt until well into 1969. Even when the immediate anxieties had passed, it was only a few years before the pound was in trouble again. Less than five years after 1967 it was allowed to float – downwards – in June 1972.

Devaluation from $2.80 to $2.40 to the pound took place on

18 November but on this occasion there was no simultaneous devaluation by other industrial countries, Denmark excepted. Bank rate was raised to 8 per cent, bank advances were limited, hire purchase restrictions on cars tightened, and cuts announced in defence spending and public investment. Export rebates and SET premiums, except in Development Areas, were withdrawn. The IMF was to be asked for a standby of $1400 million and additional credits to bring the total to $3 billion were to be raised from foreign central banks.

The government's targets were set out in a Letter of Intent to the IMF at the end of November. These included 'an improvement of at least £500 million' in the balance of payments and a surplus in the second half of 1968 of £200 million at an annual rate. There was also a target for DCE (domestic credit expansion) − a new concept, dear to the IMF, and intended to measure changes in the money supply purged of the influence of balance of payments surpluses and deficits. There would be four-monthly reviews of the economic situation by a visiting team from the IMF. After the submission of the Letter of Intent the Chancellor (James Callaghan) resigned and was succeeded by Roy Jenkins.

There was doubt from the beginning as to the adequacy of the government's measures in relation to the targets set. The devaluation also provoked heavy spending in the expectation of rising prices. But it was difficult to supplement the measures, once announced, by action to curb spending in advance of Christmas and the Chancellor concentrated in January on cutting public expenditure. After long debate he was able to announce a reduction in expenditure plans for 1968−9 of £500 million, with larger reductions in later years. These reductions effected a radical change in the trend in public expenditure on goods and services, which had climbed over the three years to the beginning of 1968 at 4.7 per cent a year in real terms and over the next two years fell at 2 per cent a year. The reductions also marked a withdrawal of Britain from military positions east of Suez and a contraction in aspirations to remain a world power.[23]

The Chancellor announced his intention to allow expansion in 1968 and 1969 at 4 per cent per annum. This came under criticism at the OECD where a 3 per cent rate was thought high enough. It was soon clear, however, that in the first quarter of

1968 expansion was well above both these figures. Consumer spending in particular, which the government expected to fall below the level of 1967, was running nearly 5 per cent above it in the first quarter and at the end of the year showed an increase on 1967 of nearly 3 per cent. The year-on-year increase in GDP, however, was 4.3 per cent in 1968 and 2.5 per cent in 1969: slightly higher than the Chancellor's target in 1968 and well below it in 1969.

The exchange markets took little comfort from the early promises of a switch in resources to improve the balance of payments and were alarmed by the high spending over the winter. The current balance of payments improved quarter by quarter but remained in deficit throughout 1968: the forecast surplus of £200 million a year in the second half of the year turned into a deficit now estimated to have been at an annual rate of £146 million although thought to have been £300 million in the estimates published in 1969. The cause of the divergence from the forecast was an unexpected buoyancy in imports which increased by 10 per cent in volume in spite of the rise in import prices resulting from devaluation. It was only when the rise in imports virtually ceased in 1969 that a balance of payments surplus emerged.

The long delay in the emergence of this surplus not only added directly to the need for foreign finance but created uncertainty in the exchange markets over the chances of maintaining the new parity. The pressure on sterling was particularly acute in the first half of 1968 when over £1000 million in foreign exchange had to be found. In four successive quarters from the middle of 1967 to the middle of 1968 the amount of foreign exchange paid out by the authorities was never less than £500 million and reached a total of £2200 million — several times higher than the official reserves then or earlier (see figure 4.2, p. 151).[24] Even in the second half of 1968, and especially in the final quarter, foreign exchange had to be borrowed from other central banks on a large scale; and for the year as a whole the amount of foreign exchange that had to be provided by the monetary authorities was twice as much as in 1967, the year of devaluation.

The pressure on sterling was out of proportion to the continuing balance of payments deficit which was estimated in 1969 at a little over £400 million on current and long-term capital account.

Speculative pressure was resumed shortly after devaluation and mounted in March when there was a large-scale movement into gold by speculators fearing a devaluation of the dollar and other currencies. This led to a closure of the international gold pool and a separation of the gold market for monetary authorities at $35 an ounce from the free market for private transactions.

The budget, introduced next day on 19 March, was more deflationary than any post-war budget. It included large increases in indirect taxes, higher rates of SET and motor vehicle duties and a levy on investment income for one year only. The additional revenue in a full year was estimated at £923 million. One result of the 1968 Budget, reinforced by the 1969 budget was to convert the PSBR from a deficit of £1844 million in 1967 to a surplus of £534 million in 1969 – the first such surplus since the days of Stafford Cripps at the end of the 1940s.

The 1968 budget slowed down the rapid expansion in progress but did not put an end to the pressure on sterling. By the first quarter of 1969 GDP had risen over the previous twelve months by a little over 2 per cent and unemployment was more or less unchanged at 2.2 per cent. From the spring of 1967 until the end of 1970 unemployment remained broadly between 2.0 and 2.6 per cent – limits which many in the early 1960s would have identified with full employment. The exchange market, however, remained subject to wild fluctuations with peaks in the forward premium on dollars in March, May and November.

The speculative pressure in these months led to further restrictive action. In May there was a tightening of monetary policy. In November fresh hire purchase restrictions were introduced. As the crisis became more acute, with expectations of a franc devaluation, the Chancellor announced a scheme of import deposits covering about one-third of total imports and requiring the deposit for six months of half the value of imported goods. He also used the regulator to raise indirect taxes by 10 per cent and obliged the clearing banks to reduce their lending to the private sector by 2 per cent in comparison with the level in November 1967.

Even these measures were insufficient to restore confidence and rumours spread of an impending break-up of the government. As late as May 1969 some observers were still in doubt whether there would be a current surplus in 1969.[25] Although the trend towards a surplus was pretty unmistakable by the end of 1968, the market was unconvinced and pressure recurred in April − May and August 1969 because of speculative transfers into deutsche marks. By the autumn, however, there could be no mistaking the emergence of a current surplus which reached about £500 million in 1969. The spot dollar rate, which had remained below par since April 1968, and was at its lowest in August 1969, at last recovered to reach par at the end of 1969 and the premium on forward dollars almost disappeared.

The impact of devaluation

The effects of the devaluation have been the subject of several studies. The impact on the balance of payments is put at between £400 million and £1000 million in three years with a majority verdict of about £700 million.[26] There is general agreement about the effect on exports but marked disagreement on imports.

The consensus on exports of goods points to an increase of between 9 and 12 per cent by volume and between 6 and 9 per cent in price: by value the estimates lie between 16.5 and 20 per cent. Since the actual increase by volume between 1967 and 1970 was 30 per cent, these estimates may be on the low side. The increase in the price of imports is put in most estimates at 12−13 per cent and the consequent reduction in volume at 5 per cent in two studies and zero in two others. The increase in the value of imports works out at between 7 per cent in the first two studies and between 10 and 16.5 per cent in the other two. Again, these may be too pessimistic. It makes no sense to assume that imports are unaffected by a rise in price by 10 per cent or more and indicates a failure to study previous trends in the volume of imports. In the case of manufactured imports, for example, where the increase after devaluation was particularly large, there was a strong upward trend and evidence of acceleration, interrupted in 1965−6 by the import surcharge. The unexpected rise in the total volume of imports by 7.5 per cent in 1967 in spite of the slackening in economic activity at a time when forecasters were predicting a much smaller rise points to just such an acceleration.

One feature of the studies of devaluation is the importance they attach to the change in invisibles. In most estimates this works out at about half the estimated change in the trade balance but in one it is the other way round. Given that the change in invisibles was not far short of the change in the trade balance between 1967 and 1970 it is likely that the contribution of invisibles to the total effect of devaluation was more than half.

What of the repercussions of devaluation on wages and prices? On one calculation the increase in hourly earnings attributable to devaluation alone was no more than 6.8 per cent and for consumer prices 5.6 per cent.[27] Over the three years 1968–70 the actual increase in hourly earnings was about 33 per cent while the increase before devaluation in the years 1964–6 was over 25 per cent. It may be quite accidental that this yields a difference of about 6.5 per cent. No firm conclusion can be drawn from the comparison but it does suggest an order of magnitude not inconsistent with the estimate quoted. Similarly the increase in retail prices of 13.4 per cent in 1964–6 compares with a rise of 19.6 per cent in 1968–70, an acceleration of 4.6 per cent that is not very different from the estimate of 5.6 per cent.

It can be objected, however, that the effect on prices is not to be measured over some finite period but takes the form of a speeding up that may continue for a long time with larger increases in succeeding years. The inflationary effect of devaluation, instead of dying away may intensify. If we look at the sequel in wage and price movements up to 1971 we get a picture of gradual acceleration consistent with this view (see figure 4.3).

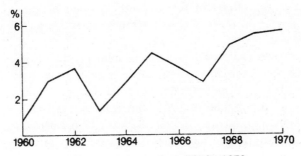

Figure 4.3   Increase in consumer prices, 1960–1970
Source: National Institute *Economic Review*

Table 4.2   Increase in hourly wages and retail prices 1966–1971[a]

	Hourly wages	Retail prices
1966	3.5	3.7
1967	7.6	2.8
1968	5.3	6.4
1969	7.3	5.0
1970	11.4	8.5
1971	12.0	8.0

[a] Measured from first quarter to first quarter.
Source: National Institute *Economic Review*

The figures in table 4.2 need to be interpreted with caution. The apparent slowing down in wage increases in 1968, for example, would vanish if comparisons were made on a fourth quarter instead of a first quarter basis. The rise in hourly wages, for example, was 5.3 per cent in 1967 and 1969 on a comparison from fourth quarter to fourth quarter and 6 per cent in 1968: that is, it was faster, not slower if we start the comparison one quarter earlier.

What the figures do show is that it was not until 1970 that the rise in wages was appreciably above rates experienced earlier in the 1960s. It is possible to interpret the acceleration as a delayed effect of devaluation. But more obviously it represented a reaction to wage restraint in earlier years and its removal in 1970. We are dealing, in other words, with three separate factors: the ordinary process of collective bargaining and the influences to which it responds; the efforts of the authorities, aided by the TUC, to restrain wage increases and the termination of those efforts; and devaluation.

There was some evidence of the influence of incomes policy in 1968 when the government made a fresh attempt to restrain wage increases. Wage rates had been remarkably steady from July 1966 until the middle of 1967. But from the second quarter of 1967 to the first quarter of 1968 they rose by 6.7 per cent. At that point the government took powers to postpone wage settlements, announced a nil norm for 1968, with a maximum increase of $3\frac{1}{2}$ per cent in exceptional circumstances, and reached agreement with the trade unions that they would not seek compensation in higher wages for price increase attributable to devaluation. In the next two quarters wage rates rose by only 1.6 per cent but how far this reflected a response to the government's policy is difficult to say. As always, wage increases tended to slow down in some phases and speed up again in others.

There can be no doubt, however, that devaluation made it more difficult to keep wage and price increases within reasonable limits. Apart from its immediate inflationary effects it helped to discredit incomes policy. As we have seen, by the time Labour left office in 1970 and incomes policy ceased, hourly wages were rising at over 11 per cent annum and prices at 8 per cent per annum – rates well in excess of the comparable rates in other industrial countries.

Industrial policy[28]

Although the balance of payments was an abiding preoccupation of the Labour government throughout its six years in power, there were many other developments in policy during those years. There was, for example, an effort to make industry more efficient and competitive through government intervention.

Conservative governments had relied largely on anti-monopoly policy and laying down rules to govern competition. They had also been involved closely with the industries in public ownership, with the defence industries, and in various ways with private industry across the board, either by way of encouraging investment or in order to promote exports and discourage imports. Industrial policy was not born in 1964. But under the Labour government it took a more deliberately interventionist form.

Labour viewed British industry, with few exceptions, as technologically backward and capable of improved performance through selective intervention by the government. A National Plan was to set targets for each industry and help was to be provided towards their achievement by prods, grants, and rationalization. In order to mobilize the resources of science and technology and assist in the restructuring of British industry the government created a new department, the Ministry of Technology in 1964; a new agency, the Industrial Reorganization Corporation (IRC) at the end of

1966; and a new source of industrial finance under the Industrial Expansion Act of 1968.

The Ministry of Technology was the co-ordinating agency in the government's efforts 'to bring advanced technology and new processes' to British industry. It was responsible for the work of the Atomic Energy Authority, the National Research Development Corporation (NRDC) and the industrial research and development activities of the Department of Scientific and Industrial Research (DSIR). From its formation in 1964 it dealt with machine tools, electronics, telecommunications and computers. Its R&D functions expanded progressively to include those of the Ministry of Aviation in 1967 and the Ministry of Power in 1969. It was deeply involved in aircraft production (e.g. over *Concorde*), shipbuilding and textiles. It made grants for research and development, placed R&D contracts, and ordered pre-production models of advanced design. It tried to spread knowledge of advanced technology by creating an industrial liaison service with the help of colleges and universities and by setting up low-cost automation centres that used educational institutions to provide demonstrations, practical courses and fee-paying consultancy services. How much all this achieved is difficult to judge. But it would be hard to argue that British industry was already taking full advantage of the opportunities open to it and needed no prompting from the government.

The IRC was directed by an independent group of businessmen and had at its disposal £150 million of Exchequer finance to lend to, or invest in, reorganized industrial units. It espoused the idea that British firms were too small in comparison with their foreign competitors and were not likely to be re-grouped into larger, more efficient units through the operation of market forces. An institutional gap was thought to exist which could be filled by the IRC, acting in co-operation with industry and financial agencies. Only schemes of reorganization that were commercially viable were to be promoted and in selecting such schemes the IRC would give preference to those that were likely to improve the balance of payments as well as improve productivity.

The Industrial Expansion Act was intended to reinforce the work of the IRC and provided it with finance for schemes approved by the House of Commons to improve efficiency and promote the use of new technology. The Act also provided additional finance for the National Research Development Corporation (NRDC), for the shipbuilding industry, for the development costs of *Concorde* and for the ocean liner, *Queen Elizabeth II.*

The IRC had an active life of about four years before the Conservative government announced in 1970 that it was to be wound up. It operated largely by encouraging mergers, and mergers under its auspices were not referred to the Monopolies Commission. This seemed to run counter to earlier insistence by the Labour government on the need for freer competition. The Monopolies and Mergers Bill introduced in 1965 was directed against mergers in the interests of maintaining competition while the IRC was seeking to promote mergers in the interests of efficiency and the balance of payments. Without clear criteria it was difficult to reconcile the two objectives. Competition might not always promote efficiency but it was doubtful whether increased size consequent on a merger could be relied upon to do so.

Between 1965 and 1973 the Board of Trade and its successor, the Department of Trade and Industry considered 875 mergers or proposed mergers of which only 18 were referred to the Monopolies Commission and only six forbidden. While the proportion of cases referred is not conclusive evidence, the deterrent effect of the 1965 Act was clearly limited and the activities of the IRC worked in the opposite direction. In all, the IRC took an interest in about 90 projects and injected £120 million into them between 1967 and 1970. In financial terms the influence of £120 million may seem small in comparison with manufacturing investment of about £7000 million over the same period.[29] But the projects sponsored involved many of the best known firms in British industry. The IRC suggested and promoted a merger between General Electric and Associated Electrical Industries, the two largest electrical engineering companies. It helped to create Ransome Hoffmann Pollard, the ball-bearings manufacturer, by a merger of three companies. It procured a reversal of the ruling of the Monopolies Commission against a merger between the Ross Group and Associated Fisheries. It intervened in several different industries including aircraft, shipbuilding, instrumentmaking and textiles to promote mergers.

While it is difficult to evaluate the total impact of industrial policy in the 1960s it is clear that it can have made only a modest difference to the trend in industrial productivity. There was a rather higher improvement than in the previous decade and it is possible that some at least of the improvement resulted from government measures. On the other hand, the years that saw the IRC in action were the years when employment in manufacturing first began to decline.

International relations

The 1960s were a period of world boom in which Europe enjoyed particular prosperity. Britain shared in this prosperity but with a lower upward trend; her European neighbours one by one drew level in their standard of living and by 1970 some were ahead of her.

Some of the changes over the decade are illustrated in tables 4.3 and 4.4. GNP grew only half as fast as in West Germany and the gap in relation to France, Italy, and, of course, Japan was even wider. If we take labour productivity in manufacturing as a basis of comparison the gap is much the same in relation to continental countries but is reversed in relation to the United States. Labour costs per unit of output rose appreciably faster than in other industrial countries when measured in national currencies but at a roughly comparable rate when account is taken of the sterling devaluation in 1967.

The final comparison shows the reduction over the decade in Britain's share of world trade in manufactures. In 1950 Britain's share had been about 25 per cent and higher than the share of France, Germany and Japan combined. In 1960 Germany was ahead and France and Japan, taken together, not far behind. By 1970 Japan, too, was ahead and Britain's share was not much above that of France or of Italy. In no year between 1950 and 1970 did Britain's share fail to decrease.

One reason for this disappointing performance emerges from table 4.4. While world trade grew fast in the 1950s and 1960s, the markets expanding most rapidly were in Europe but only a relatively small proportion of British exports (in comparison with members of the Community) went to Europe. The markets of the sterling area, to which over half British exports went in some

Table 4.3 Measures of economic performance in six leading countries, 1960–1970

	GNP in 1970	Output per man hour in manufacturing in 1970	Labour cost per unit of output in 1970	Share in world trade in manufactures (% of total)	
	(1960 = 100)	(1960 = 100)	(1963 = 100)	1960	1970
UK	134	142	132	16.5	10.8
USA	148	136	116	21.6	18.5
France	176	178	113	9.6	8.7
Germany	159	169	125	19.3	19.8
Italy	169	199	121	5.1	7.2
Japan	285	269	(112)[a]	6.9	11.7

[a] Wage cost, not labour cost.
Source: National Institute *Economic Review*, February 1972

Table 4.4 Growth of world trade, 1960–1970

	% increase in total imports (at current dollar prices)	Increase in UK exports, £ million per quarter	Proportion of UK exports to these markets	
			1960	1970
Sterling area	78	126	35.2	22.8
EEC	199	288	16.2	21.8
EFTA	119	209	11.9	16.0
World total	146	1069	100.0	100.0

early post-war years, expanded relatively slowly and Britain's share of these markets also contracted.[30] The result was a precipitate decline in their share of British exports to less than half what it had been in 1950 while the share of the EEC nearly doubled.[31] The EEC increased its total imports threefold in the 1960s and this rapid expansion not only reflected, but contributed to the growth of member countries. On the other hand, the slower growth of Britain's traditional markets in the sterling area and the less developed countries in other continents raised difficulties for British exporters quite apart from any decline in their competitive power.

A second consequence of the changed direction of trade, with 38 per cent of British exports being sold in Europe was to encourage efforts to enter the European Community and enjoy freer access to its expanding market. The increase in exports to the EEC had been an important element in the expansion of British trade in the 1950s and 1960s but it represented only a small proportion of the growth in Community imports — about $5\frac{1}{2}$ per cent of the $59 billion expansion.

Two attempts were made to join the Community. The first was announced at the end of July 1961 and the second in May 1967.[32] After the collapse of the free trade area negotiations at the end of 1959 effort had been devoted to building a bridge between the Six and the Seven, chiefly by arranging that the tariff reductions by the two groups minimized discrimination in trade between them. But it was soon clear that it would not be possible to establish a satisfactory bridge on the terms proposed by the British. Early in 1960 the Prime Minister came to accept that the right course was to apply for membership of the EEC, and this conclusion was supported by an inter-departmental committee, more on political than on economic grounds. Hitherto negotiations had been in the hands of the Board of Trade as a matter of commercial policy because the most concrete achievements of the EEC had been its plans for a Customs Union and its institutional framework while the political aspects of the Treaty of Rome still remained to be worked out. From 1960 the Foreign Office and the Treasury took a more active part.

By 1961 the government had taken soundings of Commonwealth, EFTA and American opinion, and the Prime Minister felt that he had sufficient support and sufficient chance of success to make an application for membership. The main problems were thought to consist of British agriculture, Commonwealth relations, and partners in EFTA unwilling to join the EEC. Of these problems, no final agreement was reached on the first after extensive discussion, virtual agreement was reached on the second and the third was hardly discussed. The common external tariff was to be accepted as it stood but with an offer of a 20 per cent cut in the forthcoming GATT negotiations.

On agriculture, the British proposed that Commonwealth producers of foodstuffs competing with European products should receive 'comparable outlets' to those they currently enjoyed in the British market. What had to be accepted was a general promise of 'reasonable access', coupled with assurances of Community support for international commodity agreements designed to maintain a 'satisfactory' level of world trade. So far as Commonwealth manufactures were concerned, no significant concessions were obtained in favour either of the older Dominions or of the Asian members. Had agreement been achieved on British entry it would have been on terms very different from those envisaged by the United Kingdom. Before the negotiations ended, however, General de Gaulle issued a veto in January 1963.

While negotiations were in progress, the Dillon Round of GATT negotiations was concluded in 1962. Reductions in tariffs on industrial products were made by Britain and other industrial participants that reached 20 per cent on many goods and were estimated to average 7–11 per cent. Larger reductions followed the Kennedy Round beginning in May 1963 and completed in June 1967. This was, in effect, a bilateral bargain between the USA and the EEC with Britain offering strong support to the US proposal for equal percentage cuts. It was agreed to cut in half the tariffs on many industrial products and make smaller cuts on others, yielding an average reduction for all manufactures of between 35 and 40 per cent. Two-fifths of the agreed reductions, by far the largest ever negotiated internationally, were made by the United Kingdom in July 1968 and the rest in equal doses at the beginning of 1970, 1971 and 1972.[33]

By 1966 the Labour party was in favour of entry into the EEC, 'provided essential British and Commonwealth interests are safeguarded'.[34] The Cabinet considered and rejected as not negotiable the alternative of a North Atlantic free trade area to include the US, Canada and EFTA. George Brown was given responsibility for economic relations with Europe and he and Harold Wilson toured Europe early in 1967 to sound opinion before the Prime Minister announced at the beginning of May Britain's intention to re-apply for membership of EEC.

As before, the French adopted obstructive tactics and it was soon clear that General de Gaulle would find occasion to veto the application. This he did after the devaluation of 1967 before negotiations had begun. The British application was not withdrawn but on French insistence the EEC were unwilling to allow negotiations with Britain until the summer of 1970, by which time de Gaulle had resigned (in April 1969) and the Conservatives were again in power.

Notes

1 Macmillan, *Pointing the Way 1959–61*, ch. 8; Lord Roberthall, *The Robert Hall Diaries*, vol. 2, pp. 231–2.
2 National Institute *Economic Review*, February 1962, p. 4.
3 Macmillan, *Pointing the Way*, p. 372.
4 In January 1961 the deficit was estimated at £150–£175 million; in April this was revised to £344 million; in 1990 the deficit was put at £237 million (Blackaby (ed.), *British Economic Policy 1960–74*, p. 17).
5 *Incomes Policy: the Next Step*, 1962, Cmnd 1626.
6 W. Fellner, et al., *The Problem of Rising Prices*.
7 Cairncross and Eichengreen, *Sterling in Decline*, p. 165n. The concurrent rise in imports suggests that output was at or near capacity so that excess demand fell on imports.
8 National Institute *Economic Review*, November 1963, pp. 3 and 14.
9 Ibid., February 1964, p. 11; Blackaby, *British Economic Policy*, p. 27.
10 National Institute *Economic Review*, May 1964, pp. 3, 14–15.
11 Ibid., February 1964, p. 10; May 1964, p. 4; August 1964, p. 4.
12 Prime Minister's Office, *The Economic Situation*, London: HMSO, October 1964.
13 Blackaby, *British Economic Policy*, p. 32.

14   Blackaby, *British Economic Policy*, pp. 34–5.

15   Cairncross and Eichengreen, *Sterling in Decline*, p. 185.

16   Cairncross and Eichengreen, *Sterling in Decline*, p. 177.

17   National Institute *Economic Review*, August 1965, p. 8, quoted in Blackaby, *British Economic Policy*, p. 35.

18   Blackaby, *British Economic Policy*, p. 36.

19   'Whereas by July 1962 all outstanding debts to the IMF accumulated in 1961 had been repaid, and reflation could begin "with a clean slate", by the time of the April budget in 1967 there still remained £292 million to be repaid to the IMF by the end of the year, together with a further £28 million owed to the Swiss authorities; and on top of this, there was a further £544 million to be repaid to the IMF by early 1971' (National Institute *Economic Review*, February 1968, p. 8).

20   Department of Economic Affairs, *Prices and Incomes Standstill: period of severe restraint*, Cmnd 3150, 1966.

21   R. W. R. Price, 'Budgetary policy' in Blackaby, *British Economic Policy*, 1978, p. 187.

22   On a full employment basis the 1967 Budget was about £300 million more expansionary than the 1966 Budget (ibid.).

23   Blackaby, *British Economic Policy*, p. 45.

24   The figure of £2200 million includes over £300 million to meet the losses on forward transactions entered into in 1967.

25   National Institute *Economic Review*, May 1969, p. 12.

26   For an assessment of the various estimates see Cairncross and Eichengreen, *Sterling in Decline*, pp. 197ff.

27   J. R. Artus, 'The 1967 devaluation of the pound sterling', *IMF Staff Papers*, November 1975.

28   For a detailed discussion see P. Mottershead, 'Industrial policy' in Blackaby, *British Economic Policy*, 1978.

29   Mottershead, 'Industrial policy', p. 439.

30   Britain's share of exports to the Commonwealth fell from 43 per cent in 1955 to 34 per cent in 1960 and 19 per cent in 1970 (Blackaby, *British Economic Policy*, p. 540).

31   The EEC took 11.2 per cent of British exports in 1950 and 21.8 per cent in 1970. During the 1950s the volume of exports to the sterling area more or less stood still; they were no higher in 1960 than in 1951. Exports to Western Europe, on the other hand, increased over the same period by 45 per cent and to North America by 77 per cent.

32 For a useful summary, see A. D. Morgan, 'Commercial policy' in Blackaby, *British Economic Policy*, 1978.
33 Morgan, 'Commercial policy', pp. 528–9.
34 Election manifesto, March 1966.

Further reading

Artus, J. R. 1975. 'The 1967 devaluation of the pound sterling', *IMF Staff Papers*, November, 595–640.

Beckerman, W. (ed.) 1972. *The Labour Government's Economic Record 1964–70*, London: Duckworth.

Blackaby, F. (ed.) 1978. *British Economic Policy 1960–74*, Cambridge: Cambridge University Press for NIESR.

Cairncross, A. (ed.) 1971. *Britain's Economic Prospects Reconsidered*. London: Allen & Unwin.

Cairncross, A. and Eichengreen, B. 1983. *Sterling in Decline*, chapter 5. Oxford: Blackwell.

Cairncross, F. and Cairncross, A. (eds) 1992. *The Legacy of the Golden Age: the 1960s and their economic consequences*. London: Routledge.

Cairncross, A. 1995. *Managing the British Economy in the 1960s*. London and Basingstoke: Macmillan.

Caves, R. (ed.) 1968. *Britain's Economic Prospects*. Washington, DC: Brookings Institution.

Cohen, C. D. 1971. *British Economic Policy 1960–69*. London: Butterworths.

McKie, D. and Cook, C. 1972. *The Decade of Disillusion: British Politics in the Sixties*, London: Macmillan.

Official Reports.

Incomes Policy: the next step, 1962, Cmnd 1626, London: HMSO.
Prices and Incomes Standstill: period of severe restraint, 1966, Cmnd 3150 London: HMSO.

5 The 1970s

The Course of Events

The decade of the 1970s falls into three parts. First come the years of Conservative government under Ted Heath from 1970–4, then the mid 1970s from 1974–6, first under Harold Wilson and from April 1976 under Jim Callaghan, and finally the late 1970s, after recourse to the IMF at the end of 1976, from the Lib–Lab pact of 1977 to the return of the Conservatives in 1979. These are political divisions but they coincide broadly with an economic segmentation into a period of boom in the early 1970s, a period of crisis in the mid 1970s and a period of recovery in the late 1970s.

At the beginning of the decade the economy had won free from the balance of payments difficulties that plagued the 1960s. From the beginning of 1969 until early in 1972 the current account remained in handsome surplus, funds moved into sterling and the large debts accumulated in the 1960s were gradually repaid. The last remaining debts to the IMF were extinguished in the second quarter of 1972 just as sterling once again came under severe and continuing pressure.

At first unemployment continued within the limits of 500,000–600,000 where it had remained for the previous three years. It rose slowly in 1970 and much more rapidly in 1971, reaching 900,000 at the beginning of 1972. This moved the government to take reflationary measures a little ahead of the great international boom of 1973 so that unemployment tumbled to 500,000 at the end of 1973 and output grew faster — by 7.3 per cent — than in any post-war year. The boom, which affected all industrial countries, drove up the prices of imported primary products, turning the terms of trade strongly against the United Kingdom even before the quadrupling of oil prices at the end of 1973. The rise in international commodity prices broke the rhythm of post-war economic expansion and introduced a period of crisis in which nearly all industrial countries suffered from inflation, balance of payments deficits and slower economic growth − none more so than the United Kingdom.

Meanwhile the Conservative government, after a year or so of trying to disengage from intervention in industry and abstain from any form of incomes policy, had gradually adopted a different posture, moved partly by the downturn in industry in 1971 and partly by the failure of its efforts to curb union power by legislation. Hourly wage rates which had risen at 5−6 per cent in the 1960s had begun to rise much faster after incomes policy ceased. A 10 per cent rise in 1970 had been followed by a 13 per cent rise in each of the next two years. These rates of increase were alarming enough to induce the government to make a fresh approach to the unions and introduce a new incomes policy in the course of 1972.

Other factors were at work to accelerate inflation before the boom of 1973 had made much progress. One was the removal of ceilings on bank credit and the attempt to encourage competition between financial institutions. A second was the increased pressure of demand as the economy approached capacity working. A third was the rise in import prices which by the first quarter of 1973 had already risen by 15 per cent since the middle of 1972. This in turn was partly the consequence of the decision in June 1972, after great speculative pressure, to let the pound float and the fall in its value by 9 per cent as it floated down over the next six months.

These influences were powerfully reinforced by the further rise in import prices in the year to the first quarter of 1974 by about 55 per cent. Inflation took a firm grip and by the summer of 1975 retail prices were rising at 27 per cent per annum (on a year-on-year comparison) and wages even faster. Together with the balance of payments, which by 1974 was in record deficit, inflation had become and remained the government's principal source of anxiety.

In 1974−6 the Labour government at first failed to take the measure of the dangers threatening the economy and, as the borrowing requirement grew to £12,000 million in 1975, the government lost the confidence of financial markets. The balance of payments, although improving, remained in deficit and it was necessary to engage in extensive borrowing abroad to meet the drain on the reserves. In the summer of 1976 it looked for a time as if things were on the mend. But a renewed rise in commodity prices as the world economy recovered from a downturn in 1974—5 reversed the improvement in the rate of inflation. This, and disunity within the Cabinet over cuts in public expenditure when unemployment was still increasing, produced a fresh loss of confidence in sterling. It was necessary to turn to the IMF for help and to meet conditions acceptable to the IMF. It proved in 1977 that these conditions were already being met. The first deliveries of North Sea oil began. As confidence returned, funds flowed into sterling on a colossal scale. The pressures that had lowered the pound to $1.55 in October 1976 were replaced by upward pressures that carried it up year after year until it reached $2.40 in 1980.

Inflation was at its worst in 1975 but was checked and lowered, partly by rising unemployment, which passed the million mark in the autumn, and partly by a successful incomes policy organized by the Chancellor and the TUC. Once the policy was in operation in the second half of 1975 the rise in retail prices began to slow down. From a peak of 27 per cent in August 1975 the rise in the retail price index, year on year, slowed down to 13 per cent in just under a year, picked up again to nearly 18 per cent in mid 1977 and then fell rapidly in the first half of 1978 to a low point of $7\frac{1}{2}$ per cent in June. In the 'winter of discontent' in 1978—9 inflation again began to accelerate and in the spring of 1980 it was well over 20 per cent. Inflation had been held in check but it had not been mastered. Moreover, while the inflation of the mid 1970s originated largely outside the United Kingdom and was intensified by wage pressure, inflation at the end of the decade, before the second oil shock in 1979, was more a domestic affair and was not self-correcting like a rise in commodity prices.

The current balance of payments, after the first oil shock, had been in heavy deficit in 1974. This gradually declined but did not disappear until the middle of 1977. Even with increasing supplies of North Sea oil there was a further deficit in 1979 and there was no substantial surplus until the latter half of 1980. The decade that had started with a promising surplus ended in sight of an even larger one but in between the balance of payments, as in the 1960s, was a source of almost constant anxiety.

Expansion had been halted by the rise in prices in 1974–5. Production fell in both years and there was a big rise in unemployment in 1975. When expansion was resumed in 1976 unemployment continued to rise slowly until the end of 1977 when it had reached 1,200,000.[1] It then fell by about 150,000 over the next two years as the pace quickened a little but shot up in 1980 and continued to rise for the next six years. At the end of 1979 unemployment was more than twice what it had been when the decade began.

Table 5.1 shows the movement of the main aggregates over the decade. The most striking feature of those years is the absolute fall in GDP in three of the ten years covered: small falls in 1974 and 1975 and a heavier fall in 1980. Thanks largely to the extraordinary rise in 1973 the increase in GDP over the decade was not far short of that in the 1960s, if measured at market prices, but appreciably less if measured, as it should be, at factor cost.

Of the other aggregates, the increase in exports was greater than in any other decade. It was much greater than the increase in imports although that was larger than ever before. Indeed, the faster growth of exports, in volume terms, stands out in comparison with all other decades except the immediate post-war years. The increase in fixed investment, on the other hand, was disappointingly small – not just less than in other decades but almost negligible. In five out of the ten years, fixed investment actually fell: in 1980, quite heavily when stockbuilding was also contracting heavily. The rise in consumers' expenditure was (as in successive decades since 1945) higher than in the previous decade but it came nowhere near the increase that followed in the 1980s. The growth of public expenditure on goods and services was faster than in any comparable period in spite of all the cuts in 1976 and at other times. Stocks and work in progress fell for the second decade in succession (but only because of the big drop in 1980).

Table 5.1 also brings out the fluctuations over the period. Moderate expansion in 1971–2 was followed by an extremely vigorous but short-lived upswing in 1973. Then began the troubles of the mid 1970s, with two years of declining output and a third year in which an exchange crisis coincided with domestic developments that in retrospect look remarkably healthy. Over these

Table 5.1 Changes in the allocation of resources, 1970–1979 (increase from year to year in £ billion at constant 1985 prices)

	1971	1972	1973	1974	1975	1976	1977	1978	1979	Changes between 1970 and 1979
Consumers' expenditure	5.0	10.1	8.5	-2.6	-0.7	0.7	-0.7	10.0	8.1	38.5
Public authorities' final consumption	1.7	2.4	2.6	1.2	3.5	0.8	-1.1	1.5	1.5	14.1
Gross domestic fixed capital formation	1.0	-0.1	3.4	-1.4	-1.1	0.9	-1.0	1.6	1.5	4.9
Value of physical increase in stocks and work in progress	-1.3	-0.6	6.6	3.6	-6.4	5.0	1.8	-0.5	0.5	1.4
Exports of goods and services	4.0	0.7	7.4	5.1	-2.1	6.6	5.4	1.6	3.2	31.8
Total final expenditure	10.4	12.7	29.0	-1.8	-7.5	14.5	4.6	14.2	14.9	90.9
Imports of goods and services	3.0	5.9	7.5	0.8	-4.9	3.5	1.2	3.0	7.4	27.3
Gross domestic product (at market prices)	6.0	6.7	21.5	-2.7	-2.1	10.8	3.3	11.2	7.5	62.3
Gross domestic product (average at factor cost)	3.9	6.6	17.8	-3.9	-2.1	6.7	6.7	7.9	7.7	51.2

Source: Economic Trends Annual Supplement (1990 edn) table 3

years stockbuilding fluctuated wildly – far more than in previous decades – and fixed investment, apart from 1973, was remarkably depressed. The adjustments in 1974–5 to the high rate of inflation cut consumer spending after big increases in 1971–3 and raised the proportion of income saved. Public authorities started by spending more heavily up to 1975 and beat a retreat in 1976 and 1977.

In the last years of the decade from 1976 to 1979 GDP (at factor cost) grew steadily. Then in 1980 there was a pronounced setback. All the aggregates fell in that year, the heaviest fall being in consumer spending, closely followed by stockbuilding. The reasons for the setback are discussed below (pp. 231–3, 238–41).

Domestic policy under the Conservatives, 1970–1974

The decade as a whole was dominated by the struggle to contain inflation. This was true almost throughout and it was true not just of the United Kingdom but of virtually all industrial countries. The most sensational economic events of the 1970s were the two inflationary oil shocks in 1973 and 1979, price increases that helped to bring the long secular boom of the post-war years to an end and cut the rate of economic growth severely in nearly all the advanced industrial countries. Inflation in Britain, using the GDP deflator as a measure of price changes, increased from an average of 4.7 per cent over the years between 1956 and 1973 to an average of 14.8 per cent in six years from 1973 to 1979. For the OECD group of countries the rise was more moderate but almost equally alarming: from 3.8 per cent to 8.9 per cent.

With the spurt in inflation went balance of payments deficits and higher unemployment, again on an international scale. The rise in the price of oil acted as a kind of tax, deflating the incomes of oil importers and obliging them to make extra payments of foreign exchange. The resulting balance of payments deficits were the counterpart of the large surpluses earned by the oil producers who thus accumulated large funds abroad that could be lent to the oil importers. So long as the demand for oil remained unchanged at the higher prices, the deficits and surpluses were bound also to continue. They would dwindle, however, as the oil producers absorbed larger imports of manufactures and other goods – a process that was bound to take some time. Consumers of oil were also likely in time to find ways of economizing and substituting other fuels and this might help to bring down the price of oil as well as the volume of imports, as eventually happened. The danger was that in the meantime the oil importers would each try to shift their deficit to their neighbours by deflating demand, lowering economic activity and employment, and cutting imports. This would produce a downward spiral in international trade and employment without doing much to get rid of the collective deficit. Some deflation occurred automatically from the high price of imports, as in 1951, some from deliberate government policy in an effort to check inflation; others again, of which Britain was one, tried to offset the deflation by expansionary measures, borrowing abroad to finance their balance of payments deficit.

We discuss later how these international influences, which were of particular importance in the 1970s, affected the United Kingdom. For the present we need only note how the international background changed: the rise in inflation, the emergence of a new imbalance in international accounts, the slowing down of economic growth; the higher level of unemployment. The intellectual background was changing too. There was more scepticism and distrust of the powers of government. Some of those who had campaigned for more planning at the beginning of the 1960s now campaigned for a more limited agenda for the state. The use of the annual budget for the preservation of continuous full employment was dismissed as 'fine tuning'. The need to check inflation began to be given priority over the need to avoid unemployment and those who claimed to have the antidote to inflation were given a hearing previously reserved for those who claimed to have a cure for unemployment. As fiscal policy came into disrepute, monetary policy was endowed with almost magical properties. Inflation, it was argued, 'is always and everywhere a monetary phenomenon'; control of the money supply would ensure control of the price level. It was the heyday of monetarism.

The early years of the Conservative government

At the outset in 1970 wages were rising at over 10 per cent per annum and prices at about 7 per cent — about twice the average rates in the 1960s. Incomes policy had faded out and the Conservative government, taking office in June, had no intention of reviving it. While they hoped to bring down inflation, they laid stress initially on other objectives: government withdrawal from intervention in industry; greater efficiency through the use of new techniques of administration; reducing the power of the unions; and renewing the effort to enter the EEC.

So far as intervention was concerned, the government started by refusing help to a number of enterprises in difficulties — Mersey Docks and Harbours Board (whose debenture holders then found that they did not have the government guarantee of their holding which they had assumed); Rolls Royce (which was allowed to go bankrupt but helped to continue the production of RB211 engines to meet a contract with Lockheed); and Upper Clyde Shipbuilders (which was denied assistance but after a sit-in was reorganized on a basis that allowed work to continue at all four yards involved). In contrast to this disinclination to help 'lame ducks', the government's expenditure on goods and services at constant prices increased every year from 1970 to 1973 and in 1972 and 1973 the increase was greater than in any year in the 1960s except 1967.

Four months after the election, a budget was introduced in October 1970 that was designed to be neutral in its impact on demand but made many changes in keeping with the government's philosophy of less but better government. The Regional Employment Premium was to be phased out and the Industrial Expansion Act repealed. Investment grants were to be replaced by tax allowances, as in the 1950s, and deficiency payments to farmers by levies on imported foodstuffs. Some welfare schemes were to be curtailed or made subject to higher charges and a new scheme for supplementing the incomes of the poorest families was announced.

By the time of the 1971 budget, unemployment, which had been creeping up slowly for two years, began to rise at a much faster rate, reflecting the slowing down in economic expansion since 1968. The Chancellor planned his budget so as to permit a 3 per cent growth rate in 1972 but misjudged what was required for this purpose. He reduced taxation in 1971−2 by £500 million by halving selective employment tax, cutting corporation tax and increasing taxpayers' child allowances. Most of this, however, was slow in affecting demand, and unemployment continued to rise rapidly. Further expansionary measures were taken in the summer: a large programme of public works in the development areas, larger house improvement grants, increased capital allowances for industry with a time limit, the abolition of hire purchase controls, and cuts in purchase tax amounting to £400 million. These were intended to back up an informal arrangement with the CBI to avoid or limit price increases over the next twelve months. Before the end of the year yet more reflationary measures were taken: some government expenditure over the next two years was to be brought forward and all outstanding post-war credits were to be repaid. Unemployment, however, continued to rise towards a million in the months before the 1972 budget.

The troubles of 1970–1 were not confined to the United Kingdom. In other countries, too, wage claims rose in spite of an easing of pressure and more rapid inflation was causing increasing concern. The United States in particular was running a massive deficit in its balance of payments and this precipitated drastic action in August 1971 when President Nixon suspended convertibility of the dollar and introduced an era of floating exchange rates.[2] The currencies of Germany and the Netherlands had already been floating since May, the Scandinavian countries, Italy and Japan now floated theirs and the pound was also allowed to float briefly although it was not until June 1972 that a continuing float began.

In the middle of these currency uncertainties in the autumn of 1971, the Bank of England abandoned ceilings on bank credit and introduced a new scheme that left the clearing banks freer both to compete for deposits and to offer credit to their customers. It was intended to allow more competition between the clearing banks and other financial agencies but it left the Bank with a much less direct and certain control over credit creation and the stock of money. Instead of the previous obligatory 'liquid assets reserve ratio' of 28 per cent and cash ratio of 8 per cent (from both of which the non-clearing banks were exempt) the Bank now imposed a fixed uniform $12\frac{1}{2}$ per cent reserve asset ratio on all banks, specifying the assets which were eligible for inclusion as reserves.

Whatever the merits of the scheme, its immediate effect was to allow bank advances to increase sharply. In the nine years 1963 to 1972 bank lending had grown at a little over 12 per cent per annum; in 1972 it increased by 37 per cent and in 1973 by 43 per cent.[3] The growth in the money supply quickened correspondingly. Whatever the contribution of changes in the stock of money to inflation in other years, their contribution in 1972 and 1973 is beyond dispute.

In the same month (September) as the new scheme was announced by the Bank a dispute over pay began between the National Coal Board and the National Union of Mineworkers which led to a seven-week strike with picketing at coal depots, open cast sites and power stations. In February 1972 a state of emergency was declared and industry was put on a three-day week. When a settlement was ultimately reached the average earnings of miners were raised by 17 per cent or more compared with an initial offer of a rise of 7 per cent. The government's hope that each successive settlement in the public sector would be smaller than the one before was now groundless. The rise in wages was undiminished as unemployment grew.

The later years of the Conservative government

From then on until it left office, the government pursued two allied objectives. It sought to mitigate inflation by persuading the TUC to lend support to an incomes policy or, if no agreement was possible, by imposing a statutory policy. It also aimed, from the Budget of 1972 onwards, at a rate of growth in output of 5 per cent, sufficient to bring down unemployment to half a million or less. The efforts of the government to arrive at a workable incomes policy are discussed in the next section. Its management of demand can be dealt with fairly briefly.

The 5 per cent target was set initially for a two-year period from the first half of 1971 to the first half of 1973 and extended subsequently to cover an additional year. A 5 per cent rate of growth was well above the normal rate of expansion, which was usually put at about 3 per cent but there was a good deal of slack in the economy as evidenced by the high level of unemployment. It was also arguable that, since unemployment had continued to grow in 1971 while output grew at 3 per cent, there were signs of some acceleration in the growth of economic potential. The announcement of a 5 per cent target might encourage higher investment and make it easier to introduce an acceptable incomes policy.

Over the two-year period indicated by the Chancellor the growth of output was a little in excess of 10 per cent. But in the following year to the first half of 1974 there was a slight fall which brought expansion over the three years from 1971 just below the 10 per cent level. Unemployment also fell to about 500,000 at the end of 1973 before beginning a steady climb for the next four years. To that extent the policy achieved its objectives. But there were casualties. One was the balance of payments, which came under heavy pressure in June 1972 when the pound was allowed to float after a record drain on the reserves in the second quarter. At that stage the current account was still in substantial surplus but it soon moved into increasing deficit. In the second half of 1973, before the oil shock had taken effect, the current account deficit had reached over £1500 million a year, with an addition of nearly £2000 million still to come in 1974.

The rate of inflation is often represented as a second casualty. This was not at first much affected by the increase in pressure. Even when the pound floated down by 9 per cent in the second half of 1972 the rise in retail prices was at just over 10 per cent a year later – about 2 per cent higher than in 1971 and 1972. It was only in 1974 and 1975 that inflation roared ahead and by then the enormous rise in international commodity prices in 1973 was working through to domestic prices. Even if one measures inflation in terms of wage settlements, there had been little acceleration by the end of 1973.

The main instrument of policy for raising the rate of expansion was, as usual, fiscal, with monetary policy in support. The 1972 budget made large cuts in income tax and purchase tax to increase consumer demand. The 1973 budget was broadly neutral but involved a further rise in the borrowing requirement (PSBR), a concept figuring increasingly in public controversy and discussed at some length later. To be both spending more and borrowing more seemed to some critics unsound finance, all the more because the stock of money was now expanding rapidly. There were, in any event, good grounds as 1973 progressed for taking action to check demand, since private investment was rising strongly and some of the public expenditure intended to give a boost to the economy in 1972 had been delayed and was now superimposed on a very high level of demand. The Chancellor accordingly made a small cut of £100 million in public expenditure in May and coupled it with a much larger cut of £500 million in 1974–5.

Monetary policy also became more restrictive. In 1971 interest rates had been cut and the ceiling on bank credit removed as part of the reflationary programme. In 1972 and 1973 bank credit expanded rapidly, carrying the money stock up in parallel, and the Bank of England began to raise interest rates, at first gently but in the second half of 1973 in larger steps. Between the end of June and the end of July Bank Rate was raised by 4 per cent and by November had reached a peak of 13 per cent – a level never previously reached. Special deposits were also increased and had reached 5 per cent by the end of the year.

Thus as the Conservative government entered 1974 it was struggling to contain a very rapid growth in demand, a rate of inflation that threatened to accelerate and an external deficit larger than any experienced since the war.

Incomes policy

In the later years of the Labour government incomes policy had become increasingly ineffective. Apart from the restiveness of the unions under continuous wage restraint the rise in retail prices after devaluation put an increased strain on the policy. The 1968 budget set a ceiling of $3\frac{1}{2}$ per cent on pay increases that met the criteria in the White Paper of 1967 (which were much the same as those in the White Paper of 1965). It allowed exceptions only for genuine increases in productivity but the exceptions grew in bogus productivity deals. Commitment to the policy on the part both of unions and government became steadily weaker. With the growth of labour militancy and unofficial strikes, the unions came to be seen as lacking the authority to bind their members. The same considerations made the government give priority over incomes policy to the reform of industrial relations in the hope of checking 'the industrial anarchy' of unofficial strikes.

A White Paper, *In Place of Strife*, set out in January 1969 proposals for a Commission on Industrial Relations with powers to enforce a settlement in inter-industry disputes, the registration of collective agreements, and a number of 'interim remedies', such as a cooling-off period of twenty-eight days to protect the economy from the disruptive effects of serious unconstitutional strikes. The proposals, especially those embodied in penal clauses, aroused strong opposition within the Labour party. The government, however, was determined to persevere and introduced a Bill concentrating largely on unofficial strikes rather than on long-term reform of industrial relations. The TUC, at the request of the government, produced their own counter-proposals and after lengthy negotiations the Bill was dropped in June 1969 in return for a 'solemn and binding undertaking' by the TUC as to how they would act to secure a return to work in an unofficial strike.

Nothing remained of the longer-term proposals for reform following the Report of the Donovan Commission on Trade Unions and Employers' Associations in June 1968 except the Commission on Industrial Relations which was set up in March 1969. Although there were a score of references to it in the year following the dropping of the Industrial Relations Bill it had little opportunity of establishing itself before the change of government in June 1970 and was denied the co-operation of the TUC when the Conservatives in turn introduced a Bill to reform industrial relations.

By the autumn of 1969 incomes policy was on its last legs. The government had intimated in the 1969 Budget its intention not to seek renewal of its powers over wages and prices when they expired at the end of the year. Aubrey Jones, the chairman of the NBPI, announced his retirement in October and the government when they lost office had it in mind to amalgamate the NBPI and the Monopolies Commission.

When the Conservatives took over in June 1970 they made clear their opposition to a formal incomes policy. This was indeed part of their philosophy of withdrawal from intervention in industry and it was not until unemployment began rising much more steeply in 1971 that their attitude changed. Their original position was that it was for employers to resist high wage demands but that at the same time the trade unions should be obliged to work within a legal framework that would limit their powers. In December 1970 they introduced an Industrial Relations Bill which was intended to reform collective bargaining, reduce industrial conflict and allow greater individual freedom. The Bill provided for the establishment of a National Industrial Relations Court and required all unions to register and submit their rule books for scrutiny. The Bill limited the legal immunities of trade unions in ways calculated to restrict the right to strike and required union rules to specify who could order industrial action and in what circumstances. Other clauses echoed the Labour party's proposal for a cooling-off period and secret ballots in certain circumstances.

The TUC condemned the Bill as 'striking at the very root of a union's bargaining strength', boycotted the NIRC and CIR and called for the repeal by any future Labour government of the Bill's provisions. In September 1971, at the annual conference, unions were *instructed* (not just recommended) not to register and twenty unions were expelled in 1973 for failing to de-register.

When the government sought to make use of the legislation in 1972 it proved of little value. The enforcement of a cooling-off period of fourteen days in a rail dispute merely delayed negotiations; and when the government called for a ballot this showed a large majority in favour of further industrial action. By July in a dispute in the docks over blocking and picketing of some container firms, the government made no use of their emergency powers. When they came to seek union co-operation in a renewal of incomes policy in the second half of 1972 the Act had become a serious embarrassment. Instead of seeking to weaken the unions as a means of checking inflation they now saw the advantage of strong unions in the operation of a formal incomes policy.

Experience in 1970–1 brought home to the government the advantages of an incomes policy. The absence of such a policy did not free the government from its responsibilities for wages and prices in the public sector. Nor was it likely to be possible to keep them immune from the influences at work in the private sector. Large increases in pay in the private sector, where rises of 10 per cent and more were widespread in 1970, were accompanied by even larger claims in the public sector. The government found itself caught up in 1970–1 in disputes with the unions on a series of wage claims over the specific magnitude of the increases in pay to be allowed. In three prominent cases involving the dustmen, the electricity supply workers and the Post Office workers the issue was referred to a Committee or Court of Inquiry after strike action or work-to-rule. The government might avoid direct confrontation in this way, but the awards that were made could be embarrassingly large: in the first two cases they amounted to at least 14 per cent.

The government had also tried in 1971 to operate an incomes policy from the prices side. It embarked in the summer of 1971 on the series of reflationary measures outlined above as backing for an initiative taken by the CBI. This consisted in asking their members for an undertaking to refrain as far as possible from raising the prices of British products and services and limiting unavoidable price increases to 5 per cent over the next twelve months. Undertakings were obtained from nearly two hundred of the largest British companies. The government could do no less and sought to restrain increases in the prices charged by nationalized industries. This had damaging repercussions on the success of those industries in complying with the financial targets they had been set and a consequent need to provide substantial subsidies.

These efforts did do something to slow down the rise in prices. (see figure 5.1) From the middle of 1971 to the spring of 1972

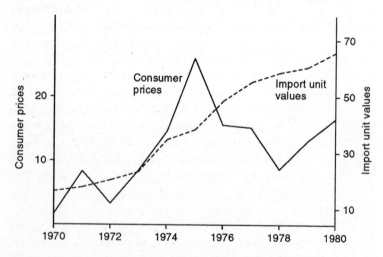

Figure 5.1   Import unit values and consumer prices, 1970–1980
Source: Economic Trends Annual Supplement 1981

the price of consumer gods and services, which had been rising at 8—9 per cent per annum, hardly changed. But with wage rates rising over the same period as fast as ever at 10 per cent per annum, the rise in prices recommenced at much the same rate as before. They continued to rise at 8—9 per cent in 1972 and 1973 but by 1974 the big increase in import prices of nearly 60 per cent in 1973 fed through into consumer prices and the rate of inflation accelerated sharply.

In their last two years in office the Conservatives became very much preoccupied with incomes policy. They made little progress in the first half of 1972 when the Industrial Relations Act came into force and was used with conspicuous lack of success in a dispute with the railwaymen. Negotiations between the government and the TUC began in July with the TUC demanding the repeal or suspension of the Industrial Relations Act and the government proposing consideration of low pay and conciliation machinery and suggesting a link between wage agreements and the cost of living. The negotiations continued until November with proposals from the government of a ceiling of 5 per cent on increases in retail prices over the next twelve months, a lump sum increase in pay for everyone with additions for price increases in excess of 6 per cent, and a commitment to a 5 per cent rate of growth for the next two years. The TUC wanted a bigger lump sum increase in wages, with a long list of budgetary concessions, price control, dividend restriction, higher pensions, increased family allowances and, of course, suspension of the Industrial Relations Act.

The Prime Minister made clear that some of the TUC proposals could not form part of an agreed incomes policy since they were for Parliament to decide. He offered a number of minor concessions which left the TUC unmoved. Had they accepted the government's proposals, there would still have been doubt whether the TUC could keep wage and salary agreements within the limit set without sanctions that were not discussed, or whether the government could have honoured a guarantee to limit price increases without fresh powers.

On 6 November 1972 a freeze on pay and prices, rents and dividends was announced. It was to last 90 days, with exceptions for fresh foods and for sharp increases in the price of materials. Excluding food, prices rose 0.7 per cent over the next three months and earnings less than 1 per cent. The prices freeze was extended to the end of April, at which point the new value added tax replaced purchase tax. Wage settlements held up on 6 November because they had a later operative date came into operation in February and March and account for some of the rise in earnings in later months.

A second stage of incomes policy lasted from April to November 1973. Pay was limited to increases over a twelve-month period in average earnings per head of £1 per week plus 4 per cent of the wage paid in the preceding twelve months. No one could be paid more than an extra £250 a year. All settlements had to be referred to a newly created Pay Board and no compensation was allowed for higher productivity – a favourite loophole in the late 1960s. Price increases had to be referred to a new Price Commission which would restrict price rises to allowable cost increases. Although the Pay Board claimed that the increase in pay under the settlements they approved averaged under 8 per cent in stage II, the recorded nation-wide increase in average hourly earnings in the twelve months covering stages I and II was 12.7 per cent including overtime.[4] In assessing the impact of the policy it is probably best to use hourly wages rather than earnings since overtime earnings must have been considerable in 1973. On an October–October comparison, hourly wage rates rose by nearly 19 per cent in 1971–2 and just under 12 per cent in 1972–3. There can be no doubt of a substantial check, especially at a time when the increase in pay was accelerating, even if the rate of inflation still remained alarmingly high.

In the summer, talks on stage II were conducted with the TUC and the CBI, but the annual Congress of the TUC approved the talks by only a small majority. In July the government announced its intention of linking pay and prices by a threshold clause. In the same month the National Union of Mineworkers gave notice of a claim for wage increases of 22–46 per cent. No doubt with this in mind the provisions of stage III were made more flexible and envisaged additional payments for working 'unsocial hours'. The Pay Board was also asked to prepare two reports, one on relativities in pay and one on anomalies.

The new pay code, introduced on 7 November 1973, limited increases in pay to £2.25 per head per week, or 7 per cent, and an individual limit of £350 per year. For every 1 per cent rise in retail prices above 7 per cent on an October 1973 base, pay could be increased by an extra 40p a week. Manufacturing firms with sales between £5 million and £50 million a year had to notify the new Price Commission created in the spring along with the Pay Board.

What followed was coloured by the dispute with the miners on the one hand and the first oil shock on the other. On 11 October the miners rejected an offer from the National Coal Board worth on average about 13 per cent just ahead of a large rise in the price of Middle East oil. (The offer was made consistent with the 7 per cent code by using the flexibility provisions to the maximum.) The miners then began an overtime ban on 12 November, by which time the electric power engineers had been on strike for some days and the Arab oil producing countries had cut oil supplies to the west by 25 per cent. A state of emergency was declared on 13 November. The minimum lending rate (bank rate) was raised to 13 per cent and in December hire purchase controls were reintroduced and a new scheme, generally referred to as 'the corset', was brought into use in order to check the growth of interest-bearing bank liabilities. The government also cut public expenditure in 1974−5 by £1200 million − an unprecedented reduction but by no means sufficient to prevent public expenditure from continuing to rise.

At Christmas oil prices were doubled as from 1 January while the cut in supplies was reduced to 15 per cent. Efforts to settle the miners' dispute continued. The TUC proposed that other unions should agree that whatever settlement was reached with the miners, they would not cite it as a precedent in their own bargaining. This was strongly supported on 16 January at a special conference of union presidents and general secretaries but the proposal was not taken up by the government. The Pay Board produced a report on relativities on 24 January and the Prime Minister suggested to the CBI and TUC the appointment of an independent relativities board to consider the miners' and other claims. The NUM, however, having decided not to strike on 10 January, decided to call a strike ballot on 24 January and, when this showed an 80 per cent vote in favour, went ahead with the strike on 10 February, refusing to wait until after the general election which the Prime Minister called on 7 February.

Last efforts were made to settle the strike by a group of industri
alists whose offer was refused. The Pay Board sat as a special
relativities board for seven days to consider the case of the miners.
But by the time its report was issued the Labour party was in
power and had settled the dispute with large increases in pay.

The Pay Board remained until July 1974 when it was scrapped
by the new government. The threshold arrangements of stage III
also continued until October 1974. With prices rising far faster
than the 7 per cent that for some reason was accepted as the basis
of stage III, increases in pay were triggered again and again between May and October. Hourly wage rates in 1974 rose by 24
per cent, in part because of the threshold arrangements made in
October 1973.

International relations

The European Community had agreed at the end of 1969 to reopen
negotiations for British entry in the following summer. With the
change of government it was the Conservatives who appeared in
Brussels in June 1970. The problems were largely unchanged
from 1967. They included agriculture and fisheries, New Zealand,
Commonwealth sugar and the length of the transition period.

A year later agreement had been reached on nearly all the major
issues on the basis of British entry in January 1973. The EEC
system of agricultural support with minimum import prices and
levies would replace the British system of deficiency payments and
British prices would be raised gradually to EEC levels. Similarly
United Kingdom tariffs would be brought into line by July 1977
with the common external tariff. New Zealand would enjoy concessions for butter and cheese during the transition period but
not for lamb and was promised 'suitable measures' for butter
thereafter. There would be special (but unspecified) arrangements
for Commonwealth sugar. Commonwealth preference for manufactures had been replaced in Britain at the end of 1971 by a
system of generalized preferences similar to the one recently
introduced by the EEC and a changeover to the EEC scheme of
preferences was made after entry. Most imports from EFTA and
the Republic of Ireland continued to be allowed duty-free entry.

The financial arrangements involved a British contribution to the Community budget rising to 19 per cent of the total budget in 1977. It had already been arranged to go over from purchase tax to VAT in 1973 so agreement to use the Community system of indirect taxation required no change. Other financial matters – exchange control, debt management, monetary policy, etc. were not immediately affected.

The Labour government, 1974–1979

The Labour government of 1974–9 suffered from a number of disadvantages. For most of its life it had no parliamentary majority and in its struggle to survive could not look more than a year ahead. When a second election in October 1974 gave it a majority of three, the majority soon disappeared. In 1976 there was a change of leader and in 1977 it had to share power with the Liberals. The Cabinet itself was bitterly divided on strategy and its divisions were a matter of public knowledge.

The problems faced by the government were formidable. It inherited a balance of payments deficit of well over £3000 million a year, import prices that were rising at 60 per cent per annum, terms of trade that had deteriorated by 20 per cent in a year, and a public sector financial deficit of over £3000 million. Inflation was accelerating, unemployment had begun to rise, and wage earners were demanding larger wage increases.

It was still the aim of the Labour government to revivify British industry and arrest its long decline in comparison with its continental neighbours. How this was to be done, however, remained obscure. Attention was focused on manufacturing industry and there was the usual emphasis on the need for more investment and research and development. The earlier hankering after planning continued but now took the form of urging planning agreements with leading firms. Not much came of this: the only planning agreements reached were with Chrysler and the National Coal Board, both of them highly dependent on government assistance.

Then there were tripartite sector working parties – a Whitehall idea – to review the problems of specific industries and contribute to an industrial strategy under the umbrella of the National

Economic Development Office. These, too, effected no radical changes and more often became pressure groups for government favours. Efforts continued to reconcile anti-monopoly competition policy with mergers designed to create larger enterprises that were assumed to be more efficient. Even when large budget cuts had to be made, money continued to be provided in pursuance of the government's industrial strategy. But employment in manufacturing declined rapidly in the first two years and was still lower, by a small margin, at the change of government in 1979. Labour productivity in manufacturing rose by only 7 per cent during the five years of Labour government − the lowest improvement in any five year period since 1945. Unemployment doubled, rising above 1 million for the first time since the war, and most of the increase was in manufacturing.

The most urgent economic problems facing the government were inflation on the one hand and the external deficit on the other. The two were connected since the main cause of the acceleration in inflation in 1974−5 was the fast rise in the price of primary products; and it was this that turned the terms of trade sharply against Britain and produced the large external deficit. To that extent the problems of 1974−5 were external in origin. Other countries, however, although affected by the same international factors, suffered less from inflation and international imbalance. Consumer prices, for example, rose by 19.2 per cent in the United Kingdom during 1974 but by only 14.2 per cent on the average in the member countries of OECD. Inflation was more pronounced in Britain than elsewhere because it was aggravated by domestic factors.

A view popular among monetarists is that the inflation was the result of the large expansion in the money supply two years previously.[5] This is not a plausible explanation of a worldwide phenomenon nor can it account for the slightly faster rate of inflation in Britain. Prices were already rising faster in Britain in 1972−3.[6] One important factor was the operation of the threshold arrangement in stage III of the Conservative government's pay policy. This had been retained by the Labour government with the result that eleven successive pay increases were triggered between May and December 1974 and wages increased in the second half of the year by 16 per cent. It must be admitted, however, that most of the rise in prices in 1974 took place in the first half of the year and that it was in 1975 that the rise in wage costs because of the threshold arrangement had its main effect on prices.

In any event, 1974 was only the beginning. The big rise in prices and wages continued in 1975. In the year to July 1975 hourly wages rose by 33 per cent and claims for still larger increases were entered. Retail prices over the same period rose by 26 per cent. The scale of these increases alarmed not only the government but the TUC who were well aware of the drastic action that the Chancellor might be obliged to take. When the government took office there had been a social contract which was intended to moderate wage increases in return for government expenditure in various directions. This had obviously been of little help.

Now, after talks between the government, the TUC and the CBI, it was proposed in July 1975 to fix a ceiling to wage increases either in the form of a percentage or a lump sum. The lump sum was preferred and the maximum increase was fixed at £6, with no increases in incomes above £8500. The Price Code continued and increases in pay in breach of the limit were to be disallowed for price increases. The government would monitor progress jointly with the CBI and the TUC and would, if necessary, take powers to make a breach of the pay limit illegal. There were also a number of provisions, including additional food subsidies, designed to temper price increases and maintain employment.[7]

The policy agreed in 1975 was highly successful. In the year to July 1976 the rate of increase in hourly wages dropped from 33 to 18 per cent and in the second half of 1976 it had fallen temporarily to a rate far below 10 per cent. The crisis that occurred at the end of 1976 was in no way associated with failure to check wage inflation.

Not that wage inflation had caused no difficulties earlier. In all his budgets Denis Healey had to take into account the danger of adding to inflation either by encouraging inflationary wage claims or by maintaining or increasing the pressure on the economy. In his first budget in March 1974, introduced only three weeks after taking office, he had contemplated deflationary measures but contented himself with a 'broadly neutral' budget which, however, added £700 million to public expenditure and £1400 million to revenue from taxation. Food subsidies were increased by £500 million and pensions raised (from higher national insurance contributions). Income tax was increased and the prices of nationalized industries were raised sufficiently to yield an extra £1000 million. An item that assumed importance later was a 2 per cent increase in corporation tax and advance payment of half the corporation tax due in 1974−5. There was to be a second budget in the autumn.

Long before the autumn, unemployment had begun to rise, suggesting that the budget was more restrictive than it seemed. Business became increasingly alarmed by a loss of liquidity and feared a major crisis. When corporation tax was raised in the budget it was assumed that profits were relatively high. This was true if inflationary increases in stock values were included. Inflation-adjusted profits on the other hand were falling rapidly since replacement costs moved up at least as fast as inflation.[8] Companies found themselves in an increasingly illiquid position and the *Financial Times* index of industrial shares, reflecting the fear of wholesale bankruptcy, fell to under 150 from a level of 300 at the time of the budget in March. In his autumn budget on 12 November the Chancellor came to the rescue by exempting 90 per cent of stock appreciation from corporation tax and easing price control. Where companies had previously been allowed to pass on only 50 per cent of additional labour costs of production (higher productivity being assumed to take care of the other half) they were now allowed to pass on 80 per cent. These concessions were expected to reduce revenue by £1500 million in 1975 and add correspondingly to the PSBR.

The PSBR, which was the total amount of borrowing likely to be undertaken over the financial year by the central government, local authorities and nationalized industries, was a concept to which increasing importance was being attached. As a measure of the impact of the public sector on financial markets it was given a place of honour in monetarist doctrine alongside the stock of money and the rate of interest. Economists interested in demand rather than money tended to concentrate on the public sector financial deficit which deducted from the PSBR and sums on-lent by the public sector to other agents.

As will be seen from table 5.2, the PSBR increased every year in the 1970s until 1976−7 − and even then the 1976 budget

Table 5.2 Budget forecasts and outcomes, 1971–1979 (£ billion)

	Public sector borrowing requirement		Public sector financial deficit[a]		Public expenditure in real terms[b]	% of GDP
	Budget estimate	Provisional outcome	Budget estimate	Provisional outcome		
1971–2	1.2	1.3	0.3	−0.7	141.8	41¾
1972–3	3.4	2.9	2.4	2.1	148.7	41¾
1973–4	4.4	4.3	2.9	3.1	160.8	43½
1974–5[c]	2.7/6.3	7.6	1.2/4.8	5.9	180.2	48¾
1975–6	9.1	10.0	7.6	8.2	180.2	49¼
1976–7	12.0	8.8	10.6	7.7	175.8	46¾
1977–8	8.5	5.8	7.6	5.8	167.1	43¼
1978–9	8.5	9.2	7.4	7.5	175.4	44

[a] The financial deficit differs from the PSBR by the amount *lent* by the public sector.
[b] Revalued at 1989–90 prices and excluding privatization proceeds.
[c] The forecasts for 1974–5 relate to the March and November budgets.
Sources: Financial Statement and Budget Reports and Autumn Statement 1990

forecast a further increase. In 1974–5 Denis Healey budgeted for a substantial reduction in the PSBR but at the end of the financial year found that there had been a large increase, not a reduction. A similar increase occurred in the financial deficit. But it was no full-employment budget. If we look at the outcome in terms of employment and output there is no doubt that 1974 was a year of falling activity. By the second quarter of 1975 unemployment was over 800,000 and still rising while GDP was 3 per cent lower that in 1973.

The size of the PSBR horrified some financial commentators who believed in balanced budgets and drew criticism from other less orthodox quarters. A zero PSBR was a much more exacting target than a balanced Budget since the PSBR counted in capital transactions as well as current expenditure, including the borrowing for capital purposes of nationalized industries and local authorities. It had been rare for the PSBR to reach zero: the only occasions were in the budgets of Stafford Cripps and Roy Jenkins and in the case of Cripps it had been necessary to supplement the negligible level of personal savings by aiming deliberately at a high level of public saving through the Budget.

New views of economic management

All kinds of ideas were in circulation as to the policies the Chancellor should follow. Monetarists wanted strict control of the money supply as the only sure way of holding the price level steady. But whether central banks had the power to control the money supply except indirectly by varying the level of economic activity was open to doubt; and there were those who argued very plausibly that it was the price level that determined how much money people held, not the other way round.

Then there was the New Cambridge school which regarded the external deficit as the mirror image of the budget deficit because, of the four sectors into which the economy could be divided – business, household, external and public – the first two were held to maintain a steady rate of surplus so that fluctuations in the surpluses or deficits of the other two must match. Cutting the budget deficit would cut the balance of payments deficit. Here it was a simple question of fact and the facts did not support the alleged constancy of the surpluses of the business and household sectors. It was not possible to assume that a smaller budget deficit would automatically reduce the external deficit.

Other theories asserted that Britain had too few producers. Kaldor, as we have seen, wanted to make more labour available for manufacturing by taxing services. Bacon and Eltis argued that too much of the labour force was employed on government account instead of in meeting market requirements. Others again pointed to the high proportion of earnings taken by the state in taxation and the loss of incentive that this implied. One way or another Britain's problem was seen to consist in finding more labour for manufacturing and providing larger incentives to effort and ingenuity.

It cannot be said that many of the controversies of the time had much relevance to current problems. So far as manufacturing was concerned, from 1974 for many years the trend in employment was down and the trend in unemployment was up. Shortage of manpower was the least of its difficulties and lack of incentive (which had many causes, not just one) was less important than lack of training. As for the budget, the Chancellor kept trying to cut the deficit, for some time with the opposite result, and when he did succeed it was not the impact of the cuts on demand that improved the balance of payments but the impact on confidence reinforced by very high interest rates.

Financing the external deficit

It was round the balance of payments and the finance of the external deficit that much of the policy of the years 1974−6 revolved. The current balance, already in deficit in 1973, reached a peak deficit of £3200 million the following year and then improved year by year until it emerged in surplus in 1977 (see table 5.3). Over the five years 1973−7 the cumulative deficit on current account was about £7000 million against which can be set a net import of long-term capital of about £3700 million − mainly for investment in North Sea oil. In 1973−5 the difference (about £5000 million over those three years) was financed almost entirely

Table 5.3 Balance of payments of the UK, 1970–1980 (£ million)

	Balance on current account (seasonally adjusted)	Finance provided by			Drawings on reserves	Total
		IMF	Other monetary authorities	Foreign currency borrowing		
1970 Q1,2	+ 495	− 112	− 1091	−	− 110	− 1313
Q3,4	+ 326	− 22	− 70	−	− 15	− 107
1971 Q1,2	+ 496	− 295	− 1107	+ 82	− 330	− 1650
Q3,4	+ 618	− 259	− 156	−	− 1206	− 1621
1972 Q1,2	+ 331	− 415	+ 1424	−	− 145	+ 864
Q3,4	− 128	−	− 560	−	+ 837	+ 277
1973 Q1,2	− 296	−	−	+ 326	− 452	− 126
Q3,4	− 710	−	−	+ 673	+ 224	+ 897

1974	Q1,2	− 1564	—	—	+ 741	− 83	+ 658
	Q3,4	− 1622	—	—	+ 1010	− 22	+ 988
1975	Q1,2	− 709	—	—	+ 630	+ 268	+ 898
	Q3,4	− 817	—	—	+ 180	+ 387	+ 567
1976	Q1,2	− 180	+ 1018	+ 581	+ 858	+ 176	+ 2633
	Q3,4	− 783	—	− 615	+ 933	+ 677	+ 995
1977	Q1,2	− 734	+ 899	—	+ 634	− 4355	− 2822
	Q3,4	+ 559	+ 214	—	+ 479	− 5233	− 4540
1978	Q1,2	+ 363	− 505	—	− 246	+ 2072	+ 1321
	Q3,4	+ 573	− 511	—	+ 59	+ 257	− 195
1979	Q1,2	− 654	− 522	—	− 92	− 1023	− 1637
	Q3,4	+ 105	− 74	—	− 158	− 36	− 268
1980	Q1,2	− 221	− 71	—	− 267	− 597	− 935

Source: Economic Trends Annual Supplement 1981 and 1990

in two ways: through a net inflow of short-term capital, much of it oil money, and through foreign currency borrowing. The latter, which was by far the more important of the two, was a device first used on any scale in 1973 under which nationalized industries and other public sector borrowers raised funds in the Eurocurrency market which they sold for sterling to the Exchange Equalization Account, the Treasury providing forward cover. Since sterling was liable to depreciate, as it did from the middle of 1975, this could be an expensive way of borrowing.

Foreign currency borrowing reached a peak in 1976 when it was necessary to find no less than £3628 million in foreign exchange to meet all the demands in that year. Although the current account continued to improve, it remained heavily in the red with a deficit (on the latest figures) of £940 million and heavy withdrawals of sterling funds amounting to £2400 million. Even on long-term there was a small net outflow. This caused acute pressure, a heavy fall in sterling and recourse to the IMF, as described below. While the help given by the IMF was indispensable, it will be observed that it provided not much more than a third of what was raised through foreign currency borrowing or from the reserves, and the loan negotiated at the end of the year was not available until 1977 when the pressure was all in the other direction.

It was not possible for the Chancellor to tackle the external deficit directly. All he could do was to exploit the various means of financing it through agreements with foreign governments and central banks and with international institutions like the IMF. One other possibility was to let the pound depreciate. From the Chancellor's point of view, however, the problem was more to keep it up instead of encouraging more inflation to ride in on the back of a falling exchange rate. The dollar exchange rate remained fairly stable but with a falling trend until the second half of 1975 when it fell in six months from $2.28 to $2.02 (see figure 5.2).

One scheme to which the Chancellor attached particular importance was for extensive recycling of the surplus funds of the oil producers. In January 1975 the finance ministers of the EEC countries agreed to press strongly for new recycling arrangements allowing the IMF to recycle up to $12 billion in 1975. Healey also felt strongly that industrial countries should not seek to reduce their trade deficits by deflation since this would give rise to beggar-

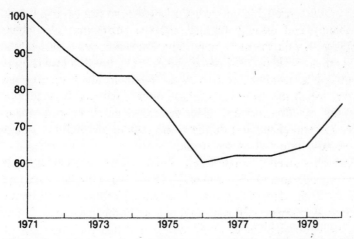

Figure 5.2   Sterling effective exchange rate, 1971–1980 (1971 = 100)
Source: Economic Trends Annual Supplement 1981

my-neighbour policies of the kind that perpetuated depression in the 1930s.

What the external deficit did force on the Chancellor was a series of cuts in government expenditure. This was not because of any effect on the balance of payments but as a kind of sacrificial gesture to 'sound financial opinion'. The budget deficit was financed almost entirely domestically and although this might require the offer of high interest rates there was no insuperable difficulty provided the rate met market expectations. Whether at that rate other borrowers were 'crowded out' is a much disputed issue. It need not happen if the market's appetite for gilts is elastic, if the level of activity and income is raised by the 'excess' expenditure, and if the stock of momey expands correspondingly. But if there is an investors' 'strike', as in the autumn of 1976, the market may be so disrupted that the level of aggregate demand falls.

It had been orthodox Keynesian doctrine that public investment should be increased if unemployment was on the increase and this had been broadened to substitute public expenditure for public investment. In 1974 the Chancellor did make a large increase in public expenditure, meaning to combine it with a fall in the borrowing requirement. When instead the borrowing requirment started leaping up, in spite of repeated cuts in mini budgets throughout 1974—6, the Chancellor hesitated to go further and plan for a still higher PSBR. By the time he introduced his 1976 Budget he expected a PSBR of £12 billion, which was 10 per cent of GDP at market prices and substantially more than total personal savings. However ready one was to draw on government finance to maintain full employment, one might hesitate to use more than the public was currently saving even if one recognized that a little inflation accounting showing the state making large capital gains on the national debt would make things look very different. More important, a Chancellor who was facing an exchange crisis could not disregard the views of those from whom he proposed to borrow.

The Chancellor's first budget had forecast a PSBR of £2.73 billion, his 1975 budget a PSBR of £9.06 billion and his 1976 budget a PSBR of £11.96 billion. On the first two occasions the borrowing requirement had turned out to be much larger than forecast and had reached £7.60 billion in 1974—5 and £10.77 billion in 1975—6. However much it was cut, expenditure seemed to creep up relentlessly. The 1976 forecast was received therefore with a good deal of scepticism. The scepticism, moreover, appeared at first to have some justification since by July estimates were being revised upwards. Even after large cuts in July and again in December after the IMF visit, the PSBR was expected to be over £11 billion. But as is shown by figures of quarterly changes, not then available, the peak rate of increase had already been reached in the first quarter of 1976 and the cuts the IMF pressed for in November were already being made six months earlier without anyone knowing.

For this there were two reasons. One was that most of the rise in public expenditure and most of the underestimation of the PSBR arose out of unexpectedly rapid inflation and a faster rise in prices in the public than in the private sector. The increase in public expenditure between 1972—3 and 1975—6 came to £27.3 billion in cash terms but only £7 billion at constant 1977 survey prices. The second reason was the introduction of cash limits for which planning started in 1974—5 and which was taking effect in 1976—7 in the form of great caution in spending as the limit was approached. Cash limits, in fact, were more deflationary than the government dared to be and the PSBR for 1976–7 ended up at £8.82 billion, not £11.2 billion as the IMF had been told.

Meanwhile the deficit in the balance of payments was taking its toll. Countries holding reserves in sterling had drawn down their balances in each of the last three quarters of 1975 and the flow of short-term funds had been outwards in the final quarter. The reserves had fallen by £800 million in the last nine months of 1975 and the rate of exchange was sliding down. The Chancellor had taken steps to reinforce the reserves by applying to the IMF for $1.2 billion under the 1975 oil facility and $800 million from Britain's first tranche. It was soon needed.

Early in 1976 there had been some discussion in the Treasury of using a lower rate of exchange to promote exports but no ministerial authority was ever secured for a controlled devaluation. Nevertheless when the Bank of England engaged in the sale of sterling on 4 March the move was interpreted by the market as an attempt to lower the exchange rate, all the more because of large sales made simultaneously by a large seller, thought to be Nigeria.[9] Next day, as if to lower the rate still further, a small cut was made in bank rate (MLR). The rumours, which were not officially denied, initiated a prolonged fall in the value of the pound from over $2 in January and February to under $1.80 in June (see figure 5.2).

While the pound was falling, the government experienced a defeat in the House of Commons and only narrowly won a vote of confidence on 11 March. Five days later the Prime Minister, Harold Wilson, announced his resignation and on 5 April was succeeded by James Callaghan. Early in May a new wage agreement was reached with the TUC for the year from July 1976 limiting increases to £2.50–£4.

Pressure on the pound was intense and the drain of foreign exchange in the second quarter reached record proportions at nearly £2 billion in three months. About half of this represented withdrawals of exchange reserves by central monetary bodies. The drain made the Prime Minister feel that the central problem was that of the sterling balances and led him to seek a revival of arrangements like those negotiated in Basle in 1968 which had guaranteed the value of sterling holdings but had been allowed to lapse in September 1973. The fact was, however, that the drain of foreign exchange in the second quarter made it virtually certain that it would be necessary, sooner or later, to turn to the IMF for a loan as Healey himself had thought likely since April. No Basle-type arrangement for sterling balances was probable without the blessing of the IMF.

Early in June the pound fell 7 cents against the dollar. A standby credit of $5.3 billion was arranged by Dr Zijlstra, the head of the Netherlands Central Bank. The credit was for three months, renewable for a further three months. As the Americans made plain, it could not be further extended and would therefore have to be repaid by early December at the latest. Some of the lenders were anxious to see the United Kingdom obliged to turn to the IMF eventually and be forced to comply with the spending cuts and credit restrictions on which it would no doubt insist.

The fundamental question that had to be resolved was how the economy was to be readjusted to the sharp change in the terms of trade. It was a change that in twelve months had added about 30 per cent more to the import bill than to exports; and since imports formed over 20 per cent of GDP, the loss of income to which adjustment was necessary was about 6 per cent, assuming no early improvement in the terms of trade. The same scale of adjustment was indicated by the size of the external deficit: it would require the injection of about 6 per cent of GDP into the balance of payments to wipe out the deficit and leave a small, necessary surplus. The adjustment could not come from additional output since the economy in 1974 was fully employed. The danger was that it would come from diminished employment and general impoverishment reducing the level of imports.

In fact the adjustment was spread over the next four years as the balance of payments gradually improved and North Sea oil began to flow. By 1978 the terms of trade had moved nearly half-way back to the level of 1972 and North Sea oil was contributing about £2.5 billion more than in 1974. Viewed in retrospect the problem was largely one of borrowing until international prices moderated and North Sea oil came on stream. But in 1974 and 1975 borrowing had to be short-term and unstable. Something more was necessary to cut imports, boost exports and limit consumption. These were changes that could be promoted by depreciating the currency and holding down the rate of wages. The high price of imports would also exert its own deflationary influence since efforts to maintain real wages through higher wage claims would be countered by higher prices to meet the higher wage costs.

There was in fact a definite check to consumer spending in 1974–7, the average for those four years working out at 2.7 per cent less than in 1973. This was not due to a fall in real wages: from the middle of 1974 to the middle of 1978 wages rose about 9 per cent faster than prices. Nor was it due to a higher level of saving since the savings ratio fell slightly over those years. The explanation must be a deflation of non-wage incomes (including the loss of income by those who lost their jobs).

The Treasury, backed by the Bank of England, was already arguing in July for cuts in public expenditure to bring the PSBR down to £10 billion. This was necessary, it was maintained, to prevent a further fall in the pound. After seven stormy Cabinet meetings, cuts of £1 billion were agreed and a further £1 billion was raised by an increase in national insurance charges on employers.

The drain subsided a little and the exchange rate remained fairly steady in July and August. But at this point inflation began to pick up speed again. The big rise in commodity prices in 1974 had been succeeded by a fall in 1975 as world production lost momentum. But from the middle of 1975 there had been an economic recovery that carried commodity prices up again in 1976 and to this had been added a fall in the sterling–dollar exchange rate of 18 per cent from July 1975 to July 1976. Retail prices rose 4 per cent in the final quarter of 1976 where they had risen by a little over 3 per cent in each of the first two quarters. What impressed financial markets more was a large increase in bank lending in the third quarter; but this, too, was probably related to the rise in commodity prices, as well as to expectations of higher interest rates.

Monetary policy

For some reason monetary policy had remained remarkably relaxed in Labour's first two years, with bank rate (or MLR) falling from 13 per cent to 9¾ in April 1975, rising to 12 per cent in October and then falling again to 9 per cent in March 1976. It was then put up sharply to $10\frac{1}{2}$ per cent, under intense pressure on the pound, in April and to $11\frac{1}{2}$ per cent in May. Special deposits, which had been up to 5 per cent in January 1974 were never more than 3 per cent from May 1974 to September 1976. Supplementary deposits ('the corset') had been used in the second half of 1974 but were removed in February 1975.

In September faced with renewed pressure on the pound and a buyers' strike in the market for gilts, the Chancellor began rather belatedly to tighten monetary policy. Bank rate was raised on 10 September to 13 per cent, the first increase since May. However, the pound continued to fall and there were rumours that it was intended to let it reach $1.50 before stabilizing. At the end of the month, before and during the Labour Party Conference, at which some highly unrealistic motions were passed, the pound fell by $7\frac{1}{2}$ cents in two days. The Chancellor, who decided at the last moment to attend the Conference rather than fly to the IMF Annual Conference in Manila, announced that he would be applying to the IMF for a loan of $3.9 billion, the largest loan ever made by the IMF.

Notwithstanding this announcement, the pound remained under pressure throughout October. Bank rate was raised to 15 per cent on 7 October and special deposits, which had been raised from 3 to 4 per cent on 16 September, were raised again to 6 per cent. On 18 November the corset was reintroduced and exchange control was tightened. Meanwhile on 25 October the dollar rate had fallen to 1.55. From then on it recovered, beginning the long climb that took it to 2.40 in 1981. The tightening of monetary policy stopped the outflow of short-term funds and started an inflow to the United Kingdom. The funds advanced in June were repaid in December without drawing on the IMF loan which was not granted until 5 January.

The IMF Agreement

The IMF had begun by asking for cuts of £4 billion in two years, stricter control of the money supply and a fall in the exchange rate. The terms presented to the Cabinet on 23 November were a cut of £3 billion in the PSBR to come from lower expenditure, higher taxation and the sale of BP shares. The Cabinet, then engaged in a long series of meetings over three weeks to discuss alternative strategies, rejected these terms, only two ministers supporting the Chancellor. The IMF subsequently proposed cuts of £2.5 billion over two years and on 2 December this was agreed, the Prime Minister having finally made it clear that he was in support of the Chancellor. Cuts would be made of £1 billion in 1977−8 and a further £1 billion in 1978−9, the remaining £$\frac{1}{2}$ billion coming from the sale of BP shares. The agreement implied a reduction in the PSBR in 1977−8 to £8.7 billion − a figure below the £9 billion that the Prime Minister had represented to the IMF earlier in November as the lowest the Cabinet would accept but virtually identical with the actual (but as yet unknown) PSBR in 1976−7.

The agreement had not been reached without prolonged efforts to moderate the terms and attempts to seek support elsewhere. They were modest in comparison with the cuts of £5 billion that the IMF was rumoured to be seeking and not much more than had been contemplated when a PSBR of £9 billion in 1977−8 was proposed in July. They certainly did not prevent a steady expansion in 1977−8, with a moderate rise in unemployment in 1977 and a moderate fall in 1978. The experience of these years compared favourably with that of the three preceding years.

More dramatic was the immediate turn-round in the flow of funds. Instead of constant downward pressure on the pound, there was now constant pressure upwards. It had begun before agreement was reached. But it was only in 1977 that the transformation became fully apparent with an addition to the reserves in the course of the year of £9.5 billion − an almost unimaginable improvement by previous standards. The exchange rate was for a time 'capped' i.e. held at a more or less fixed rate by official purchases of foreign exchange. But when this threatened to add too much to the money supply (for which a target had been fixed in July 1976) the authorities decided to 'uncap' the pound in September 1977 and it then rose to $1.93 in the first quarter of 1978 and $2.02 in the first quarter of 1979.

The role of public expenditure

Looking back on these years, interest is usually concentrated on public expenditure. Both in the 1960s, and even more in the 1970s, there was an initial sharp increase in the proportion of GDP spent by the government, succeeded by a reduction that carried with it an improvement in the balance of payments (table 5.2). There were those who thought the original increase entirely proper as a means of countering rising unemployment and the subsequent cuts very much mistaken since bound to make unemployment rise faster than ever. Those who thought in those terms regarded general deflation as an inappropriate way of reducing a balance of payments deficit and wanted import quotas or some other form of protection.

So far as unemployment was concerned, the big increase took place in 1975 when the PSBR was rising fast while there was relatively little increase after the middle of 1976 when the PSBR was decelerating. This may seem paradoxical: how could GDP fall when the public sector was running a deficit of over £10 billion? And how could it expand again in the face of cuts of at least £7 billion. The answer is largely to be found in the behaviour of stockbuilding which fell by £4 billion between 1973 and 1975 and rose by nearly £3 billion between 1975 and 1977. Some of the movement in the PSBR, moreover, was a simple reflection of contraction or expansion in GDP rather than itself the cause of the change in GDP. But the experience of the mid 1970s was widely held to sound the death knell of demand management on Keynesian principles. Budget deficits did not ensure full employment and expenditure cuts could be made with impunity.

A more direct approach to the external deficit raised other difficulties. Import quotas, although a legitimate device, had fallen out of use except for limited purposes for many years. It was possible to use selective import controls against specific products, especially textiles coming from developing countries, but the use of quotas on any scale against fellow members of the EEC was out of the question. Other industrial countries such as Germany found it possible to balance their international accounts without quotas. Others again ran deficits like the United Kingdom but with no prospect of seeing them extinguished by North Sea oil.

Was it wise for the United Kingdom to take the lead in a worldwide move to protectionism when what was needed was greater competitive power? An import deposit scheme such as had been used by Roy Jenkins (and by other countries) might have helped to check imports but was unlikely to have brought imports into balance with exports. It would have caused difficulties with the IMF and it was only the IMF that could lend enough and put an end to the exchange crisis. Why call in a battalion when what was needed was an army?

Much of what happened in the United Kingdom in the mid-1970s was paralleled in other industrial countries. In nearly all of them, America being an outstanding exception, public expenditure rose just as fast as in the United Kingdom in proportion to GDP between 1972 and 1976 but continued to grow over the next two years when the proportion in the United Kingdom fell back nearly halfway to the 1972 level. The British proportion in 1978 was lower at 44 per cent than in Belgium, France, Germany and Italy, and far below the Netherlands and Sweden. In the four years 1972−6 GDP rose faster in the United Kingdom than in Germany and the United States but more slowly than in the other continental countries just mentioned. The largest differences were in inflation: between 1972 and 1976 Italy came top with a rise of 84 per cent, Britain second with 79 per cent and Germany lower with 25 per cent. Belgium, France, Italy and Sweden were all in balance of payments deficit on a scale comparable with Britain by 1976. But none of them ran a reserve currency and were exposed to the risk of large-scale withdrawals; all of them had substantial reserves of foreign exchange.

While the exchange crisis was in progress the Prime Minister had sought international assistance in guaranteeing the value of sterling balances and had sent Harold Lever on a mission to Washington in mid November to obtain President Ford's backing. The American line, however, was that this must wait until the United Kingdom had reached agreement with the IMF. Accordingly, discussion was now resumed and on 10 January the Bank for International Settlements in Basle announced a funding scheme allowing holders of sterling balances to convert into foreign currency denominated securities of 5−10 years' maturity. This would be backed by a $3 billion standby facility from eight countries to the Bank of England and there was also to be a seven-year $1500 million Eurocurrency loan from the West German banks.

Monetary policy began to ease in January 1977, with reductions in special deposits and a continuing decline in interest rates. From 15 per cent in October 1976 bank rate fell gradually to 12 per cent at the beginning of February, 8 per cent in May and 5 per cent in October 1977. This was in large measure a response to the inflow of funds and the strength of sterling. The IMF loan had been drawn on for $1.2 billion early in January but as the reserves mounted there was little need to draw on it further: the only drawings after January were for $384 million in May and again in August, making a total less than half the size of the loan.

The Chancellor had still to secure the approval of the House of Commons for his revised expenditure plans. When these came before the House on 17 March 1977 left-wing abstentions produced a rejection of the White Paper on Public Expenditure and Mrs Thatcher called for a vote of no confidence. This took place next day and went in favour of the government which had secured the support of the Liberals in a Lib−Lab Pact which lasted until the election in 1979.

At the end of March Healey introduced a budget that was on balance expansionary (that is, in its tax provisions and taking no account of expenditure cuts). Income tax reductions added up to £2¼ million in a full year, and of this nearly £1 million was conditional on acceptance of the government's pay policy. In July, however, it was announced that the cut in income tax, previously envisaged at 2 p, would be limited to 1 p. The July budget changes added £100 million to the PSBR but remained within the limit agreed with the IMF. A further attempt to bring pressure on excessive increases in pay was a provision that companies breaking the rule against more than one increase in twelve months would be disallowed in their permitted profit margin the amount of the offending pay rise.

Incomes policy

The government's pay policy had in fact worked remarkably successfully over the previous year. In July 1976 the unions had been assured that if they accepted lower pay, competition would soon force prices to follow suit. But in the twelve months since then while hourly wages had risen by 5.3 per cent retail prices had risen by 17 per cent. On the other hand, in the following year to July 1978 hourly wages rose by 14 per cent and retail prices by 8.3 per cent. In those years of slow growth between 1974 and 1979 real wages grew slowly and erratically. Measured in terms of weekly wages deflated by the rise in consumer prices (not just retail prices), the rise in real wages between 1970 and 1974 was 19 per cent, an unusually rapid increse. Between 1974 and 1979 the increase was no more than 8 per cent. As we have seen, real wages tend to move with productivity and if we use as a measure of productivity output per manhour in manufacturing, the relationship holds in the first period, the increase from 1970−4 being 18 per cent. But from 1974−9 it is only 4.2 per cent − well below the rise in real wages. If, as we should, we use total output per head as the measure of productivity these percentages are reduced and the margin between real wages and productivity widens. It is fairly clear that inflation was hard on profits and kind to wages although what was given by inflation was taken away by slow growth. Real wages grew much faster before 1974 than after; and when they grew most slowly they outpaced productivity growth by an unusually large margin.

In July when the next stage in incomes policy came up for discussion with the TUC, it was agreed to limit wage increases to 10 per cent. As we have seen, this was exceeded but not by a very large margin, the rise in hourly wages over the year to July 1978 averaging 14 per cent.

North Sea oil had started to flow in 1975 and by 1978 the output was already worth about £2½ billion. The entire output went to improve the balance of payments either in exports or in displacement of imports. Already in the second half of 1977 oil production had helped to convert a substantial balance of payments deficit in the first half of the year into a surplus in the second half. It was a surplus that disappeared briefly in 1979 but flourished for six years thereafter until a new boom began in 1986. For the first time since the war and in strong contrast to the 1970s the 1980s opened with a large and growing surplus and an enviable freedom from the expectation of balance of payments difficulties.

Monetary and fiscal policy continued to be eased as the year went on. Interest rates were lowered until they reached 5 per cent in October. The corset was removed in August. The tax concessions in the spring and in July were supplemented in yet another mini budget in October increasing tax allowances by £1000 million. All this, as Healey explained in a further Letter of Intent to the IMF in December 1977 was in keeping with the undertakings given to the IMF a year before. Healey was able to quote figures for the PSBR and DCE (domestic credit expansion) to show that the increases in 1977–8 would work out within the limits set. The PSBR instead of reaching £8.7 billion ended up in 1978 no higher than £5.7 billion and DCE, for the growth in which a ceiling of £7.7 billion had been fixed, increased by no more than £3.3 billion. The Chancellor did not even set targets for 1978–9 but contented himself with expressing an 'expectation' that the PSBR would not exceed £8600 million.

Throughout the years 1976–9 output grew at a little over 2.5 per cent with an absolute fall of about the same magnitude in 1980. The rate of growth was not sufficient to prevent a gradual increase in unemployment in the first two of those years, from a level already above 1 million but there was a gradual fall in the next two, when growth was slightly faster, that brought unemployment back to its initial level. While total output grew steadily there were large fluctuations within the total. In 1976 the pace was set by exports and a high rate of stockbuilding with much smaller increases in the other aggregates except imports which, however, rose much less than exports. In 1977 the movement of resources to the advantage of the balance of payments and at the expense of the domestic economy is even more marked. Exports and, to a lesser extent, stockbuilding continued to make the pace with only a small rise in imports and a fall in all the other aggregates. In 1978 and 1979 the situation was very different. Exports fell off, imports increased and the difference between the two turned negative. Stockbuilding also fell away. The running was made principally by consumer spending with some support from fixed investment and the expenditure of public authorities on goods and services.

The change in 1978–9 reflects the government's reflationary policies. At the end of 1977 Healey had made tax concessions and announced additional spending plans adding up to £1 million in 1977−8 and £2.2 billion n 1978−9. Much of this was for tax allowances to individual tax payers but £1 billion in 1978−9 represented additional expenditure. In his 1978 Budget Healey injected an additional £2500 million, mainly as before through more generous tax allowances. These repeated injections chiefly affected consumer spending.

The government, however, was no longer able to take for granted that the Finance Bill would be enacted automatically. As a minority government it had been obliged to accept amendments to its budget proposals in 1977. These included an amendment requiring indexation from 1978 of personal income tax reliefs; and the increase that Healey had made in allowances in October 1977 was an advanced implementation of this provision. His remissions of tax in 1977−8, although very large ($£3\frac{1}{2}$ billion) were almost entirely offset by additional revenue from increases in indirect taxes (the national insurance surcharge and the regulator) and from fiscal drag (i.e. the automatic increase in revenue at existing rates when incomes and prices rise).

After the success of its efforts to give a lead to wage restraint in 1975−6, the government reviewed the position each July with the TUC (but not the CBI) and formulated new guidelines. In July 1976 it set a limit of £2.50 or 5 per cent or £4 a week for those earning respectively up to £50, £50−£80 and over £80 a week. In July 1977 it set a 10 per cent limit and in July 1978 suggested a ceiling of 5 per cent. In 1976−7 the policy had the full backing of the TUC but in 1978 the TUC denied the government support except in banning two wage increases in the same year.

The winter of 1978−9 was one of turmoil in the labour market. The 'winter of discontent' started in November when workers at Ford's won a 17 per cent increase in breach of the government's pay policy. The government sought to use sanctions against Ford and were defeated in the House of Commons on the issue, narrowly surviving a vote of confidence next day. Since the pay policy lacked the necessary support workers felt free to strike for pay beyond the limits set and a long series of strikes began. In January 1979 a million and a half workers in the public sector took part in a one day protest strike and the Cabinet was obliged to relax its policy and agree to offer more to low paid workers, promise comparability with private industry and impose tougher price controls on manufactures. Shortly afterwards the TUC signed a concordat with the government to bring down inflation to 5 per cent in three years. But in the first six months of 1979 retail prices rose by 11 per cent and hourly wage rates by just under 10 per cent – a far cry from the government's target.

Notes

1   On the definitions used in 1990. Earlier definitions yield a higher figure.
2   His measures also included an import surcharge of 10 per cent and a freeze on prices, wages and dividends for 90 days.
3   Using the figures for 'bank lending' in *Economic Trends Annual Supplement 1981*, p. 187 and comparing first quarter totals.
4   Blackaby, *British Economic Policy*, p. 381. Blackaby attributes the divergence to 'settlements postponed by the freeze, the move to equal pay, payments by results systems, increases in overtime and the permitted continuance of incremental awards' (ibid., p. 382). It is not clear why he brings in overtime since he puts the increase in earnings at $13\frac{1}{2}$ per cent *excluding* overtime. He claims (correctly) that the rise in earnings was 'significantly lower than during 1972'. On an October to October comparison, *including* overtime, the reduction was from 15.1 per cent to 12.7 per cent.
5   W. Rees-Mogg, 'How a 9.4 per cent excess money supply gave Britain 9.4 per cent inflation', *The Times*, 14 July 1976.
6   Consumer prices rose by 10.5 per cent in Britain and by between 7.9 and 9.2 per cent in France, Germany, Canada and the United States (but by 12.5 per cent in Italy).
7   *The Attack on Inflation*, Cmnd 6151, July 1975.
8   MacDougall, *Don and Mandarin*, pp. 222–4.
9   The Nigerian government announced on 9 March that it had diversified its predominantly sterling reserves.

Further reading

Artis, M. J. and Cobham, D. (eds.) 1991. *The Labour Government 1974–79*, Oxford: Oxford University Press.

Ball, S. and Seldon, A (eds.) 1995. *The Heath Government 1970–74: a Reappraisal*, London: Longman.

Beckerman, W. (ed.) 1979. *Slow Growth in Britain*. Oxford: Oxford University Press.

Cairncross, A. and Burk, K. 1992. *Good-bye Great Britain: The IMF Crisis of 1976*. London: Yale University Press.

Dell, E. 1991. *A Hard Pounding: Politics and Economic Crisis 1974–76*, Oxford: Oxford University Press.

Gardner, Nick 1987. *Decade of Discontent*, Oxford: Blackwell.

Hall, M. 1983. *Monetary Policy since 1971*, London: Macmillan.

Holmes, M. 1982. *Political Pressure and Economic Policy: British government 1970–74*, London: Butterworth.

Holmes, M. 1985. *The Labour Government 1974–79: political aims and economic reality*, London: Macmillan.

Wass, D. 1978. 'The changing problems of economic management', Lecture to the Johnian Society, Cambridge.

Official Reports

The Attack on Inflation, 1975, Cmnd 6151, London: HMSO.

6 The 1980s

With the change of government in May 1979 came a major shift in policy. The Conservative government's dominant aims were to master inflation through control of the money supply and to pull back the frontiers of the State with an increasing emphasis on privatisation. These were pursued with great pertinacity, but often with more rhetoric than success, in circumstances that included a second oil shock in 1979, an international slowdown and recession, war in the Falklands, a prolonged miners' strike and international economic recovery from 1984 onwards. We begin with an overview of events from May 1979 when the Thatcher government took office until the end of 1990 and the resignation of Mrs Thatcher. This is followed by a more detailed chronological account of developments. The chapter concludes with some reflections on the changes over the decade.

The Thatcher years: an overview

The year-to-year changes over the decade in the main elements in demand are shown in table 6.1. If we set aside the initial depression in 1980–1, we are left with a continuous expansion from 1982 onwards and a bigger rise in output than in any previous decade. The impression this gives, as we shall see, has to be qualified in various ways, notably by the low level from which recovery started, the persistence of massive unemployment throughout and the emergence in the later years of the decade of an extremely large external deficit.

Table 6.1 Changes in the allocation of resources, 1979–1989 (increase from year to year in £ billion at constant 1985 prices)

	1980	1981	1982	1983	1984	1985	1986	1987	1988	1989	Change between 1979 and 1989
Consumers' expenditure	0.2	0.2	2.0	9.1	3.4	7.5	13.7	12.4	17.6	10.1	76.0
Public authorities' final consumption	1.1	0.2	0.6	1.4	0.7	–	1.4	1.0	0.4	0.6	7.3
Gross domestic fixed capital formation	-3.0	-5.1	2.6	2.6	4.6	2.3	1.1	5.8	10.0	3.7	24.6
Value of physical increase in stocks and work in progress	-6.7	0.2	1.9	2.6	-0.3	-0.3	-0.1	0.4	3.0	-1.5	-0.7
Exports of goods and services	–	-0.7	0.7	1.8	6.0	5.7	4.8	6.1	0.3	4.9	29.6
Total final expenditure	-9.2	-5.7	8.1	17.9	14.3	15.2	20.9	25.7	31.2	17.9	136.4
Imports of goods and services	-2.8	-2.3	3.8	5.4	8.7	2.5	6.8	8.3	14.6	9.0	54.0
Gross domestic product (at market prices)[b]	-6.4	-3.4	4.3	12.5	5.6	12.8	14.1	17.4	16.6	8.9	82.3
Gross domestic product (average at factor cost)[c]	-6.0	-3.2	4.8	10.6	5.2	11.3	11.1	14.0	15.7	7.2	70.6

[a] Totals differ from sum of the components.
[b] Expenditure – based.
[c] Average estimate.
Source: Economic Trends, December 1990

The decade 1979–89 can be divided roughly into two equal periods in which production expanded at very different rates, both in the United Kingdom and in other industrial countries. In the first five years (1979–84), the increase in total output was only 3.8 per cent in the United Kingdom but recovered over the next five years (1984–9) to 20.4 per cent. The comparable figures for the OECD countries as a group (including the UK) are 10.5 per cent for the first five years and 18.8 per cent for the second. Thus the United Kingdom recorded less than half the growth in the rest of OECD in 1979–84 and slightly faster growth in 1984–9.

To grow more slowly than other industrial countries has been the usual experience in Britain since the war. What was unusual in 1979–84 was the very slow growth in other countries; but Britain's growth was even slower – slower than in any previous quinquennium. In 1984–9 the United Kingdom's better performance was again in relation to a rate of growth in OECD countries that was low by past standards. Countries like France and Germany, which had experienced rates of growth of 5 or 6 per cent annually in the 1950s and 1960s, averaged no more in the 1980s than 2.1 and 1.9 per cent respectively. They achieved higher rates of 2.8 and 2.7 per cent in the second half of the decade but these were still comparatively low rates on past experience.

Britain's performance from 1985–9 appeared to augur well for the future. Growth at 3.8 per cent annually for five years was well above the rate across the Channel. Even in the five years to 1973, the nearest comparable period, growth was not so fast. But there were grounds for caution in extrapolating success since it was coupled with an unsustainable boom. The rate of expansion in those years was fed on a rundown in unemployment of at least a million – most of it in 1988 – and an increase in pressure on industrial capacity that sent the balance of payments into enormous deficit and pushed up the rate of inflation. By 1989 the expansion was slowing down and in 1990 was moving into an unmistakable recession.

Expansion was sustained by high consumer spending. This had risen strongly in 1978–9 but in 1980–1 increased hardly at all. From 1983, however, with a pause in 1984, it rose to a more normal level until in 1986–8 it was swept up into a consumer boom on a scale never before experienced – indeed in

1988 the increase in consumer spending was more than the rise in GDP. This was possible only because imports, too, grew in 1988 by almost as much as GDP. Underlying the boom in consumer spending was a borrowing spree that can be regarded as negative saving and brought down the ratio of savings to personal income from 8.2 per cent in 1986 to 5.4 per cent in 1988. The fall in the saving ratio − it had been 13.5 per cent in 1980 − had been one of the main forces sustaining demand throughout the decade, but by 1988 the enthusiasm of consumers for getting into debt had overshot the mark and was no longer a helpful development.

If the rate of increase in consumer spending was an all-time high, the rate of increase in public expenditure on goods and services was lower than for decades. In every year but one there was a small increase in public expenditure on goods and services but the rise over the decade was as low as in the 1950s and involved a large reduction in relation to the growth of GNP. Fixed investment, after a dip in 1980−1 recovered to a level higher than in any year in the 1970s except 1973 and in 1987−8 was far above anything seen since the war. Stockbuilding was negligible over the decade, as it had been in the 1970s, and rather more stable than in other decades. Exports, after a marked check in 1980−2, had four good years in 1984−7 before giving way under the pressure of domestic demand in 1988 and recovering again once the pressure was reduced. Imports, which were checked even more than exports in 1980−1 − but for different reasons − rose at a remarkable rate thereafter. Between 1980 and 1990 the increase of nearly £60 billion (at constant 1985 prices) was more than twice the increase in any previous decade.

For the whole of the decade until the last few years there was no balance of payments problem to impose itself on domestic policy; no balance of payments crisis of the usual kind. For that North Sea oil was in part responsible. The output of North Sea oil reached its peak in 1985−6 and the downturn that followed coincided with the return of a chronic external deficit. But there was also a second factor at work: the persistent underemployment of the economy. This reduced the spending power of consumers below what would have been earned at full stretch and hence limited the demand for imports. When the slack in the economy began to be taken in and incomes expanded, much of the additional spending power went on imports and the brighter economic prospects led to readier borrowing and released more purchasing power to inflate the demand for imports. The United Kingdom found itself in a position in which full employment, already distanced by anti-inflationary policies, was still further distanced by pressure on sterling.

Full employment had ended in the 1970s when a world in which it was politically unthinkable that unemployment could remain above 600,000 had given way to a world in which for years unemployment remained at over twice that level. In the 1980s unemployment rose to at least five times the highest level in the 1960s, and a level about as high as was ever experienced in the 1930s, without any marked political upset (see figure 6.1). The basis of the figures was changed repeatedly − always in a downwards direction − and they now relate only to claimants of unemployment benefit aged 18 or over. It is not easy, therefore, to know how high the total would have risen on the basis used in earlier decades; but estimates of up to 3.8 million have been made, and compare with the official estimate of 3.1 million for 1986.[1]

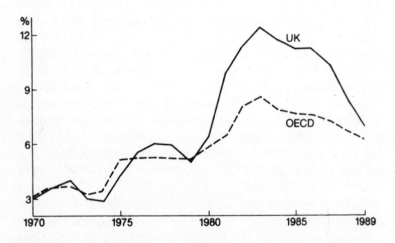

Figure 6.1   Unemployment in the UK and OECD, 1970−1989
Source: Economic Outlook, OECD, June 1990

The rise was almost entirely due to a contraction in manufacturing employment – as indeed was true also in the 1970s. It would appear to be the usual experience that fluctuations in employment are concentrated on the manufacturing sector. Employment in manufacturing had already fallen from nearly 9 million in 1966 to a little under 7 million at the beginning of 1980. There was then a continuous fall until 1987 and after a slight recovery in the boom of 1988 the fall was resumed in 1989. By 1990 nearly two million fewer workers were employed in manufacturing than ten years earlier; and the manufacturing sector, which accounted for so large a proportion of exports and was of equal importance in furnishing alternatives to imports, had shrunk by that time to 22.5 per cent of total civil employment from 31 per cent at the beginning of 1980 (and 38.3 per cent in 1965). Three-quarters of the fall of 2 million in manufacturing employment occurred in the first three years of the decade, 1980–2.

The rise in unemployment in the 1980s was the outcome of policies designed to curb inflation. Since the government was dtermined not to embark yet again on an incomes policy, and had little hope of carrying the TUC with it if it had, it had to leave wages and prices to market forces and rely on a contraction in demand to keep prices down. But a contraction in demand was at least as likely to act on output as on prices.

Some contraction may have followed the second oil shock when oil prices rose more in absolute terms, although less proportionately, than in the first oil shock. But the course of events in 1980–1 was very different from the course of events in 1974–5. There was no disastrous change in the terms of trade: while import prices rose by 18 per cent, export prices rose nearly as fast, by 16.5 per cent. There was no enormous deficit in the balance of payments: on the contrary, there was a surplus in 1980 of £2.8 billion compared with a deficit in 1979 of over £500 million. The rate of exchange did not fall: it rose from $2.15 in October 1979 to $2.42 in October 1980.

There is no doubt that North Sea oil contributed to the very different outcome of the second oil shock. It is estimated to have contributed a net £6 billion in 1980 and £9 billion in 1981 compared with £3.8 billion in 1979.[2] That represents a large acquisition of foreign exchange in relation to the size of swings in the balance of payments. For ten years from 1977 until 1987 North Sea oil, or the prospect of North Sea oil, freed Chancellors of the Exchequer from the compulsions of a balance of payments deficit.

But does that mean that, as some have argued, it took the place of a large chunk of manufacturing industry, dispensing with the need for an equivalent output of manufactures?[3] The question can be answered at two levels.

First of all, there is no reason to suppose that there was any direct link between the arrival on the market of North Sea oil in increasing quantities and the decline of manufacturing. In particular the volume of exports of manufactures hardly altered between 1979 and 1980 and dropped by only 4 per cent in the next three years. This is trifling in relation to the drop of 1.7 million or 24 per cent in manufacturing employment between these two dates.

Was it perhaps a rise in imports of manufactures that hit British manufacturing industry? Again, the changes look relatively small. Between 1979 and 1981 (when most of the drop in manufacturing employment occurred) imports of manufactures fell. They rose in 1982 to 5 per cent and in 1983 to 17 per cent above the 1979 level. But this was no faster than in the 1970s: in the four years before 1979 imports of manufactures increased by 50 per cent. Whatever the impact of North Sea oil on the balance of payments and on the exchange rate, it was not the cause of the disastrous contraction in manufacturing employment in 1980−2.

The main cause lay in the use of very tight money to fight inflation. Bank rate had risen over the winter of 1978−9 to 14 per cent and after reductions in March and April 1979 was back at 14 per cent in June. In November 1979 it was increased to 17 per cent and remained at that level for nearly eight months and at 16 per cent for nearly four months more. For twenty-one months from June 1979, bank rate was 14 per cent or more. Nor was 1981 very different: interest rates were again at 14 per cent or more over the winter of 1981−2. These rates were higher and more sustained than in earlier periods of tight money. They hit business at a time when inflation was adding to its borrowing requirements and forcing companies to seek assistance from the banks on a much increased scale. In each of the three years 1980−2 stocks were run down − something that had never never happened since the war in two successive years, much less three.

Financial stringency is the obvious explanation, as it is also of the check to the growth in final expenditure. A decumulation of stocks by nearly £8 billion in three years was a powerful drag on production, which was nevertheless higher in 1982 than in 1980. Fixed investment also reflected financial stringency, dropping by over £8 billion between 1979 and 1981 and recovering a little in 1982.

To go back to North Sea oil. A second line of argument associating it with a setback to manufacturing contends that in the long run the rise of a new line of exports must be balanced by a decline in other exports. But there is nothing inevitable about this. A weak balance of payments may be succeeded by a strong balance of payments with a lasting surplus, as has happened in the case of Japan. The emergence of a surplus, if the oil adds to the country's prosperity, may be coupled with increased saving and higher investment abroad.

There were in fact several different ways in which North Sea oil might have been used in the management of the economy. The most obvious use would have been to buttress the balance of payments while the economy was held at a higher level of employment and output. Alternatively, it might have financed a higher level of domestic investment: but since this would have boosted domestic output, the outcome would have been a variant of the first possibility. What in fact happened was that the external surplus generated by the combination of oil production and a depressed level of economic activity was largely channelled into foreign investment. By the mid 1980s the United Kingdom ranked second to Japan in the scale of its foreign investment, with a portfolio of over £100 billion. Towards the end of the 1980s, however, some of this was being drawn upon as the balance of payments moved back into deficit. To the extent that the deficit represented higher imports of equipment of all kinds, domestic investment was finally gaining from North Sea oil.

What, finally, of inflation, the main concern of the government, as it had been of its predecessor? Initially there was a renewed surge to very high rates (see figure 1.1, p. 30). In the year before the Conservative government took office, retail prices rose by 10 per cent; in the year after, the rise was 22.7 per cent. This partly reflected a rise of 18 per cent in import prices over the year and all the consequences of the second oil shock (oil prices rose by 150 per cent in two years); partly high wage settlements, including some in the public sector that the government felt compelled to honour. An additional factor, responsible for a $3\frac{1}{2}$ per cent rise in prices was the government's ill-timed effort to switch from direct to indirect taxation with a rise in VAT to 15 per cent from rates of 8 and $12\frac{1}{2}$ per cent.

In 1980 the rate of inflation had begun to drop. It continued to fall as demand slackened and was down to 4.5 per cent in 1983. For the next five years it fluctuated, with a low point of 3.4 per cent in 1986, but was never more than 6 per cent. In 1988, however, the rate of inflation crept up steadily, quarter by quarter and by the middle of 1989 had reached over 8 per cent. By the end of the decade, in the autumn of 1990, it was back to the level of 10 per cent from which it started in 1979.

A chronology of developments

A change of economic philosophy

The government which took office in May 1979 was dominated by ministers with a very different economic philosophy from that of earlier governments. In some respects they shared the views of the Heath administration in its early days. They were strongly against state intervention in industry and wanted to abolish controls, subsidies and other attempts to prevail over market forces. They intended to cut public expenditure and reduce taxation. They hoped to return an unspecified amount of publicly owned industry to private enterprise. Producers and consumers were to be left as free as possible to conduct their own affairs.

Those who held responsibility for economic policy combined these ideas with others of a different character. They regarded the prime aim of macro-economic policy as the maintenance of a stable economic environment, with stability in the value of money enjoying top priority. The level of employment on the other hand (and hence the level of output, although this was never added) was fundamentally a matter of micro-economic policy since it was represented as varying with the wage at which labour could be hired. If workers insisted on 'pricing themselves out of a job' it was not for the government to create more jobs at the cost of inflation and so destabilize the economy.

The aim of financial stability, moreover, was to be achieved by control over the stock of money. It was regarded as the product of monetary policy which was the sole and sufficient instrument for the avoidance of inflation. Fiscal policy might be a useful prop to monetary policy: the less the government had to borrow in order to pay its way the less it would be likely to turn to the banks to take up its debt or force up interest rates by putting more debt on the market. But there was to be no question of budgetary 'fine tuning' in an effort to manage demand on a short-term basis. Government economic policy should be governed by long-term objectives − eventual extinction of inflation, provision of the right environment for economic growth, the improvement of industrial efficiency, and so on.

These ideas were sometimes carried to extremes. If inflation could be effectively controlled by limiting the growth in the stock of money, there was no need for other action. Higher wages, for example, would be powerless to raise the cost of living and efforts to arrive at a satisfactory incomes policy would be redundant. Since the government had no wish to make use of incomes policy anyway and regarded it as futile or worse this was comfortable doctrine. It was much in vogue in the first year of Conservative government when, in compliance with a pre-election pledge, it felt obliged to implement some very high wage and salary awards made by the Clegg Commission. The same logic allowed the government to dismiss other causes of rising prices − higher indirect taxes and falling exchange rates, for example − as without effect on the price level so long as the money supply was unaffected. To rely on the anonymous pressure of monetary stringency had vastly more appeal than confrontation with the trade unions, or higher direct taxation or struggles to maintain the exchange rate.

Unfortunately those who held those ideas had presumed too readily that control of the money supply was well within the power of central banks. They were to find that they were mistaken. Even if all their ideas had been logically beyond attack − which was very far from being the case − it did not prove possible to give effect to them by holding to a fixed path of monetary expansion.

The monetary targets which were to govern policy were first missed, then changed and finally abandoned. The story of economic policy in the 1980s is largely the story of a reversion from new concepts of economic management to older concepts initially rejected.

As the rate of inflation fell back to a more moderate pace in 1983 it ceased to enjoy the absolute priority it had been given at the start. No attempt was made to reduce it to zero and it was allowed to creep up again without the immediate and dramatic tightening of monetary policy adopted in 1979. The various monetary targets that were supposed to guide policy faded into the background. From an early stage, too, fiscal policy re-emerged partly as an alternative to dearer money but to some extent also as an instrument of demand management in its own right. The rate of exchange, at first left to the market to determine, became a major concern of policy as it had been in the past.

By the end of the decade the management of the economy had swung back a long way towards earlier aims and methods. A higher importance was still attached to overcoming inflation, there was no thought of incomes policy, and there was a more ready acquiescence in high and rising unemployment. But the problems facing the government were much more akin to those of earlier decades, especially with the reappearance of a large balance of payments deficit. Monetary policy was no longer regarded as an instant cure for inflation. The instruments at the government's disposal for managing the economy had shrunk; it was dependent, to an extent not true of any earlier government since 1945, on its control over short-term rates of interest when that control in turn was qualified by the rates of interest set by other monetary authorities.

The initial disasters, 1979–1980

Six weeks after taking office in May 1979 the Chancellor (Geoffrey Howe) introduced his first budget. Its main feature was a switch from direct to indirect taxation involving a cut in the one and an increase in the other by about £$4\frac{1}{2}$ billion in a full year. Income tax was lowered from 33 to 30p, the top rate of income tax was cut from 83 to 60 per cent, and personal tax allowances were improved in various ways. On the other hand, VAT was raised to a flat rate of 15 per cent from rates varying between 8 and $12\frac{1}{2}$ per cent, and petrol duty went up by 7p a gallon. Public expenditure was cut by £1.5 billion and monetary policy was tightened by an increase in bank rate from 12 to 14 per cent. The Chancellor also announced his intention of selling state-owned assets to the value of £1 billion (mainly BP shares) during the financial year. The net effect of the budgetary measures was deflationary: they set a lower target for the PSBR and for monetary growth. On the other hand, they had a decidedly inflationary impact on prices.

The measures seem to have flowed from the determination to cut the top rate of income tax drastically and so, it was hoped, give entrepreneurial energies more encouragement. This in turn dictated the 3p cut in the standard rate as a political *quid pro quo*; and to make up for the revenue sacrificed and leave a lower budget deficit, an additional £$4\frac{1}{2}$ billion was required from the only possible source − indirect taxation. It was not a move calculated to dampen inflationary expectations.

The impact of the budget on the cost of living was compounded by a rise in the prices charged by the nationalized industries. These industries had been subsidized in the past in order to allow them to delay price increases and were now left free to put up their prices. This, it has been estimated, added a further $2\frac{1}{2}$ per cent to retail prices.[4] In conjunction with the extra $3\frac{1}{2}$ per cent resulting from higher indirect taxes and the Clegg Commission wage awards discussed below, it contributed to a sharp steepening of the trend in retail prices. Between the first quarter of 1979 and the third, retail prices rose by 12 per cent and in the ensuing six months by a further 8 per cent. In the year following the May 1979 budget, prices rose by over 20 per cent.

That all these measures making for higher prices were taken by a government intent on curbing inflation may have owed something to the almost religious conviction that limitation of the money supply would of itself put an end to inflation. But could the money supply be held down by any known technique, and if so, how? The question was not one to which the government had given much thought. Presumably it took for granted that the Bank of England already knew. Later, it argued for control of the monetary base without appreciating the force of the arguments against such control: for example, the loss of control over interest rates that it involved. Although a Green Paper on *Monetary Control* appeared in March 1980 proposing base control, the proposal was soon abandoned. In the end the government virtually gave up the effort to control the money supply, which grew over the decade at an average annual rate of 16 per cent.

One of the first moves of the government was to abolish exchange control. It was first relaxed in July and withdrawn completely in October (dealings with Rhodesia apart). It was a controversial move but there was a case for encouraging more foreign investment at a time when disinvestment was occurring in the form of extraction of North Sea oil − and the rate of exchange was far too high. Financial institutions were likely to take advantage of the absence of control to diversify their portfolios once they could acquire foreign securities without having to pay a premium for the necessary 'investment currency'. It would appear, however, that it took a long time for a full adjustment to be made. Whatever outflow of capital occurred, it did not prevent a further rise in the effective rate of exchange by well over 10 per cent in the eighteen months following abolition of exchange control.

The removal of exchange control reacted on monetary management. For example, it weakened the effectiveness of the 'corset', a device reactivated in June 1978 for checking the growth of bank deposits. The Chancellor had announced in the budget that this would be withdrawn at the end of the year but it was retained until June 1980. The banks had already found ways round the corset restriction by 'disintermediation' (arranging loans from one customer to another off bank balance sheets). Now that banks were free to operate in the euro-markets, the restriction was further weakened. But as was plain when it was removed, it continued to limit monetary growth to a greater extent than had been expected.

In November 1979 the *Autumn Statement* carried the usual economic forecasts for the following year. These showed an expected fall in output of 3 per cent in 1980, a rise in unemployment to 2 million in 1981 and a deterioration in business profits and financial prospects. No previous official forecast had shown a prospective fall in output, much less one of 3 per cent. In fact the forecast proved to be remarkably accurate. Output fell by between 3 and 4 per cent between the second half of 1979 and the second half of 1980; unemployment rose to well beyond 2 million before 1981 was more than a few months old; industrial and commercial companies had a negligible financial surplus in spite of heavy cuts in stocks and found themselves obliged to borrow heavily from the banks and elsewhere. The Chancellor paid little attention to the forecast and the Financial Secretary refused to accept it. As for drawing the usual conclusion that the PSBR would be swollen by unemployment benefit and loss of tax revenue, they insisted on aiming at a reduction in the PSBR in the 1980 budget.

They were much more concerned at the growth of the money supply, which at that time meant £M3, a broad money indicator consisting mainly of sterling bank deposits and currency in circulation. This had increased by about 7 per cent in the six months between the first and third quarters of 1979 − far slower than the expansion in money incomes and not a great deal more than the upper limit of 11 per cent per annum set for monetary growth in the budget but enough to alarm the authorities. Sales of government debt had also fallen off in the third quarter. Another factor in the situation was a large rise in euro-dollar interest rates reflecting concern on the part of the American authorities, also over monetary growth. From 10 per cent in the middle of 1979, euro-dollar deposits were paying over 15 per cent by October, a higher rate than on sterling certificates of deposit.

Anxious to demonstrate their determination to exercise rigorous monetary control, the authorities put up bank rate in November by an unprecedented 3 per cent from 14 to 17 per cent.[5] Even so dramatic a move failed to check the rise in broad money (£M3)[6] which rose over the next year by 16 per cent. But it had unmistakable effects on the growth of output, which had already slowed down since the middle of the year. Between the second half of 1979 and the second half of 1980 GDP fell by 4 per cent − a much bigger fall than in any other post-war year. Simultaneously, the rate of exchange shot up over the next fifteen months by 15 per cent (figure 6.3, p. 247). In the two years between the first quarters of 1979 and 1981 the appreciation of sterling was about 25 per cent although, to make matters worse, sterling labour costs had risen much faster than labour costs abroad.

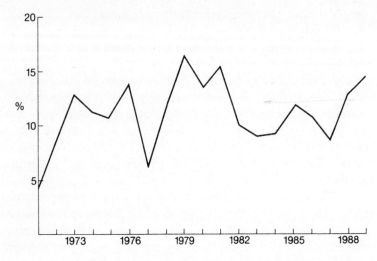

Figure 6.2   Yield on Treasury Bills, 1971–89 (last Friday of each year)

The rise in interest rates (figure 6.2) roughly coincided with the second oil shock which had international effects not unlike those of the first oil shock. That is, the industrial countries suffered a renewal of inflation, deficits in their international accounts and a downturn in economic activity. Oil importing developing countries, with less flexibitility in their economy, were faced with an even more difficult problem of adjustment and incurred still more external debt.

The rise in oil prices and its impact on other industrial countries led many observers to conclude that the same forces accounted for the rise in the sterling rate of exchange and the recession in Britain. So far as the rate of exchange is concerned this is very doubtful. No doubt the currency of an oil producer became more attractive when oil prices doubled. The extra earnings from oil exports (or larger economies in imports) must have helped to sustain the balance of payments. But if the high price of oil was the crucial factor why should the exchange rate begin to fall in 1981 as rapidly as it rose in 1980? There had been a shift to a less restrictive monetary policy before the end of 1980 that accords more closely with the turning point in the sterling exchange rate.

Indeed, as we shall see, the relaxation in monetary policy arose out of acceptance by the authorities that it was tight money, not oil prices, that underlay the rise in the exchange rate. The same conclusion is suggested by experience in 1986 when the price of oil was halved but the fall in the exchange rate was quite modest.

When we turn to the recession there is no escaping the difference between British and foreign experience. The recession in Britain was both earlier and deeper. In no other major industrial country except the United States (which also had raised interest rates in 1979) did GDP fall in 1980; and in none (except possibly Canada) was there a fall in GDP of as much as 4 per cent. The collective GDP of OECD countries rose by $1-1\frac{1}{2}$ per cent in 1980 and 1981 and fell only in 1982 by an almost negligible amount. While Britain was subject to the same international influences as other industrial countries, her position as an oil producer might have been expected to shade, not intensify, their effects on the British economy. It is difficult to resist the conclusion that a misguided persistence in tight money exposed Britain to misfortunes other industrial countries escaped.

The medium-term financial strategy (MTFS)

The monetary policy which intensified the recession in 1980 derived from the monetary target set in the 1980 budget. This repeated the range of $7-11$ per cent in the 1979 budget in spite of the wide margin that had separated that target from actual performance − a 15 per cent increase in £M3. The target was now incorporated in a medium-term financial strategy (MTFS) first expounded in the 1980 budget. This was intended to guide government policy over the next four years.

The medium-term strategy was contrasted by the government with short-term demand management which was derided as a mere reaction to changing circumstances. The strategy was also contrasted with efforts to control real variables such as employment and output. It was a *financial* strategy aimed primarily at reducing inflation and making use of *financial* instruments of policy with no reliance on administrative controls. The aim of the strategy was to force down the rate of inflation by combining a tightening of monetary policy with a gradual reduction in the budget deficit designed to allow interest rates to be lowered. The rate of exchange was not mentioned: it would be allowed to float without intervention and respond to market pressures.

The government proposed to work towards an annual growth in the stock of money of about 6 per cent, reducing the initial range of 7−11 per cent by a percentage point in successive financial years until the range became 4−8 per cent in 1983−4. The measure of monetary growth selected initially was £M3 but when it turned out year after year that the actual and target increases were wide apart there was a natural tendency to look for a more predictable indicator. The most reliable was M0 (i.e. notes and coin in circulation) but it was also the least meaningful: nobody could take seriously the idea that the cost of living was determined by the small change people elected to carry around.

The medium-term financial strategy envisaged a triangular relationship between broad money (£M3), the PSBR and interest rates. It did not seek to control monetary growth by 'exclusive reliance on interest rates' but assumed that a reduction in the PSBR would serve the same purpose as an ancillary method of control. Such a reduction would make it possible to keep interest rates at acceptable levels whereas a high PSBR was thought to bring with it high nominal interest rates and financing difficulties for the private sector. The strategy also recognized that 'the speed with which inflation falls will depend crucially on expectations both within the United Kingdom and overseas'.[7]

This way of looking at things made fiscal policy a mere corollary of monetary policy when traditionally the management of the economy has rested mainly on fiscal policy with monetary policy as an adjunct to deal with pressure on the balance of payments. The triangular relationship, moreover, treated changes in the money supply and in the PSBR as isolated phenomena arising from no known cause and divorced from the accompanying changes (e.g. in economic activity or the creation of financial assets) by which they are always attended. The actual relationships were more complex.[8]

One obvious criticism of the MTFS was its neglect of the rate of exchange which had hitherto been one of the main concerns − if not *the* main concern − of monetary policy. The

Treasury and Civil Service Committee in February 1981 drew attention to this omission and suggested that the exchange rate should be taken into account in setting interest rates. It was not long before the authorities were obliged to act on this advice.

Critics have pointed out that the medium-term financial strategy assumed the truth of three key propositions which many, if not most, economists would reject: 'that there was a predictable and causal relationship between the growth of £M3 and the rate of inflation; that public sector borrowing was the prime determinant of M3; . . . and that public sector borrowing levels were the prime determinant of interest rate levels'.[9] Experience was to show that all three propositions were extremely doubtful. In a few years, attention was focused on other monetary indicators of less intrinsic interest, and on the PSBR rather than on the money supply. A zero PSBR and a stable rate of exchange both came to rank ahead of monetary targets.

The strategy did not get off to a very good start. The targets were missed by a wide margin and production fell far more heavily than the government expected. The PSBR had already exceeded the budget estimate in 1979–80. In 1980–1 it turned out to be £12½ billion instead of the £8½ billion planned.[10] Government expenditure which was to have fallen had again increased. The money supply was also a long way off its target with an increase of over 18 per cent – well above the pace of expansion the year before. One miscalculation contributing to this result had been the removal in June 1980 of the 'corset', a quantitative restriction on the growth of bank deposits which was thought to have lost most of its usefulness. In July and August the money supply increased first by 5 and then by 3 per cent, i.e. by not much less than the MTFS target of 9 per cent for the whole of the financial year. Yet although all the elements of the MTFS went astray, money was very tight, unemployment was rising rapidly and inflation was easing.

By the autumn of 1980 it had become clear that business was in serious difficulty. Even a firm like ICI announced that it had made a loss in the third quarter and many reputable firms were on the verge of bankruptcy. Ministers were still disturbed by the continuing expansion in £M3 and overlooked the influence on bank lending of distress borrowing by companies in difficulties.

They also tended to make light of difficulties which they took to be the inevitable consequence of the production of North Sea oil: the rise in the exchange rate and the decline in manufacturing industry were both ascribed to this irresistible development. It was only when they called in Professor Niehans, a Swiss economist, to make a study of the high exchange rate and he put the blame firmly on dear money that they were persuaded to relax their monetary policy.[11] It is true that bank rate was brought down to 16 per cent in July 1980 but it was not until November that it returned to the 14 per cent from which it started in November 1979. Even these reductions, belated though they were, could not be reconciled with the monetarist views with which the government started since they involved lowering interest rates when the monetary target was being exceeded.

Meanwhile the heavy fall in output, which reached 16 per cent in manufacturing (more than in the slump of 1929–31)[12] was changing the atmosphere in the labour market. Wage bargains became increasingly moderate as the unemployment total mounted. Weekly wages which had increased at over 17 per cent in 1979 were rising at just over six per cent three years later. This had little to do with the money supply but a great deal to do with the collapse of demand. So far as financial stringency was at the root of the lower wage settlements, nobody would have detected the stringency from observation of the monetary indicator featured in the MTFS (£M3). Nor was it ever suggested that if the strategy worked, it would be by destroying the jobs of two million workers.

The 1981 budget

The 1981 budget provided the government with an opportunity to reconsider its policy. Unemployment was soaring by 100,000 a month; vacancies had almost vanished; manufacturing industry had shed 10 per cent of its labour force in a year and large numbers of firms were being forced out of business; the rate of exchange had risen to a level of $2.40 to the £1 at which industry could not hope to survive on a competitive footing.

Once convinced that interest rates were too high and the main reason for the high exchange·rate, the government was prepared to do its best to get interest rates down. But it regarded a lower borrowing requirement as indispensable for this purpose: all the more because it had allowed the PSBR to overrun the 1980 budget estimate by no less than £4 billion (table 6.2). Although the CBI was urging an increase to £15 billion or more, the Chancellor decided on a tighter fiscal policy to accompany the intended easing of monetary policy and budgeted for a PSBR of £10½ billion, £2 billion more than budgeted for in 1980 but over £2 billion less than actually experienced in 1980−1. There would be no overt increases in taxation but the indexation of tax allowances for inflation, called for by the Rooker−Wise amendment of 1977, would be suspended and this came to the same thing. Bank rate, however, was cut from 14 to 12 per cent and interest rates were reduced as the year progressed. The monetary target for 1981−2 remained at 6−10 per cent as envisaged in the version of the MFTS in the 1980 budget.

Raising taxes and tightening fiscal policy in a depression in order to cut the money supply outraged many economists who foresaw a large further rise in unemployment. A short letter of protest signed by 364 of them appeared in *The Times*.[13] The alternative would have been for the government to engage in more borrowing, as the Labour government had done in similar circumstances after 1973.

In many respects, indeed, the situation after the second oil shock resembled the situation after the first and to that extent Sir Geoffrey Howe faced the same problem as Denis Healey in 1975−6. The fall in manufacturing output was at first of similar severity but after a year experience diverged, the fall continuing in the second half of 1980 but not in the second half of 1975. Howe had the advantage of a surplus in the balance of payments and was in a position to welcome any loss of confidence that lowered the value of sterling. Healey on the other hand had a record deficit and was therefore obliged to pursue policies calculated to preserve the confidence of financial opinion abroad in deciding how big a deficit he could run. For Howe the question was rather: how much could he borrow without risking such a drop in the price of gilt-edged that private investment would hold back in alarm or sterling would rise still higher? The chances are that he could have borrowed as high a proportion of GDP as

Table 6.2 Budget forecasts and outcomes, 1979–1989 (£ billion)

	PSBR[a]		PSFD[b]		Privatization proceeds	Public expenditure in real terms[c]	% of GDP[d]
	Budget estimate	Out-turn[e]	Budget estimate	Out-turn[e]			
1979–80	8.3	9.9	7.2	8.1	0.4	181.1	44
1980–81	8.5	12.5	8.5	11.7	0.2	184.3	$46\frac{1}{2}$
1981–82	10.6	8.6	6.3	5.5	0.5	187.0	$47\frac{1}{4}$
1982–83	9.5	8.9	6.6	8.5	0.5	192.0	$47\frac{1}{8}$
1983–84	8.2	9.7	8.9	11.7	1.1	195.3	$46\frac{1}{8}$
1984–85	7.2	10.1	8.5	13.5	2.1	200.3	$46\frac{3}{4}$
1985–86	7.1	5.6	9.8	7.9	2.7	200.2	45
1986–87	7.1	3.6	12.2	8.2	4.5	203.2	44
1987–88	3.9	-3.4	9.4	1.2	5.1	203.1	$41\frac{3}{4}$
1988–89	-3.2	-14.5	1.4	-9.0	7.1	198.2	$39\frac{1}{4}$
1989–90	-13.8	-7.9	7.3	-4.6	4.2	203.0	$39\frac{1}{2}$

[a] Public sector borrowing requirement including privatization proceeds.
[b] Public sector financial deficit.
[c] Revalued at 1989–90 prices.
[d] Excluding privatization proceeds.
[e] The out-turn figures keep being revised and some are now very different from those first issued.

Source: *Financial Statement and Economic Report*, various issues; *Autumn Statement* 1990 and 1991; *Annual Abstract of Statistics* 1991

Healey did, i.e. up to 10 per cent of GDP, when in fact he limited himself to 4 per cent. Howe himself, however, took a more categorical line: 'To aim at a significantly higher public sector borrowing requirement' he argued in his budget speech, 'in other words to ease the stance of fiscal policy – would serve only to fuel the fire of inflation'. This appears to imply that a larger deficit would have involved increasing the money supply and that this would inevitably have raised prices. But with a small increase in the money supply to match a higher level of activity, there is no obvious reason why increased expenditure in a world of rapidly rising unemployment should force up prices.[14]

Reducing the overvaluation of sterling

It was one of the aims of the 1981 budget to make it possible for interest rates to come down and reduce the pressure forcing the exchange rate up. The exchange did fall from early in the year and by the autumn was not much higher than it had been at the change of government in May 1979 (figure 6.3). The fall was

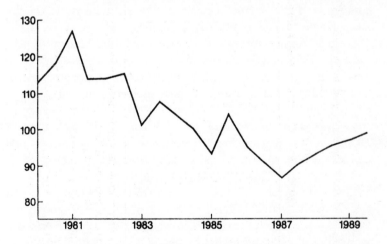

Figure 6.3   Sterling effective exchange rate (half-year averages), 1980–1989
Source: Bank of England *Quarterly Bulletin*

accelerated by efforts on the part of the American authorities to limit monetary expansion there by raising interest rates. This hardened the dollar and by September the dollar—sterling rate was down to $1.77 from a peak of $2.43. The effective exchange rate was also down at one point by nearly 20 per cent. The authorities reacted against so rapid a fall and were also concerned at the rate of monetary growth which had reached 18 per cent per annum. They felt obliged to change course and instead of making further reductions in interest rates followed American rates upwards. Bank rate was raised in two stages in September and October 1981 from 12 per cent to 16 per cent so that after all the efforts to bring it down it was back at the level of July 1980 that had caused such alarm a year earlier.[15]

This episode was the beginning of a changed attitude to the exchange rate and a greater concern for stability in the exchanges in the use of interest rates rather than exclusive concentration on the domestic money supply. For the next year the rate of exchange was held within fairly strict limits, interest rates being allowed to fall gently so long as this was not in conflict with stability of the exchange rate and did not involve an excessive increase in the money supply. By the autumn of 1982, however, there was renewed concern over the competitiveness of British industry within the target range of exchange rates. In its *Autumn Statement* in November 1982 the Treasury forecast a zero surplus in the balance of payments in 1983 in spite of the large contribution made by North Sea oil. It also focused attention on the lack of competitiveness of British industry and the loss of share of British industry both in overseas and domestic markets since 1977.[16] In the absence of any visible signs of recovery, the Treasury, as in the spring of 1976, was dwelling on the attractions of a lower exchange rate and was unable to conceal its thinking from the markets.

Although the Prime Minister and the Bank of England were against a deliberate devaluation, the market soon took over and a slide in the pound began in November 1982. The pound fell from $1.70 in October to $1.49 in March 1983 and the effective rate fell over the same period by nearly 15 per cent. The authorities offered only limited resistance. Interest rates were raised in December and January, the base rate being put up from 9 to 11 per cent while — a more significant development — the reserves were drawn upon to the tune of $2 billion from November to March. The 1983 budget and the approach of an election in May allowed the pound to recover and for most of 1983 it remained about 7 per cent below the level in the first half of 1982.

Fiscal policy, 1982–1984

Fiscal policy in the meantime remained tight. Public expenditure had been the subject in the summer of 1981 of a battle in Cabinet which the Chancellor had lost. He had sought agreement to cuts of £5 billion in the total for 1982–3 with no prospect of a fall in unemployment from a total of 2.7 million, and this had moved some ministers to rebellion. In November it was announced that public expenditure would rise by £5 billion above the total originally planned for 1982–3.[17] In compensation, council house rents were to be increased, unemployment pay (in real terms) was to be reduced, and national insurance contributions were to be raised so as to claw back about half of the extra £5 billion.

By the time the 1982 budget was introduced unemployment was over 3 million and the frequent assurances that recovery was on the way had proved to be illusory. On this occasion income tax allowances were increased by 2 per cent more than was required by indexation and the national insurance surcharge was cut by 1 per cent. On the other hand, indirect taxes were increased and the estimated borrowing requirement was again reduced, this time to £9½ billion. Fiscal policy remained restrictive but interest rates were allowed to fall slowly from October 1981 to November 1982.

The 1983 budget was much like that of 1982. Income tax allowances were increased by 14 per cent, indirect taxes were raised and the national insurance surcharge was again reduced. The money supply target was back at 7–11 per cent. The PSBR was lowered again to £8 billion.

How one should view the budgets of those years depends partly on one's theoretical framework and partly on whether one judges by what was planned or what actually happened. Some economists regard the budgets of 1982 and 1983 as deflationary because the PSBR was reduced. Others argue that 'taken together' they 'substantially reversed' the fiscal contraction of 1981. A Keynesian would start, not with the PSBR, but with the PSFD (the public sector financial deficit) which is a better measure (although far from ideal) of the impact of the budget on demand since it omits government lending operations. From this point of view there was indeed a reversal of fiscal contraction in 1982 and 1983. The PSFD fell from £12.5 billion in 1980–1 to £8.6 billion in 1981–2 and then reverted to £8.9 billion in 1982–3 and £9.7 billion in 1983–4 (table 6.2).[18] But the outcome of the budget as reflected in the PSBR or PSFD is a poor guide to the government's fiscal stance as measured by the net effect of budgetary measures on final expenditure.

After the election, with Nigel Lawson replacing Geoffrey Howe as Chancellor in June, there was a second attempt by the Treasury to arrest the growth of public spending. Cuts of £500 million, mainly in defence, were announced in July together with a proposed sale of £500 million in BP shares. The new Chancellor, like his predecessor in 1982, called for further cuts of £5 billion with a view to opening the way to tax reductions later. Once again, he had to be satisfied with half what was asked for. From then onwards, as Sir Leo Pliatzky has pointed out, 'the Treasury gave up, for practical purposes, the attempt to cut total public expenditure, but adopted a new strategy of stabilizing it in real terms',[19] relying on a growth in GDP to bring in additional tax revenue and permit tax cuts later in the life of the government. When even stability in real terms proved unattainable (see table 6.2), the Treasury settled for a gradual fall in the ratio of public expenditure to GDP.

Lawson also set on foot a review of monetary policy. Although £M3 remained in use as a monetary target, little notice was taken of it and alternatives were now to be examined. In departing from the indicator to which he had once attached such importance he blamed 'the far-reaching effects of structural changes resulting from the removal of exchange controls and direct controls on bank lending'.[20] He now ranged himself with Sir Alan Walters in favouring 'narrow' money indicators such as M1 or preferably M0. Since M1 like M3 had a large interest-bearing component it was, he argued, more subject to distortions than M0 which consisted mainly of notes and coins in circulation and was a better 'measure of transactions-related balances'. Whether a target that was easily hit was preferable to a target that had some meaningful causal relationship to changes in the price level was left undiscussed.

In the 1984 budget the MTFS was restated, on this occasion covering a five-year period, with M3 and M0 serving as parallel targets. But neither target was to receive the attention given to the exchange rate. This had been well maintained in the first half of 1984 but began to slide later in the year with the prolongation of the miners' strike, coupled with a marked appreciation of the dollar which continued into the first quarter of 1985. There had been no attempt to prevent the fall in the exchange rate which accorded with the wish of the Treasury for a more competitive rate. Interest rates, it is true, had been raised from a little over 9 per cent to 12 per cent in July but this was occasioned by doubts about the growth in the money supply. They were allowed to fall back gradually in line with rates on euro-dollar deposits in the second half of 1984 and were near their pre-July level by the end of the year while the exchange rate fell steadily. By December the effective rate had fallen by about 10 per cent and the dollar rate was down to $1.15 and still falling.

The exchange crisis, January 1985

Except in the 1982−3 episode the policy had been to leave the currency to float free of official intervention apart from smoothing operations. But as the rate fell towards $1 in January 1985 there was a strong reaction. The Bank of England intervened to raise its dealing rates when the pound fell to $1.10 and shortly afterwards bank rate, which had been scrapped in August 1981 to allow market forces freer play, was resurrected for a day and fixed at 12 per cent in mid January. The American President (Reagan) was then persuaded to allow co-ordinated intervention by central banks (the Group of Five) to hold down the dollar. Even so, the pound remained weak and the bank was obliged to raise interest rates to 14 per cent at the end of January 1985.[21]

The rate of exchange gradually recovered from a low point of $1.04 in February as the dollar began to weaken. By the autumn of 1985 it was back to the level of early 1984 both against the dollar and against a basket of currencies. It was an episode that made a deep impression on the Treasury. It occurred when both M0 and M3 were for the time being within their target range and was the culmination of the long fall in the exchange rate in 1985, much as the IMF crisis in 1976 succeeded a long fall then. As in 1976 the fall marked a loss of confidence by financial markets in government policy. There had been confusion in press briefing. Correspondents were told on 11 January that the government was unperturbed by the fall and had no intention of intervening on the very day the Bank of England signalled an increase in interest rates. There was a deeper source of concern in the growing deficit in trade in manufactures, the falling price of oil, and the approach of a decline in the production of North Sea oil from a peak in 1985–6.

At that stage the Chancellor was able to deny that he was 'pursuing a policy of unavowed alignment with the European Monetary System' and claimed to look to the effective exchange rate index for 'the best single measure of the external value of the pound'. But it was not long before it clearly *was* the unavowed policy to track a single currency, the deutsche mark. It was also not long before the external deficit on current account, of which the first signs appeared in 1986, were giving cause for concern.

Special employment measures

In the 1970s the rise in unemployment led to the introduction of a variety of job creation schemes of which the most important was the Temporary Employment Subsidy. Employers deferring redundancies could draw a subsidy of £20 per week for a maximum of a year on each full-time job maintained. The scheme was particularly successful in such labour-intensive industries as textiles, clothing and footwear but largely at the expense of the same industries in the European Community. It infringed the Treaty of Rome and the Community ordered it to be wound up. It was replaced by a Temporary Short-time Working Compensation Scheme, a work-sharing arrangement involving an outlay in 1980–1 of £365 million. Of the other schemes still in being in 1980–1 the two most important were the Job Release Scheme, which offered a weekly allowance to workers retiring early and not yet in receipt of their state pension, and the Youth Opportunities Programme.

From 1980, expenditure on these schemes – work sharing, job release and youth opportunities – was greatly expanded and a work-creating Community Programme Scheme providing part-time work for the long-term unemployed was also much enlarged.

By 1981–2 expenditure on these schemes had already grown fourfold in four years to a total of £1.6 billion. The main change thereafter was the conversion of the Youth Opportunities Programme into a Youth Training Scheme starting in September 1983 at a cost of £1 billion a year. This was originally intended to combine a year of work experience with training for sixteen-year olds not in full-time education so as to remove teenagers from the dole and help to avoid skill shortages when the economy recovered. In 1985 a second year was added to allow more advanced job-related training. It had originally been proposed that refusal of a place should lead to the withdrawal of supplementary benefit but after representations this was reduced to the forfeit of six weeks' benefit.

Schemes of this kind were of course no substitute for full-time jobs at normal pay. But if, as looked likely, large-scale unemployment was going to persist for many years such schemes could serve as palliatives and might be regarded as a useful social investment.

Curbing inflation, 1979–1986

The main aim of government policy had been to curb inflation. Did it succeed? Whatever index one uses shows a steep decline after the initial upsurge in prices in 1979. Inflation is often measured by the increase in prices over a twelve-month period and by that measure retail prices rose fastest in the second quarter of 1980 with the increase reaching a peak of 21.9 per cent in May. A year later, in May 1981 this had fallen to 11.7 per cent and two years later, in May 1983, to 3.7 per cent. But already in the six months from May to November 1980 the rise in prices was down to an annual rate of 8.2 per cent. From May 1983 the trend was upwards again for two years to a fresh peak of 7 per cent in May 1985. The lowest rate reached in the 1980s was 2.4 per cent in the summer of 1986. Thereafter there was a gradual rise, accelerating in 1988–9 and rising to over 10 per cent in the summer of 1990 before beginning to come down again.

In retrospect it is clear that inflation was subdued but not extinguished. It is clear also that the major factor in bringing down the rate of inflation was the recession of 1980–2. This is true not

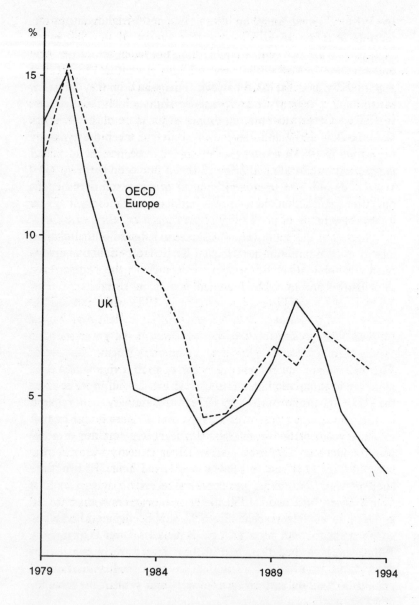

Figure 6.4   Increase in consumer prices in the UK and OECD Europe, 1979–94

Source: OECD *Economic Outlook*

only of the United Kingdom but of other industrial countries too. Consumer prices in OECD countries increased in 1980 by an average of 12.9 per cent. By 1983 this had fallen to 5.2 per cent and continued to fall until it reached 2.5 per cent in 1986. There was nothing peculiar to the United Kingdom in the course of inflation over those years except the height to which inflation rose in 1980. All countries suffered the initial pressure of the oil shock at the end of 1979 and enjoyed the relief of the big drop in oil prices in 1986. All countries also enjoyed the benefit of falling commodity prices after 1980 – over 20 per cent between 1980 and 1982 – as the international recession lowered demand. So long as wage inflation did not break out in the way it did in 1974–5 a drop in the rate of price inflation was more or less inevitable. A rise in unemployment at 100,000 a month disposed of that danger.

It is at this point, however, that British experience contrasts most strongly with continental experience. On the standardized definitions used by OECD unemployment in Britain rose from 5.0 per cent in 1979 to 12.5 per cent in 1983 while the OECD average rose only from 5.0 to 8.5 per cent i.e. by less than half as much. It was presumably not the intention of the government to produce such a catastrophic rise in unemployment. But unless that was so, and unless nothing short of such a rise would have checked wage inflation, it is hard to ascribe the fall in inflation to deliberate government policy. A less deflationary policy might have been just as successful, if perhaps over a rather longer period.

The transformation in the labour market was certainly remarkable. In October 1979 workers in the car industry were entering claims for a 30 per cent increase in wages and index linking of the settlement. In November farmworkers received pay increases of $19\frac{1}{2}$–$24\frac{1}{2}$ per cent and in December mineworkers settled for 20 per cent. In the new year the electricity supply engineers and water supply workers both received pay increases of over 20 per cent. The government had also given effect to awards recommended by the Clegg Commission of a rise of 19.6 per cent for nurses, 18.2 per cent for school and college teachers and similar increases for other groups.

A major strike in the steel industry in January 1980 proved an early test of strength. The steel workers were offered a rise of 2 per cent in November 1979, later revised upwards to 6 per cent. After a three-month strike a committee of enquiry awarded an 11 per cent rise with a 'lead-in' on $4\frac{1}{2}$ per cent for a productivity deal and changes in working practices. As happened later in the coal industry, the strike was followed by closures which were not resisted.

From the summer of 1980 wage inflation began to fall off. In July 1980 wage rates were 20 per cent higher than a year previously. By December 1980 the increase was down to 14.5 per cent and a year later to 8.2 per cent. The peak may have been a little later than the peak in price inflation but it was not the slowing down in price inflation that produced the lower wage settlements. On the other hand, the moderation in pay increases did contribute to the fall in inflation.

The interesting question is whether this moderation is to be attributed to labour legislation, or government pressure, or to the natural consequence of high and rising unemployment. Government legislation in those years was more concerned with secondary picketing and the closed shop than with direct limitation of the powers of the unions. Something was undoubtedly due to the government's attitude to wage claims in the public sector. Cash limits, for example, were intended in part as a weapon against increased costs (including higher wages) by enforcing a reduction in employment and other inputs if wages and prices rose faster than the limits postulated.

In October 1982, *after* the fall in inflation, the government set a pay target of 3.5 per cent in the public sector in 1983. By providing funds on this basis it could face unions with a choice between sustaining employment and more pay. But the most powerful factor in reducing wage settlements in 1980−1 must have been the rise in unemployment and the bankruptcy of many firms. It was only later, as excess capacity was absorbed and shortages grew, that the success of the government in moderating wage settlements on a continuous footing was put to the test.

Legislation aimed at reducing the power of the unions, which the government assumed were more militant than their members, began with the Employment Bill introduced in December 1979. This was directed against picketing of premises not directly involved in a trade dispute and called for secret ballots before decisions to strike. Two years later this was supplemented by the Trade Union Bill. This provided that unions could be sued under civil law for unlawful action by their officials or members; trade disputes were more narrowly defined as disputes between an employer and his employees; and industrial action against non-unionized companies was declared unlawful. While this legislation had some effect, the reduced bargaining power of workers had far more. A good illustration was the decision of the trade union leaders at Ford's in February 1984 to call off for lack of support a proposed strike against the closure of the Dagenham foundry. Later in the year an even more powerful illustration was the lack of support from other industries for the year-long miners' strike and the divisions among the miners' representatives themselves. In 1973 the miners had first declared a ban on overtime that caused stocks of coal to run down. In 1984 they called a strike after large stocks had been built up and when abundant North Sea oil was readily available.

Bargaining power, however, varies with the level of employment whereas legislation does not. The power exercised by the unions might therefore reassert itself as attitudes changed once labour again became scarce.

The beginning of recovery

Production had ceased to fall at the end of 1980 although this was not what the statistics showed at the time. It would appear that GDP increased between the last quarter of 1980 and the last quarter of 1981 by about $1\frac{1}{2}$ per cent and in about the same proportion in 1982 − not enough to prevent the continuing rise in unemployment in those years. The increase in GDP in 1983 was much more evident and may have been as large as 4 per cent. In 1984 there was some slowing down as a result of the miners' strike, which is estimated to have knocked $1\frac{1}{2}$ per cent off the increase in that year and inflated correspondingly the growth in 1985. Taking 1984 and 1985 together, the estimated rise in GDP averaged a little under 3 per cent per annum. It 1986 it was back up to 4 per cent and maintained a fast pace in 1987−8, averaging about $4\frac{1}{2}$ per cent before falling in 1989 to about 1 per cent and beginning to fall in the middle of 1990.

What brought about the recovery? The biggest single factor, as in most recessions, was a slowing down in the fall in stocks which was the biggest drag on demand. The fall in stocks, which had been particularly heavy from mid 1980 to mid 1981, did not come to an end until the first quarter of 1983, but it went on at a very much slower pace in the second half of 1981 and there was actually some stockbuilding in the first half of 1982. Fixed capital investment touched bottom in the first quarter of 1981 and although it was over a year before there was any appreciable recovery, the cessation of the fall had the same effect as an actual increase. Exports, too, increased a little in the second half of 1981 but they made no further progress in 1982 and the first half of 1983. Consumer spending acted as a stabilizer, rising almost imperceptibly in 1980 and 1981, beginning to accelerate in the second half of 1982 and then increasing strongly in 1983. Government expenditure on goods and services, contrary to what one might expect, increased every year from 1979 to 1984.

What this adds up to is that the recovery, like the depression, was mainly in investment and took the form initially of the normal cyclical rebound. Looked at in perspective, the expansion in fixed investment that began in 1978−9 was checked over the next four years by financial stringency and contracting markets, reached a low point at the beginning of 1981, gradually revived and then expanded rapidly after 1982.

Developments after 1983

The years after 1983 brought a continuing economic recovery in which employment expanded for seven successive years although unemployment did not turn down until the end of 1986, when it fell rapidly for three years. The prolonged rise in output from the low point in 1981 carried it up by over a third to a peak in 1990. The running was made partly by fixed investment, which reached an earlier peak in 1989, higher by over two-thirds than in 1981, and partly by consumer spending, which outstripped the growth in output and by 1990 was 43 per cent higher than in 1981.

The expansion in investment was entirely in the private sector. Investment in the public sector, once not far short of half the total but by 1990 not much above a tenth, remained little changed for most of the decade and at no time exceeded the level in 1980.

In the private sector the most conspicuous expansion was in distribution and services where at peak in 1988 fixed investment was nearly three times what it had been in 1981. The increase was, however, quite general and covered housing and manufacturing as well as the various categories of asset to which the totals relate. In manufacturing, however, even an increase of two-thirds above the low point in 1983 failed to raise investment above the level of the early 1960s. Contrary to the trend in fixed investment, stock building, except in the boom, remained low or, in the early years, negative. In relation to turnover there was a steady fall throughout the decade that reduced the stock/output ratio in the economy as a whole by 20 per cent and in manufacturing by 30 per cent.

The expansion in consumer spending was boosted after 1983 by a marked fall in personal savings. In contrast to the mid 1970s there had been no fall in consumer spending in the recession of 1980−1: in 1983 there was an increase of no less than 4.2 per cent (well above what the official figures indicated at the time). About half of this reflected higher disposable income as recovery proceeded but nearly half was attributable to a fall from 11.4 to 9.8 in the percentage of disposable income saved. It was a fall that had been in progress, although more slowly, over the previous two years from a peak of 13.5 per cent in 1980; and it was a fall that was to continue until a low point of 5.4 per cent was reached in the consumer boom of 1988.

A central part in this fall in the savings ratio was played by the housing boom that reached a peak in 1988 in the south of England and a little later in the north. House prices rose to extraordinary levels in relation to current incomes. The rise in prices and the prospect of its continuance enhanced the attractiveness of house ownership and added to housing demand. In the 1970s when inflation was very rapid house prices rose fivefold − faster even than earnings − and although the rise was rather slower in the 1980s it again outstripped earnings, rising from under $3\frac{1}{2}$ in the early 1980s to about $4\frac{1}{2}$ times earnings in 1988 (and more than five times earnings in London). These increases in price − for example, by nearly 75 per cent between 1985 and 1988 − were encouraging to borrowers so long as they could count on substantial capital appreciation to set against their mortgage interest bill. In 1988, for example, capital appreciation on the average home exceeded the average mortgage interest bill of £2800 by nearly

£5000, i.e. the real cost of borrowing was negative.[22]

The housing boom was facilitated by easy access to finance. The building societies began to offer 100 per cent mortgages and the clearing banks also entered the field in the 1980s as major lenders on mortgage for house purchase. Borrowing proceeded freely and on a remarkable scale. Building society mortgages alone (not all of them used to buy houses) grew from under £10 billion in 1980 to nearly £50 billion in 1988. The contraction of debt for house purchase did not by itself reduce personal savings but the additional funds released made possible higher spending and the need to service additional debt appropriated income that might otherwise have been saved.

After 1988 the process went into reverse. High rates of interest on outstanding mortgages put pressure on consumer incomes while house prices either fell (in the south east particularly) or rose more slowly (in the north). Borrowing fell off and the savings ratio recovered to nearly 11 per cent at the end of 1990. Just as the fall in the savings ratio earlier helped economic recovery so the later increase in the ratio contributed to the downturn after 1988. The enormous increase in consumer debt gave to fluctuations in the short-term rate of interest a power over consumer spending that it had not formerly enjoyed.

Fluctuations in the savings ratio were not, however, linked only with housing. They were affected by the withdrawal of hire purchase controls in July 1982 and by financial deregulation in general. Moreover, while the rise in house prices was perhaps the most conspicuous source of the rise in asset values and personal wealth in the 1980s other assets also rose steeply in price and encouraged borrowing and spending. The *Financial Times* index of industrial ordinary shares, for example, stood at 440 in January 1980 and had reached 1855 by July 1987 – a rise averaging 21 per cent per annum. A few months later there was a sharp drop in share prices, not unlike that of 1929, which brought the index down to under 1300. By 1989, however, the whole of the drop, and more, had been made good. In Britain and elsewhere the drop had caused fears of an immediate recession and helped to dissuade governments from tightening their policies, as in retrospect might have been appropriate. Within a few months of the 1987 fall in stock exchange prices the economy was in the middle of the 1988 boom.

To go back to the beginning of the decade, once recovery started it gradually gained momentum. There was a slowing down at three stages, the first in the Falklands war in the spring of 1982, the second in the year-long miners' strike beginning early in 1984 and the third in the latter half of 1985 when expansion in fixed investment and exports was halted by high interest rates associated with efforts to stem the fall in the exchange rate. These periods apart, growth was continuous from 1981 and latterly comparatively fast.

Employment was at first slow to respond and did not begin to rise until the spring of 1983. Unemployment continued to rise until 1986 but vacancies had reached a low point five years earlier and had already more than doubled. The rise in employment was at first quite brisk, slowed down in 1985−6, and became rapid in 1987−9 with an increase over those three years of 2¼ million. Unemployment reached a peak now officially put at 3.4 million but there have been so many changes of definition in the 1980s − all in one direction − in the measurement of unemployment that it is difficult to know what the peak would have been on earlier definitions. The fall to $1\frac{1}{2}$ million in 1990 exaggerates the actual reduction after 1986 since large numbers were removed from the register after interview. Undoubtedly, however, there was a fairly rapid fall for over four years until unemployment began to increase again late in 1990.

The boom was in no way impeded by government. The rate of interest which had been directed so exclusively against domestic inflation in 1979−80 was used to steady the rate of exchange at the beginning of 1985 and again at the beginning of 1986 but was then allowed to fall, with minor setbacks, to a low point of $7\frac{1}{2}$ per cent in May 1988 and only then was pushed up, little by little, to 12 per cent in August and 13 per cent in November. In 1989, when the rate of expansion had greatly slowed down, the rate was raised again in May and October, first to 14, then to 15 per cent and no reduction was made for a year until Britain's entry into the Community's Exchange Rate Mechanism in October 1990. By that time, curiously enough, high interest rates were seen as operating, not on the money supply but on consumer spending, chiefly through the absorption of purchasing power in mortgage payments.

Equally, no use was made of fiscal policy to moderate the expansion in demand. The standard rate of income tax was lowered by 1p in the 1986 budget, by 2p in the 1987 budget, and again by 2p in the 1988 budget, bringing it down to 25p compared with 33p when the Conservatives took office in 1979. The lower rate of tax was more than compensated for by the buoyancy of the revenue as incomes increased in the boom. At the same time the sale of publicly owned assets in nationalized industries brought in amounts rising to over £5 billion in 1987−8 and £7 billion in 1988−9. As a result it was possible to repay debt amounting to £3½ billion in 1987−8, £14½ billion in 1988−9 and £7 billion in 1989−90.

It should not be imagined that the repayment of debt by the government enriches the country if it is accompanied by the sale of assets in the nationalized industries. If the assets are sold at a cut price and with substantial selling costs the net balance of the public sector is to that extent weakened. To obtain a comprehensive picture we need to take account not only of debt repayment but of public investment, the erosion of the national debt by inflation, pension liabilities to which the government may add, and so on. Adding to, or repaying debt can be a relatively small item in the calculation of changes in the public sector's net assets or liabilities.[23]

The recovery of production had one important consequence on which the government had not reckoned. It was accompanied by a marked rise in productivity, especially in manufacturing. There is of course a large cyclical element in changes in productivity since when production expands employment usually lags behind. This inflated the apparent improvement between 1980 and 1989 just as it exaggerated the slowdown in productivity growth in 1979−80 and in 1989−90. For manufacturing the average annual rise in labour productivity both over the ten years 1979−89 and over the last five years of the period was just over 4.2 per cent. That rate compares favourably with the growth of productivity in other members of the Community over the same periods and with past experience in the United Kingdom. But when the necessary qualifications are made, it is not a great deal higher than might have been forecast in a long period of uninterrupted recovery in a country where productivity was appreciably lower than in neighbouring countries.

The growth of productivity in other sectors of the economy shows no similar improvement. For the whole economy the average rate of growth in labour productivity was 1.8 per cent annum in both periods quoted above. The figures, although not altogether reliable, yield a rate lower than in some earlier periods.

The government continued to announce in successive budgets the latest edition of its medium-term financial strategy. The PSBR, as planned, fell year by year but in fact fluctuated above and below the planned total: above in 1983—4 and 1984—5 and below in the next few years when the proceeds of privatization issues increased rapidly. Monetary policy was hitched increasingly closely to the rate of exchange and although monetary targets were announced, they changed their identity from time to time (like the unemployment figures) and were no longer the basis of policy. It was not until 1987 that £M3 was formally dropped but it had long been true that targets were selected to fit the growth in something that could be called 'money' rather than that money was made to hit a fixed target.

The downturn that began in 1989 with unemployment still over $1\frac{1}{2}$ million raised awkward questions about future prospects. On the one hand, the rise in the inflation rate in the boom to over 10 per cent in 1990 from $2\frac{1}{2}$ per cent in mid 1986 pointed to domestic inflexibilities that stood in the way of regaining anything approaching full employment. At the same time, the emergence of an external deficit that appeared to be in excess of £20 billion in 1989 pointed to an international imbalance that would not be easily overcome.

The domestic inflexibilities were threefold. There was, first, a problem of industrial capacity. The contraction in 1980—1 had been extensive and had virtually extinguished whole tracts of British industry. Coal, steel, shipbuilding, locomotive building and many other sectors of heavy engineering had almost disappeared from some of their traditional locations. As a result, the opportunities they offered of full-time work for men had greatly diminished and had not been balanced by the appearance of fresh opportunities in the newer industries. The expanding demands for labour were for women or part-time workers while full-time jobs for men never rose very far. Between 1983 and 1987, for example, while total employment was rising by $1\frac{1}{2}$ million, the number of men in full-time paid jobs actually fell. The increase in male employment of 400,000 was confined to self-employed and part-time workers. Over a million of the additional jobs were for women and of these, two-thirds were for part-time employment.

There was, secondly, an inflexibility in adjusting sufficiently quickly to changes in demand. The rapidity of expansion in 1987–8 revealed shortages and bottlenecks that might have yielded to a slower rate of growth in demand. This applied not only to investment in additional capacity but also to the training of the labour force so as to permit of greater adaptability. It is difficult in the light of past experience to suppose that major bottlenecks were bound to emerge, irrespective of the prior amount of investment and training, as soon as unemployment fell to $1\frac{1}{2}$ million. The expansion could have carried on longer had it been at a rather slower pace.

A third inflexibility was in wage settlements. It is true that much of the inflation after 1986 was at the top and not the bottom end of the income scale. But the main source of the inflation since productivity continued to rise and there was relatively little change in import prices, was the increase in wages. The habit of pressing for more than was currently being produced was not easily shaken off.

These inflexibilities did not stand in the way of a later attempt to make fuller use of the available manpower. But the external deficit might well do so. The loss of industrial capacity at the beginning of the decade and the failure of British industry subsequently to out-compete the rising volume of imports meant that imports of manufactures were growing twice as fast as exports. This was not a situation promising an early end to the enormous external deficit. On the contrary it implied that fresh efforts to expand domestic activity would send the deficit rocketing upwards; and it suspended over the economy the threat of an early exchange crisis if any hitch occurred in the large-scale inflow of funds by which the deficit was financed.

Among the issues that came to the fore in the later years of the decade were relations with Europe: the single European market due to be inaugurated in 1992, membership of the Exchange Rate Mechanism and the possibility of a common European currency. For the United Kingdom these were difficult decisions. One need only look at the slide in the value of the pound over the decades (or indeed in the 1980s) and at the large external deficit that had somehow to be removed, to feel some uneasiness at the prospect of a sterling rate of exchange that could be changed only with difficulty, still more one that could never under any circumstances be changed. There was much talk of the changes that the ERM had wrought in inflation in other countries, but little talk of the rise in unemployment that accompanied them. There was also a natural hesitation to entrust to a European central bank powers over the economy that had never been entrusted to the Bank of England.

Rolling back the frontiers of the state

It was part of the government's philosophy that the role of the market should expand and the role of the state contract. There were three main ways in which it sought to give effect to this philosophy: cutting public expenditure; deregulation; and privatization.

Cutting public expenditure

There had been talk in opposition of cuts in public expenditure of £8 billion but nothing of the kind occurred. Some items − pensions, defence, law and order, for example − were more or less ruled out on electoral or other grounds. Large cuts in items such as health and education were impracticable. It was possible to whittle away some current expenditure but the only large immediate economies were in capital expenditure (which hardly met the desire to prune out waste). The biggest reductions were in housing, subsidies and miscellaneous items. Charges could be introduced or increased. Welfare payments could be linked to prices instead of earnings. But even with subsidies, progress was slow: many subsidies both to private industry and to the nationalized industries were still being paid well into the 1980s.

The fact is, however, that public expenditure in real terms did not fall after 1979 but increased. Expressed in constant prices, the total increased rapidly after 1978−9 and was nearly 16 per cent higher by 1986−7. Over the next three years, no further increase took place (table 6.2).

How was it then that the public had the feeling of constant pressure to make cuts and inadequate maintenance of the physical and social infrastructure? The answer in the early years of the decade lies partly in the additional outlay required in unemployment and supplementary benefit, which more than offset economies in other directions. In later years the comparatively rapid increase in GDP outstripped the growth in public expenditure so that the proportion that public expenditure bore to GDP fell even in years when the absolute total continued to rise. In 1978–9 the proportion had been 44 per cent. By 1982–3 it was $47\frac{1}{2}$ per cent. Only after that year did a rather hesitant fall begin, gathering speed in the boom after 1986, and reaching $39\frac{1}{4}$ per cent in 1988–9.

There was no frontal attack on the welfare state. In spite of efforts to whittle down benefits by curtailing eligibility and restricting conditions, the government found itself obliged not only to spend heavily on the unemployed but to make increased provision for health, education and other services. Expenditure on the social services and housing (excluding capital expenditure) increased from £36 billion in 1978–9 to £93 billion in 1987–8 or by roughly 30 per cent in real terms compared with an increase over the same period in GDP of about 20 per cent. It was an increase, however, that fell short of developing needs and the claims flowing from those needs.

Current government expenditure on goods and services increased much less – by a little under 10 per cent in real terms over the years 1979–88. The increase was spread out fairly evenly over the period with a small rise every year except perhaps in 1985.

Investment by central and local government, which had fallen all through the Labour party's period in office, continued to fall in the first four years of Conservative rule. By 1982 it was 40 per cent lower than in 1979, about half the fall being in housing. After 1982, however, there was some recovery to a peak in 1986 not far short of the 1979 level and then a renewed decline. Investment by nationalized industries, on the other hand, fell rather little except in the depression in 1981–2 and it was only after 1983, as privatization assumed larger proportions, that there was a heavy and continuing fall.

Cutting public expenditure was intended to pave the way for cuts in taxation that would somehow release entrepreneurial energies. Hence the reduction in the top rate of tax to 40 per cent and the lowering of the standard rate to 25p from 33p in 1979 were regarded as major achievements from the angle of productive efficiency, not just as acts of income redistribution. But before tax remission could go very far there had also to be a reduction in the borrowing requirement. As it happened, there was no conflict by 1988 between lowering the standard rate to 25p and running the PSBR down below zero to a point at which debt could be repaid. But this rested on an unusual combination of boom, and sale of public assets and the future of the standard rate at 25p was not altogether assured

Tax reform

With the efforts to curtail public expenditure went attempts to improve revenue collection by tax reform. These chiefly affected company taxation and local authority finance.

Among development in the middle years of the decade was a reform of company taxation in 1984. This abolished tax relief for stock appreciation which had been introduced at the end of 1974 to save many companies from insolvency. With the fall in inflation such relief was less necessary and it had proved imposs-ible to devise acceptable accounting rules to deal with the prob-lem. Investment allowances, often very substantial, were swept away at the same time and in compensation corporation tax was reduced over a two-year period from 50 per cent to 35 per cent. Whether this had any part in the check to private fixed investment in 1986 is uncertain but there is no sign of any drag on investment in later years.

A later development in taxation was the introduction of the poll tax or community charge. A Green Paper on alternatives to dom-estic rates had been issued as far back as December 1981 and had listed various alternative proposals including a sales tax, a local income tax and a poll tax. It was not until six years later that a Bill was introduced providing for the introduction of a poll tax in Scotland in 1989 and in England and Wales in 1990. The tax proved highly unpopular and led to widespread refusals to pay involving a large, unplanned loss of revenue for many local authorities.

Deregulation

There was great enthusiasm for deregulation. An enormous number of quangos were abolished. Exchange control went within a few months and hire purchase controls after three years. The banks were given more freedom: direct limitation of bank lending ceased. These were all controls which had played their part in the management of the economy and although they might have lost some of their effectiveness, they were far from ineffective and supplemented the few other instruments of control at the government's disposal. Unless the economy was self-regulating, which it proved not to be, the government ran the risk of lacking the weapons necessary to stabilize it. The effects of decontrol were felt particularly in the consumer boom when almost the only check the government could resort to was the use of very high interest rates. Where in the past these were expected to operate primarily on producer investment, and to a lesser extent (usually coupled with hire purchase controls) on investment in durable consumer goods, their modus operandi in 1989−90 was on saving: the need to refrain from consumption in order to meet high mortgage payments.

The removal of these controls had important consequences. The removal of exchange control, for example, made it more natural to hold a mixed portfolio of foreign and domestic securities: it had previously been necessary to buy investment currency at a premium over the official exchange rate in order to acquire foreign securities or to borrow abroad for the purpose. The removal of the premium and of obstacles to transfers of money between different financial centres made for increased diversification of holdings, quite apart from any expectation of higher returns (including capital gains) on foreign securities. In the case of direct investment it had long been possible to proceed on the basis of foreign borrowing but here, too, the acquisition of foreign assets (including takeover bids) became a more straightforward and calculable investment. Investment abroad in both forms was greatly stimulated and a large portfolio of foreign investments was built up. Unfortunately the surge in foreign investment did not occur when the exchange rate was on the way up in 1979−81 and was still in full spate when the balance of payments moved into deficit after 1985.

The removal of hire purchase controls also diminished the government's power over unwelcome developments later in the decade. An important check to consumer spending was no longer available and it was in part the removal of control over consumer credit that allowed the consumer boom to reach such proportions. The government contended that the control had little point in the absence of exchange control because credit could be readily obtained from abroad; but this does not seem a very plausible argument in relation to the vast majority of purchasers whose access to foreign credit is negligible.

Deregulation extended beyond the removal of controls to efforts to allow the producer more freedom of action and the consumer more freedom of choice. In this sense it included privatization conceived of as a way of allowing producers to respond more freely to market forces. Schools and hospitals, for example, were to be allowed to opt out of the state system of education and health without forfeiting financial support from the state. There were also proposals for voucher systems allowing the consumer to choose schools and hospitals; even the universities were to be encouraged to bid for more students.

Thus deregulation was not to be just the negative act of withdrawing regulations: it was intended also as a positive means of encouraging competition, exposing producers and consumers to market forces, and allowing them access to wider opportunities.

Privatization

Not much was made of the idea of privatization in 1979: it did not figure in the Conservative party's manifesto. But the idea caught on and became popular. What started out on a modest scale developed into a major element in the government's policy.

From the government's point of view, privatization had a threefold advantage. It opened the door to enterprise and brought a large tract of industry more immediately under the discipline of market forces. This might mean that industry became more efficient; but it was likely to mean also that less account was taken of social considerations which it was difficult to bring into the reckoning of private firms. The sale of shares in the nationalized industries could also help to create a share-owning democracy just as the sale of council houses helped to widen the class of property owners. Finally, the proceeds accruing to the government made it easier to bring down the government's borrowing requirement and brought forward the prospect of a balanced budget and lower taxation.

It must be said that, as had happened with nationalization, the case rested heavily on ideology and rhetoric rather than on careful assessment of alternative industrial structures, industry by industry. That the nationalized industries had made enormous losses falling on the taxpayer was not in question. This was largely for two reasons that concerned the government rather than the industries themselves. On the one hand, they had been obliged to hold down prices for long periods as part of the previous government's fight against inflation; on the other hand, they had been obliged to maintain output (e.g. in coalmining and in rail transport) in places and at levels that were plainly unremunerative. The resulting losses did not necessarily reflect on their efficiency; but they did point to the vulnerability of the nationalized industries to government pressure that could be attacked as misconceived.

The essential question was not about past losses but about future efficiency; and here it was not easy to be sure in advance that large private monopolies would outperform large public monoplies. There was some danger that the pricing policy of the private monopolies would follow the opposite course to that wished on the public monopolies. So far as privatization enabled competition to get to work and force prices down, well and good. But in the case of large public utilities such as British Telecom, competition might prove wasteful or ineffective. The government appointed a regulatory watchdog, OFTEL, and required a downward movement in prices at a rate in keeping with the presumed trend in productivity. Privatization did not always bring complete freedom from the attentions of government.

Privatization got off to a slow start. It was not until 1983–4 that the proceeds of sales of assets in public enterprises were appreciably above £$\frac{1}{2}$ million a year; and most of what was raised in the first four years came from the sale of BP shares, licences to prospect for oil and sales from stockpiles of oil. From 1983–4 onwards, there was a rapid expansion year by year to £7 billion in 1988–9 with steel, water and electricity undertakings still to come in the next three years.[24]

Privatization took various forms. First of all there were sales of BP shares. The Labour government had already raised £½ billion in 1977 in accordance with its agreement with the IMF, but had retained a majority shareholding in BP. Over £8 billion was raised by the Conservative government in three successive issues in 1979, 1983, and 1987, the last of these being much the largest and disposing of all remaining shares.

Secondly, there were a large number of private sales of companies, some of them management buy-outs, some sales to a commercial buyer. These included half a dozen warship-building yards in 1985−6, holdings of the National Enterprise Board in ICL, Ferranti and other companies, the National Bus Company (much the biggest), the Royal Ordnance Factories, Sealink, and a number of other enterprises.

Public offerings, apart from BP, included the major public utilities − gas, electricity, water and telecommunications − and a wide range of large undertakings such as British Steel, Cable and Wireless, British Airways, Britoil and Rolls Royce. In some cases the government retained a substantial holding (49 per cent in the case of British Telecom), usually offering the rest for sale later (e.g. Associated British Ports, British Aerospace, Britoil, Cable and Wireless). In many of the companies privatized the government retained a 'golden share', giving it power to veto changes in some of the articles of association and allowing it to resist a takeover threat. The government could, however, elect not to use its voting rights, as in the case of BP's takeover of Britoil, and the 'golden share' has been reduced in several cases e.g. Amersham International, Enterprise Oil and Jaguar. Retention of a 'golden share' gives the government no say in the running of the business or share in the profits.

Privatization was expected to bring about a large increase in the number of shareholders. This it certainly did initially. The applications for British Telecom shares included 1 million from persons who had never before owned shares. On several occasions over 1 million applications were received. Many of those applying hoped to make a quick profit and sell within months. After three years, for example, only 40 per cent of British Telecom's original shareholders still held their shares and only about 65 per cent of investors in British Airways held their shares after six months.

But it was estimated in 1987 that the number of shareholders in Britain had grown from 3 million in 1979 to 9 million eight years later. Nearly half of those shareholders held shares exclusively in privatized companies or in the Trustee Savings Bank.[25] Privatization had certainly contributed to an important change in share ownership although the rapidly rising proportion of shares owned by institutions and financial intermediaries was perhaps of greater ultimate significance.

By the end of 1987 the government had raised about £25 billion through privatization and about 1 million jobs had been transferred from the public to the private sector. These transactions, while in progress, had important repercussions on the financial position of the government. At first the proceeds of asset sales were a small proportion of the government's borrowing requirements but by 1987−8 the total was comparable in amount with the PSBR, i.e. almost enough to save the government the trouble of borrowing. Whatever underlay the initial urge to privatize, the later enlargement of the programme must have owed something to the enthusiasm of the Treasury for what proved to be a powerful reinforcement of their financial position.

Notes

1   For the effect of the changes in definition see Worswick *Unemployment* pp. 16−18; Feinstein and Matthews, National Institute *Economic Review*, August 1990, pp. 82−3; and Charter for jobs, *Economic Report*, May 1987.

2   F. J. Atkinson, S. J. Brooks and S. G. F. Hall, 'The economic effects of North Sea oil', National Institute *Economic Review*, May 1983, p. 39.

3   P. J. Forsyth and J. A. Kay, 'The economic implications of North Sea oil revenues', Institute of Fiscal Studies, 1980.

4   W. Keegan, *Mrs Thatcher's Economic Experiment*, p. 127.

5   There had, however, been a jump of $2\frac{1}{2}$ per cent in November 1978.

6   See Appendix 3, p. 314.

7   *Financial Statement and Budget Report 1980−81*, p. 16.

8 For a fuller discussion see J. C. R. Dow and I. D. Saville, *A Critique of Monetary Policy*, pp. 113−14.

9 W. Keegan, *Mrs Thatcher's Economic Experiment*, pp. 144−5.

10 Earlier, the PSBR in 1980−1 was estimated at £13½ billion.

11 Keegan, *Mrs Thatcher's Economic Experiment*. pp. 159−62.

12 National Institute *Economic Review*, May 1981, p. 4.

13 *The Times*, 30 March 1981.

14 The issue was much discussed at the time and subsequently. See, for example, the symposium on government borrowing and economic policy in the National Institute *Economic Review*, August 1985.

15 Strictly speaking, there was no minimum lending rate (or bank rate) after August 1981 but the Bank of England continued to use open market operations to keep short-term interest rates within an undisclosed band. The base rates of the London clearing banks reflected what Bank rate would have been had it been published.

16 It was pointed out that between 1977 and the first half of 1982 there had been no increase in the volume of British exports of manufactures while world trade in them had risen by 18 per cent; and that over the same period a fall in UK production of manufactures by 14 per cent had accompanied a rise of 40 per cent in imports (*Autumn Statement* 1982, quoted by W. Keegan, *Mrs Thatcher's Economic Experiment*, pp. 179−80). Three years later imports of manufactures had risen by another 40 per cent and the share of British exports of manufactures in world trade was still falling.

17 By that time the Cabinet had been reconstructed in order to shed some of the rebels.

18 These figures differ radically from those originally published, which show a drop from £11.6 billion in 1980−1 to £5.5 billion in 1981−2 with subsequent increases to £8.5 billion and £11.7 billion, respectively.

19 Sir Leo Pliatzky, *Paying and Choosing*, p. 33.

20 Speech by the Chancellor at the Mansion House Dinner 1983, quoted by W. Keegan, *Mr Lawson's Gamble*, p. 124.

21 For a fuller account of the exchange crisis see W. Keegan, *Mr Lawson's Gamble*, ch. 7.

22 John Plender, 'Housing hiatus', *Financial Times*, 30 March 1991.

23 For an attempt to assess the changes since 1957 in net liabilities

see John Hills, 'Counting the family silver', *Fiscal Studies*, May 1989.

24   For details see Howard Hyman, 'Privatisation: the facts' in C. Veljanovski (ed.), *Privatisation and Competition: a market prospectus*.

25   H. Hyman, 'Privatization', pp. 209–10.

Further reading

In addition to the works cited above the following should also be consulted:

Godley, W. 1990. 'Prosperity and foreign trade in the 1990s: Britain's strategic problem', in *Oxford Review of Economic Policy*, autumn.

Hills, John 1989. 'Counting the family silver: the public sector's balance sheet 1957 to 1987', in *Fiscal Studies*, May.

Maynard, G. 1988. *The Economy under Mrs Thatcher*, Oxford: Blackwell.

McInnes, J. 1987. *Thatcherism at Work*, Milton Keynes: Open University Press.

Middleton, P. 1989. 'Economic policy formulation in the Treasury in the post-war period', *National Institute Economic Review*, February.

Minford, P. 1983. *Unemployment: causes and cure*, Oxford: Oxford University Press.

Pliatzky, L. 1989. *The Treasury under Mrs Thatcher*, (Chs 11–14), Oxford: Blackwell.

Smith, D. 1987. *The Rise and Fall of Monetarism*, Harmondsworth: Penguin Books.

Walters, A. A. 1986. *Britain's Economic Renaissance*, Oxford and New York: Oxford University Press.

Walters, A. A. 1990. *Sterling in Danger*, London: Collins/Fontana.

7 Epilogue: the Early 1990s

The previous chapter took the story up to 1990 and drew a picture of an uncertain future, with inflation at a high rate, and unemployment beginning to rise as the boom of 1987–9 subsided and a formidable deficit emerged in the balance of payments. In this chapter we give a brief account of the sequel, concentrating on the symptoms of imbalance in the economy: inflation, unemployment, and the external deficit.

Inflation

With the onset of depression, inflation fell steadily. It had reached a peak of 10 per cent in the course of 1989 if measured in terms of consumer prices but by 1994 was down to well under 3 per cent. The fear of inflation, however, still retained a firm grip on the monetary authorities. They keep issuing warnings of faster price rises ahead and began to raise interest rates in the second half of 1994. No doubt they were influenced by recollections of the recurrence of higher inflation in the 1980s after it had fallen to a low level. There was every likelihood of a rise in international commodity prices as they returned to a more normal level with the recovery of world industrial production. But at the end of 1994 there was little immediate danger of *accelerating* inflation. In many countries inflation was lower than in Britain and in one or two, such as Switzerland and Canada, consumer prices were actually falling.

The main changes in the economic aggregates since 1986 are summarized in table 7.1. This covers the cyclical swing from boom in 1987–8 to depression in 1991–2 and the beginning of recovery in 1992–4. An expansion in GDP that reached over 5 per cent in 1988 became more moderate in 1989–90 and was followed in 1991 by a reduction in GDP of nearly 2 per cent. There was a further small fall before recovery began in the second half of 1992.

Table 7.1   Changes in the allocation of resources, 1987–1994 (increase from year to year in £billion at constant 1990 prices)*

	1987	1988	1989	1990	1991	1992	1993	1994
Consumers' expenditure	15.6	23.4	10.8	2.1	–7.6	–	9.3	9.1
Public authorities' consumption	1.0	0.8	1.5	2.8	2.9	–	1.1	1.9
Gross domestic fixed capital formation	8.6	12.8	6.3	–3.9	–10.2	–1.1	0.3	3.1
Value of physical increase in stocks and work in progress	0.5	3.4	–2.4	–4.5	–2.8	2.9	1.5	2.8
Exports of goods and services	6.6	0.6	4.6	6.3	–1.0	4.1	4.5	12.6
Total final expenditure	32.3	41.0	21.9	2.8	–18.7	6.0	16.8	29.4
Imports of goods and services	8.8	15.4	10.2	0.7	–7.9	8.7	4.2	9.0
Gross domestic product at factor cost	19.6	21.9	10.5	2.7	–10.0	–2.4	9.9	18.6

*These estimates supersede those in table 6.1, which are at 1985 prices and have since been amended by the CSO.
Source: *National Institute Economic Review*; *Monthly Digest of Statistics*.

The most remarkable feature of the upswing in 1987–8 was the extraordinary increase in consumers' expenditure, which, as pointed out in chapter 6, exceeded the growth in GDP, and was only possible because of the large excess of imports over exports in 1988. It is also remarkable to see the extraordinary fall in consumers' expenditure between 1989 and 1991 – almost equalling the fall in GDP – and the rapid recovery in consumer spending in 1993 – again on a scale comparable with the recovery in GDP. Instead of being the most stable element in demand, consumer spending was one of the most volatile. Exports show fairly steady growth, with two marked dips in 1988 and 1991; while imports, after rapid expansion in the boom years, 1987–9, fell off heavily in the years of depression that followed and would seem to have been checked again – in volume at least – by the fall in the pound in 1992–3. Spending by public authorities on goods and services had little impact on activity except to moderate the depression slightly. Fixed investment was a powerful contributor to the boom but contributed little to the recovery. On the other hand the resumption of stock-building in 1993 was an important element in the early stages of recovery.

There is no evidence in the record of those years of any appreciable change in the underlying rate of growth of the economy. Between 1986 and 1994 the annual growth in GDP was at 1.9 per cent on average – rather less than in the 1980s but quite creditable since years of falling production are included. Neither 1986 nor 1994 was a year in which industry was working at full stretch. Unemployment was appreciably lower in 1994 and already falling, whereas in 1986 it was at a peak, so that the pressure of demand was somewhat greater in 1994 and the pressure on capacity also somewhat higher.

The End of the Boom

The recovery in the 1980s has already been discussed. It continued steadily from 1982 but without eating into unemployment until 1986, and then accelerated, developing into an unmistakable boom in 1987–8, even if unemployment was still over two million at the end of 1988. Circumstances combined to encourage spending and investment of all kinds. Profits had risen steadily, the average rate of return on the assets of industrial and commercial companies rising from 4.3 per cent in 1981 to 10 per cent in 1988. This helped to finance fixed investment, which expanded by nearly one-third between 1986 and 1989. At the same time consumers spent more freely, cutting their saving rate from 13.5 per cent of disposable income in 1980 to 5.7 per cent in 1988. Borrowers had less difficulty in raising funds: first-time buyers of houses could raise 86 per cent of the purchase price from building societies in 1986 compared with 76 per cent in 1980,[1] while in the business sector deregulation eased access to capital for businesses seeking to expand. Householders in particular borrowed heavily – and by no means exclusively for house purchase – doubling the ratio of consumer debt to personal disposable income in the course of the 1980s. The increase in debt was accompanied by a rise in asset values: house prices nearly doubled between 1985 and 1989 while the value of net personal wealth (house property and financial assets) doubled in the same four years.

Early in 1989 the boom began to fade. Indeed, the peak rate of expansion was in the second half of 1987. A gradual slowing down began and by the second half of 1990 output was actually falling while unemployment, rather belatedly was beginning to increase; vacancies, apparently a more reliable indicator, had reflected the slowdown much earlier. The decline in production became steeper in the first half of 1991 and continued more slowly for another year before the first signs of recovery appeared in the second half of 1992.

As the boom faded, the expansionary influences that fanned it went into reverse. Instead of making capital gains, borrowers were conscious of an increasing burden of debt and avoided capital commitments. In the upswing the growth of debt had been matched by a parallel increase in asset values. But there was no guarantee that values would continue to keep pace with the debt burden. The whole process of expansion was vulnerable to a tightening of monetary policy, in which higher interest rates would deflate capital values and at the same time leave borrowers with larger interest payments to make. A tightening of monetary policy became all too likely as the boom developed. By 1988, as we have seen, consumer prices were rising uncomfortably fast and the current account, was sliding into heavy deficit: from a rough balance in 1986 it was nearly £15 billion in deficit in 1988 and heading for a deficit of over £20 billion in 1989. If rapid inflation and a record external deficit had not been enough to push up interest rates, the slide in the exchange rate by 22 per cent in 1989 would have done the trick. The weakness of the currency was the main influence behind the rise in short-term interest rates from 8 per cent in June 1988 to 12 per cent in August and 15 per cent in October 1989, where they remained for the next twelve months.

Higher interest rates affected investment, which ceased to expand and fell by 15 per cent between 1989 and 1992. Householders, for example, had to meet larger mortgage payments, which many had difficulty in making with the result that a large number of houses were repossessed and put on the market. House prices fell after 1991 for the first time for a generation and housing starts in the private sector fell from 321,000 in 1988 to 120,000 in 1992, under the influence of higher loan charges and the risk of loss.

Investment in other assets was affected in a similar way by a reluctance to incur fresh debt, and hence by a diminished outlay on new assets. The fall in fixed investment in the business sector, however, was much less severe than in housing; and in the public sector there was a small but perceptible increase after 1988. By the middle of 1993 fixed investment in total had ceased to fall but remained well below the peak level reached in 1989.

The rise in interest rates in Germany, on which rates in Europe tend to pivot, exerted a wide deflationary influence. The recession in Britain was prolonged by the difficulties of her European neighbours, and particularly Germany, following the collapse of the Communist regimes in Eastern Europe. The financial burden of reuniting East and West Germany was a heavy one and, when the German government proved reluctant to meet the full cost out of higher taxes, the Bundesbank was impelled to keep a tight grip on credit so as to ward off inflation and maintained rates of interest at a level higher than for sixty years. The United Kingdom, in need of funds from abroad in order to cover its external deficit, felt compelled to keep interest rates above the German level, so that the monetary authorities in Britain were unable to respond to the fall in production by cutting interest rates by as much as they would normally have done. We return to this point, below, in considering the pressures on the exchange rate.

The rise in German interest rates, to which rates in Europe soon responded, began in the middle of 1988, when rates had been around 3.8 per cent throughout the previous year. They were over 8 per cent by the end of 1989, and went on rising after the British boom had long faded, reaching 9.7 per cent by the third quarter of 1992. The result was to spread deflation throughout the European Monetary System and to force the members to maintain rates of interest inappropriate to a deepening recession. The depressed state of European markets provided a further obstacle to economic recovery in Britain.

High rates of interest had played an important part in putting an end to the boom and bringing on recession. Lower rates of interest were to play an equally important part in sustaining recovery. But freedom to lower interest rates was compromised by membership of the European Monetary System, which Britain had joined in October 1990. In order to examine the main forces governing economic recovery we have to turn from domestic influences to changes in external economic policy. Many of the key economic problems in the 1990s involved relations with Britain's

European neighbours and it was these relationships that were coming to dominate political debate.

External Economic Policy

External economic policy had to be framed from 1989 onwards in a turbulent world. First came the successive changes of regime in Eastern Europe, starting in the late autumn of 1989 and culminating in the reunification of Germany in October 1990; the disintegration of the Soviet Union; and the various efforts to reform the political and economic system throughout the Communist bloc. In August 1990 Iraq invaded and annexed Kuwait. Sanctions were imposed at once by the United Nations and in mid-January the Gulf War began, continuing to the end of February. Next came the break-up of Yugoslavia, beginning in June 1991 with Slovenian and Croatian claims to independence and resulting in the long struggle between Serbs and Muslims in Bosnia in 1992–5. In Africa and the West Indies further problems arose in 1993–4 in Somalia and Ruanda, Haiti and Cuba.

Important issues also arose within the European Community. Of these the most important concerned the European Monetary System and Exchange Rate Mechanism, dating from 1979; the Single European Act of December 1985, with its commitment to a Single European Market by the beginning of January 1993 and its vision of monetary union as a logical consequence; the Delors Plan of 1989, giving expression to this vision in proposals for a common currency and a European Central Bank; and finally the Maastricht Treaty, signed in February 1992, which embodied the Delors proposals. The United Kingdom remained aloof from the Exchange Rate Mechanism until 1990; signed and ratified the Single European Act; was represented by the Governor of the Bank of England on the Delors Committee, which, at Mrs Thatcher's suggestion, was presided over by the President of the Commission and consisted of the assembled central bank governors of the Community; and signed the Treaty of Maastricht subject to a number of opt-outs, of which monetary union was perhaps the most important.

The idea of monetary union was not new in the 1980s. It dated back to the Werner Report, adopted by the Council of Ministers in March 1971 before Britain joined the Community. It had come to nothing then because within two months of its adoption the German and Dutch governments decided to float their currencies in spite of opposition from other members of the Community, especially the French.

The idea was revived later in the 1970s, when a preliminary move was made in 1979 to set up a European Monetary System operating the Exchange Rate Mechanism (ERM). This included all the main European currencies except the pound sterling; the peseta and the escudo joined later and the Scandinavian countries (which were not members of the Community) pegged their currencies to the écu (European Currency Unit), the pivot of the system.

The Exchange Rate Mechanism requires member countries to intervene in the foreign exchange market and pursue appropriate monetary and other policies if their currency diverges too much from parity. Needless to say, this applies only to a downward divergence: strong currencies are under no obligation to change their policies. Intervention is supported by a swap arrangement between the two central banks involved and this intervention is 'unlimited and unconditional'. Such intervention relates to very short-term pressure on the exchanges but a credit mechanism comprising short-term monetary support and medium-term financial assistance also forms part of the ERM. Since 1987, under the Basle–Nyborg agreements, the swap arrangements may be drawn upon for up to 75 days, conditionally and to a limited extent, before exchange rates reach the danger point. Soft-currency central banks thus have access to foreign currency credit from counterpart hard-currency central banks. It was through the use of swap arrangements on a lavish scale with the Bundesbank that the Banque de France was able to resist speculative pressure over the winter of 1992–93.

In the mid-1980s, when the ERM had been functioning successfully for several years, a fresh attempt was made to re-launch European integration beginning with the Single Market Programme. This was designed to remove the remaining barriers to the free movement of goods, capital and labour between member countries and open up competition across national boundaries. It was believed in Brussels, however, that the liberalization of trade and financial flows through the Single Market Programme would make the EMS unstable and eventually unmanageable, and that it was necessary to push on quickly to full monetary union. There were also those who argued that a gradualist approach, requiring convergence in macroeconomic performance in accordance with specified tests, would break down by producing anticipatory exchange rate adjustments. It would be very difficult to combine, for any length of time, fixed but adjustable exchange rates, autonomy in national monetary policy, and the free movement of capital.

These fears proved to be well-founded. As the world depression deepened in 1992 the Bundesbank raised its discount rate to 8.75 per cent and put other members of the ERM under pressure to raise interest rates too or see their exchange rate fall to the floor. The pressure grew over the next two months and by mid-September became almost irresistible. On 8 September the Finnish markka was allowed to float, then the Swedes had to raise their marginal lending rate to 75 per cent. Next the Italian lira was devalued on 13 September and withdrew from the system after the Bundesbank had spent DM24 billion in a week to keep the lira afloat at a rate that the Bundesbank regarded as 'unsustainable'. Sterling, which had been sliding gradually towards the floor, and was under DM2.79 by the beginning of September, gave up the struggle on 17 September and withdrew from the ERM. Again the sums spent in defence of the parity were enormous but they proved to be insufficient. A similar struggle over the franc succeeded only after even more enormous reinforcement by the Bundesbank and the use by the Bank of France of over half its reserves. Eventually half the members of the ERM were obliged to devalue or withdraw. By the end of January 1993, Spain, Portugal and Ireland had devalued, Italy had devalued, withdrawn and re-entered, and Britain had withdrawn with no indication of when, if ever, it would rejoin. Among the non-members linked to the system Finland and Sweden had both been forced to devalue.

These events had a tremendous effect on opinion. On the one hand there were those on the continent who drew the conclusion that there was now nothing for it but to put an end to the exchange rates between European currencies by moving to a common currency. If some members of the EC were unwilling to join, then a two-tier arrangement would be unavoidable, with the common currency circulating only within the countries forming a monetary union. On the other hand, a country such as Britain that was enabled by devaluation to bring down interest rates, enjoy a stock exchange boom and the beginnings of economic recovery and yet continue to reduce inflation, hesitated to abandon for ever the possibility of devaluation.

The British government had no liking for monetary union. Mrs

Thatcher had stood out for years against even the first step in that direction – entering the ERM – and did not submit the issue for Cabinet discussion. The proposal to join was pressed on her in October 1989, by Nigel Lawson (Chancellor) and Geoffrey Howe (Foreign Secretary), without effect shortly before Lawson resigned and Howe was moved to a less influential post. A year later, however, she gave her agreement seven weeks before she in turn resigned and was succeeded by John Major, with Norman Lamont taking over as Chancellor.

The circumstances in 1990 were far from propitious. Unemployment was already rising steeply, the balance of payments was in heavy deficit (implying overvaluation of the currency), prices were rising at 10 per cent per annum and bank rate had remained at 15 per cent for a year. However, on 8 October the move was made to a fixed rate with a parity of DM2.95.

The pound soon slipped below par and remained there. Over the next two years, as unemployment rose and production fell, there was increasing pressure on the government to adopt a more expansionary policy. Suggestions were made that a lower rate of exchange would be helpful but the Chancellor rejected all such proposals emphatically at the end of 1991 and even more emphatically in 1992.

In February 1992 the Maastricht Treaty was signed and the second reading of the Bill to ratify it (with its various opt-outs) was passed by a large majority on 21 May, six weeks after the Conservatives had been returned to power, a little unexpectedly. At that stage there was little clear evidence of a sharp division of opinion in Europe over the Maastricht proposals but on 2 June the Danes rejected them in a referendum, to the consternation of the Treaty's supporters. There was also growing doubt about the outcome of a French referendum on 20 September and the vote in favour proved to be wafer-thin.

Events in the exchange markets demonstrated the power of market opinion. As Keynes remarked in 1931, 'once the market comes to expect devaluation, the game is up'. On 17 September sterling was withdrawn from the ERM after a formidable loss of reserves, and the French narrowly escaped following suit, thanks to massive help from other central banks. The immediate consequence of sterling's withdrawal was not unlike the sequel to the devaluation of sterling in 1931. There was a sharp drop in the exchange rate but it soon steadied and allowed interest rates to be brought down progressively. The intended rise in bank rate to 15 per cent never occurred, a cut of 1 per cent was made within a week and by the spring of 1993 bank rate had fallen to 6 per cent. The stock exchange started to rise almost at once and continued to rise until early in 1994, when it was already 50 per cent higher than 18 months previously. Unemployment rose for a few months but then began to fall slowly and steadily while the rise in output, of which there were faint signs even before devaluation, picked up speed in 1993–4. There remained, however, a vast amount of unemployment and a consequent loss of output.

The recovery was increasingly export-led. As table 7.1 shows, exports had begun to increase in volume in 1992 but were outpaced by imports. In 1993 the increase in exports remained small; imports, however, were checked so that the net effect of foreign trade was expansionary. It was not until 1994 that the expansion in exports was, without question, the dominant influence on the economy, the volume of exports in the middle of 1994 being over 20 per cent in excess of that a year earlier. Since world trade was growing fast, it was only at this stage that Britain's share improved: between the autumn of 1992 and the spring of 1994 it had shown no change. Although consumer spending recovered in 1993, other parts of the economy remained depressed. The recovery broadened out in the first half of 1994 with higher levels of investment and stock-building, but in comparison with exports the domestic market was slow to expand. In the year to mid-1994 output from the service industries was up by about 2.5 per cent; in the construction industries output grew by 3 per cent and fixed investment only slightly faster. The discrepancy between these rates and the rate at which exports were growing was unlikely to continue for long; but it looked as if, even with some slowing down in export growth, the balance of payments might be in surplus in 1995 for the first time for ten years.

Fiscal Policy

The increased emphasis laid by policy-makers on inflation and the diminution in the emphasis on unemployment went with greater reliance on monetary policy and much less on fiscal policy. It is not at all obvious that control of inflation should take precedence in all circumstances over employment policy or that monetary policy is always a better instrument for promoting economic stability than fiscal policy. At low rates of inflation one might look for some return to the practice of demand management and greater willingness to contemplate budget deficits. The emergence of a public sector borrowing requirement of up to £50 billion may not be testimony to either of these changes but it certainly reminds one of old times before the days of monetarism.

The budget has certainly undergone as enormous swings in the past ten years as at any time since the war. In the late 1980s tax revenue was swollen by the rapid and prolonged growth of GNP, with some offset in 1986 as a result of the sharp drop in oil prices. The boom in revenue made it possible to combine large reductions in rates of personal taxation with a fall in the PSBR to a negative quantity in the years from 1987 to 1989, and so to repay a substantial amount of the national debt. In the early 1990s cyclical factors worked the other way. Rising unemployment and falling output reduced the revenue and added to government expenditure, producing a renewed borrowing requirement. This grew to a peak of £50 billion in the financial year 1993–4 and was expected to continue on a diminishing scale for some years thereafter.

In 1986 the basic rate of income tax was 30 per cent, with a top rate of 60 per cent. Cuts in successive budgets brought these rates down to 25 per cent and 40 per cent by 1988. There were also increases in personal allowances as well as important changes in national insurance contributions that cut payments by most contributors. The 1990 budget replaced local rates by the Community Charge (or poll tax), which proved to be so unpopular that it was first subsidized in the 1991 budget by a payment by the government of £140 per adult and then withdrawn in the 1992 budget and replaced by a Council tax. To meet the cost of the subsidy in 1991 the standard rate of VAT was increased from 15 to 17.5 per cent – part of a trend towards higher indirect taxation and lower direct taxation.

Other changes during this period were the replacement, in 1990, of joint income taxation of husband and wife by taxation of each separately; and in 1991 the first of a number of measures limiting mortgage interest relief at source to the basic rate of tax of 25 per cent. A further tax concession was the introduction in the 1992 budget of a 20 per cent band on the first £2000 of taxable income (subsequently raised to £3000 in 1993 and 1994). On the other hand, the 1993 budget initiated substantial increases in indirect taxation and national insurance contributions by employees. The latter were raised from 9 to 10 per cent from April 1994. Excise duties were also raised, particularly on petrol and tobacco, but lowered slightly on alcohol, especially on spirits. In the 1994 budget the Chancellor sought to increase the rate of tax on domestic fuel from 8 per cent to the current VAT rate of 17.5 per cent but his proposal was defeated by 8 votes. He then announced, two days later, increases in indirect taxes to bring in the additional £1 billion that higher fuel taxes would have raised.

While the changes in tax and national insurance between 1985 and 1992 have been estimated to add an average of nearly £14 per week to household income and to leave 90 per cent of the population better off, the changes from 1993 to 1995 left 80 per cent of the population worse off, with an average loss in household income of nearly £10.[2] So far as the distribution of income is concerned, the total effect over the ten years from 1985 has been to concentrate gains on those with high incomes while those at the bottom of the income scale have lost out. The tax burden has been reduced on the top half and raised on the bottom half of personal incomes; with the largest downwards changes in tax at the very top and the largest upwards changes at the very bottom.[3]

A major change occurred in the tax system in 1993 when public expenditure was brought within the ambit of the budget, so that it can now be considered in conjunction with tax revenue. The annual budget, which was formerly introduced in March or April, is introduced at the end of November, and the Autumn Statement has been replaced by a more elaborate *Financial Statement and Budget Report* issued when the budget is presented.

Economic Recovery

Economic recovery in Britain had begun in the second half of 1992 and gathered momentum in 1993–4 mainly under the influence of a surge in exports (table 7.1). Stock-building was resumed and fixed investment ceased to fall. The recovery in consumption although appreciable, was held in check by higher taxation, the 1993 budgets leaving consumers with real incomes after tax no higher than a year earlier. What was in progress was thus the kind of export-led growth that had for so long been held out in Britain as the path to prosperity – a path not followed since 1950. On the continent, economic recovery lagged behind that of Britain, production continuing to fall there in 1993. In 1994, however, recovery became general, with an acceleration in growth in all the leading industrial countries. Fixed investment ceased to fall in the leading European countries and there was some rebuilding of stocks. In 1995, however, fears of inflation revived and interest rates began to climb to higher levels. In Britain this checked the recovery in fixed investment while the growth of exports continued. As other contributions to economic recovery were jeopardized by fears of renewed inflation and rising interest rates, the maintenance of a rapid growth in exports loomed increasingly large in 1995 as the precondition for a continuing growth in output at a rate sufficient to prolong the fall in unemployment that had been in progress since early in 1993.

Notes

1   Nigel Pain and Peter Westaway, 'Housing, Consumption and Borrowing: An Assessment of Recent Personal Sector Behaviour in the UK', *National Institute Economic Review*, August 1994, p. 53.
2   C. Giles and R. Johnson, 'Tax Reform in the UK and Changes in Progressivity of the Tax System, 1985–95', *Fiscal Studies*, August 1994, pp. 78–80.
3   Ibid.; figure 6.

8 Half a Century in Retrospect, 1945–1995

Earlier chapters have dealt with the changes within each decade; in this chapter we begin by looking at the changes from decade to decade before reviewing some of the outstanding changes since 1945.

Table 8.1 summarizes the decade by decade changes in the main economic aggregates. GDP grew faster in the 1980s, thanks to an uninterrupted expansion for eight years from the low point in 1981. The 1960s enjoyed the next largest increase and the 1950s the lowest, if, as we should, we use GDP at factor cost as the appropriate measure. The immediate post-war period shows only a small increase, largely because of the withdrawal of some two million women from the labour force when the war ended. Over the fifty years from 1945 to 1995, GDP in real terms roughly trebled.

Of the components of aggregate demand, consumer spending, as one might expect, registered the largest increase. There was a big rise as soon as the war was over, then a very modest increase from 1948–51 in comparison with the growth in GDP. In the next four decades consumer spending grew not only in absolute terms but as a proportion of GDP, with a pause in the 1960s when the proportion hardly changed. The increase in consumer spending was particularly large in the 1980s, but thereafter there was a fall for a time and little real growth over the five years 1989–94.

The next biggest expansion was in imports and exports. Imports increased throughout the period and by the 1980s were growing nearly twice as fast as exports – an obviously unsustainable position. Exports showed no such consistent growth. After a post-war spurt, they grew little in the 1950s as continental countries offered increasing competition.

Table 8.1 Changes in the allocation of resources, 1945–1994 (increase in £ million at constant 1985 prices)

	1945–50	1950–60	1960–70	1970–79	1979–89	1989–94	1945–94
Consumers' expenditure	16.0	26.8	33.3	38.5	76.0	9.7	200.3
Public authorities' final consumption	−34.8	6.0	10.4	14.1	7.3	6.3	9.3
Gross domestic fixed capital formation	13.2	12.8	20.5	4.9	24.6	−11.3	64.7
Value of physical increase in stocks and work in progress	4.5	5.0	−1.8	1.4	−0.7	0.6	9.0
Exports of goods and services	18.1	8.1	22.1	31.8	29.6	22.6	132.3
Total final expenditure	16.8	60.9	84.7	90.9	136.4	27.9	417.6
Imports of goods and services	3.4	12.7	18.5	27.3	54.0	11.9	127.8
Gross domestic product at market prices	13.6	47.8	59.6	62.3	82.3	(16.0)	281.6
Gross domestic product at factor cost	13.6	40.3	58.6	51.2	70.6	15.0	249.3

Source: Economic Trends Annual Supplement (1990 edn) table 3, and estimates based on *National Institute Economic Review*, February 1995.

In the next two decades they more than kept pace with imports but in the 1980s, in spite of North Sea oil, there was a smaller increment than in the 1970s. A large balance of payments deficit emerged, not unlike the even more formidable deficit in 1945, but very different in origin. Since the peak of £22.5 billion in 1989, however, the deficit has dwindled and by the end of 1994 was quite moderate.

The growth in fixed investment fluctuated from decade to decade. As with exports, there was an initial spurt and a falling off in the 1950s. Fixed investment shows up rather well in the 1960s, rises little in the 1970s, and expands in the 1980s to the highest level since 1945. The expansion in the 1980s was confined to the private sector, public investment falling heavily; within the private sector there was no increase in investment in manufacturing industry. From 1948 to 1988 the increase in fixed investment was nearly fivefold and the ratio of gross fixed investment to GDP had reached 19 per cent from a level in 1948 of only 11 per cent. In the 1990s, however, investment fell off and remained depressed when activity revived.

Table 8.2 Proportion of GDP (at market prices) taken in taxes, social security contributions, etc.

	%
1948	35.2
1958	29.7
1968	34.8
1978	33.5
1988	36.7

Source: Economic Trends Annual Supplement 1990

Stockbuilding was the most volatile element of all but the fluctuations are concealed in totals by decade. In relation to GDP the secular trend was toward economy in stocks but this was not true of retailing where stocks rose in relation to sales by about 15 per cent between 1960 and 1990. In manufacturing, on the other hand, total stocks as a proportion of output fell over the same period by nearly 10 per cent.

Finally comes the use of resources by public authorities. This is very different from public expenditure, since it excludes all transfers in the form of grants and benefits, and represents only current expenditure on goods and services. The figures are less variable than one might expect and are dominated by the enormous drop at the end of the war. From then onwards they increase slightly more rapidly in successive decades until the 1980s when, however, they still show a perceptible increase. As with public expenditure in total, all the efforts that went to reduce government consumption of resources did no more than check its growth. This can be illustrated in another way by tracing the proportion of GDP taken in taxation, social security contributions and rates (or council tax). The proportion dipped in the 1950s and again in the 1970s but in 1988 was higher than ever (see table 8.2).

International comparisons

While a trebling of GDP since 1945 represents faster growth than in any comparable period of time it falls well short of performance in other industrial countries. The contrast emerges strikingly from table 8.3. In 1948 the United Kingdom had recovered more rapidly from the war than continental Europe where production was still a little below the level of 1938, itself a year of depression. In the next six years production on the continent grew annually at 6.6 per cent compared with a rate of 3.2 per cent in the United Kingdom – less than half the continental rate. In the next six years to 1960 the rate of growth on the continent remained more than double that of the United Kingdom. In both cases, however, growth was somewhat slower than in the years 1948–54: 5.1 per cent per annum on the continent and 2.4 per cent in the United Kingdom.

It was often suggested at the time that the high rates achieved on the continent in those years of recovery from war would prove unsustainable and that there would eventually be some convergence between British and continental rates. There was in fact some slight convergence in the 1960s when continental growth in GDP averaged a little less than before at 4.8 per cent per annum while British growth accelerated to 2.9 per cent per annum. There was a much closer convergence in the 1970s. The rate of growth fell steeply everywhere in that decade but much more heavily on the continent than in the United Kingdom, the annual averages for

Table 8.3   Increase in GDP in OECD Europe and the United Kingdom, 1938–1989

	GDP^a (1954 = 100)		% Growth rate	
	OEEC (excluding the UK)	UK	OEEC	UK
1938	69.6	73.0	–	–
1948	68.0	83.0	–	–
1954	100.0	100.0	6.6	3.2
1960	134.7	115.0	5.1	2.4

	GDP^b (1980 = 100)		% Growth rate	
	OECD Europe	UK	OECD Europe	UK
1960	47.0	62.7	–	–
1970	74.8	83.7	4.8	2.93
1979	98.5	102.2	3.1	2.24
1989	117.4	127.6	1.8	2.24

^{a} GDP is measured at factor cost. The GDP of the UK has been converted to dollars and deducted from the figures for OEEC. All figures are at 1954 prices and exchange rates.

^{b} The figures for OECD Europe include the UK and are at 1980 prices; those for the UK are at 1985 prices and have been re-based to 1980.

Source: For OEEC and UK to 1960, OEEC *General Statistics*, July 1962; for OECD Europe 1960–1989, OECD National Accounts 1990; for UK 1960–1989, *Economic Trends Annual Supplement 1990* and *Economic Trends*, December 1990

1970–9 working out at 3.1 per cent and 2.24 per cent. For the first time since 1945 GDP fell in the continental Europe in the year 1975. In the United Kingdom, where there had already been a fall in 1974, the fall in GDP extended, also for the first time, over two years, 1974 and 1975.

Table 8.4   Growth in output, factor inputs and total factor productivity, 1950–1973

	Output	*% Growth per annum* *Factor inputs*	*Total factor productivity*
UK	2.8	0.7	2.1
USA	3.6	2.0	1.6
Canada	4.9	3.1	1.8
Japan	9.3	3.7	5.6
Germany	5.7	1.9	3.8
Italy	5.3	1.3	4.0
France	4.9	1.4	3.5

Source: S. Broadberry, 'The impact of the world wars on the long-run performance of the British economy', *Oxford Review of Economic Policy*, Spring 1988.

In the final decade, between 1979 and 1989, growth was at last faster in the United Kingdom than on the continent. Again, this reflected a falling off in the continental countries, this time to an average annual rate of 1.8 per cent; it was not due to an improvement in British performance which, taking the decade as a whole, showed no change on the previous decade. As we have seen, however (above, p. 228), this masks a real improvement from 1984–9, offset by slow growth over the previous five years.

These comparisons would not be greatly altered if they were in terms of output (and hence also income) *per head*. There was very little change in the size of the employed population over the entire period either in the United Kingdom or on the continent but so far as labour input did change, it grew slightly more on the continent than in the United Kingdom. Capital investment, which also affects the comparison, was very much greater on the continent. It is difficult to separate out the influence on the growth of output of additional labour and capital from the influence of other factors such as technical progress, better education, improvements in management and organization, economies of scale, and so on. But those who have been bold enough to engage in 'growth accountancy' are agreed that, when allowance is made for differences in labour and capital inputs, the margin between Britain and other industrial countries over the post-war period narrows appreciably. One such calculation by Broadberry for the years 1950–73 is shown in table 8.4. It will be seen that although output grew a good deal faster in Canada and the United States than in the United Kingdom, what is called 'total factor productivity' (i.e. Output per unit of labour and capital) grew faster in Britain. Similarly, the margin in comparison with other European countries and Japan is reduced once account is taken of the difference in factor inputs.

Some people have argued that slower growth in the United Kingdom was an inevitable concomitant of lower capital investment. But as the example of Canada and the United States shows, the matter is not quite so simple: investment grew twice as fast in Canada and 50 per cent faster in the United States without raising total factor productivity faster than in Britain. So far as fast growth in output and investment go together, it is probably wiser to regard high investment as reflecting fast growth rather than as resulting in it.

Faster growth abroad in output meant a faster rise in the standard of living. A study by D. T. Jones in 1976 suggested that whereas there had been a margin in 1955 of about 15 per cent in living standards in favour of the United Kingdom in comparison with West Germany and France and one of 40 per cent in comparison with Italy, Germany and France had caught up by 1961 and were some 30 per cent ahead by the middle 1970s while Italy had caught up by 1973.[1] A more recent calculation by Feinstein for 1984 suggests a rather better relative performance by the United Kingdom (see col. 1 of table 8.5); and since 1984, as we have seen, production has risen faster in the United Kingdom than on the continent so that by 1990 the margin was narrower than in table 8.5.

Table 8.5 also brings out the high degree of convergence in GDP per hour worked by 1984. As Feinstein points out, it was not only the United Kingdom that was being overtaken during the post-war period but countries like the United States and Sweden as well. Higher output in the United States and Japan is buttressed by longer hours than several of the European countries, including the United kingdom, and by a relatively high participation rate, i.e. there is less leisure in the United States and

Table 8.5   GDP per head of population, per worker and per hour worked in 1984 [a]

	GDP per head of population US $ (000)	GDP per worker US $ (000)	GDP per hour worked (UK=100)	Hours worked per person per year	Participation rate %
USA	15.83	34.78	124	1630	45.5
Sweden	15.37	30.11	120	1460	51.0
Germany	13.26	32.32	112	1680	41.0
France	12.64	32.30	121	1550	39.1
Japan	12.24	25.47	69	2150	48.0
Belgium	12.15	32.62	116	1640	37.2
Netherlands	11.71	33.98	121	1640	34.5
UK	11.07	26.07	100	1520	42.4
Italy	10.04	27.23	101	1570	36.9

[a] GDP values expressed in US/dollars at 1984 prices and converted from national currencies at purchasing power parities, not official rates of exchange.

Source: C. H. Feinstein, 'Economic growth since 1870: Britain's performance in international perspective', *Oxford Review of Economic Policy,* Spring 1988.

Japan but a higher volume of output. While it would be interesting to know in which sectors of the British economy growth has been fastest and in which the rate compares most favourably with other countries, the complexities of the data make it difficult to reach firm conclusions.[2]

Changes in the international position of the United Kingdom

One of the most important changes over the period has been in the international position of the United Kingdom. In 1945 it was still possible for Britain, however much weakened by war, to present itself as a world power. It was the head of a large Commonwealth with which it carried on half its trade and the centre of the sterling area when perhaps half the world's trade was conducted in sterling. It enjoyed a 'special' relationship with the United States, then at the peak of its power. These advantages did not necessarily translate into gains in economic welfare and arguably involved more economic burdens than benefits. But they conveyed economic as well as political power and allowed Britain to exert that power on an international scale. Without the international standing that Britain enjoyed it would have been impossible for her, for example, to contract the enormous wartime debts represented by the sterling balances.

Long before 1990 the sterling area had disappeared and the British Commonwealth had completely changed its character. It had become impossible to conceive of the kind of Commonwealth Conference of July 1949, meeting to concert common measures of commercial policy in the interests of the sterling system. The proportion of British trade with Commonwealth countries had shrunk by 1990 to under 10 per cent while at the same time trade with the European Community had grown to over 50 per cent. Between 1950 and 1970 (i.e., before entry into the Community) exports to the six countries of the Community had grown from 11.2 to 21.8 per cent of total British exports and by 1992, with the expansion of the Community to twelve instead of six countries, the proportion had risen to 56 per cent. Another important trend was the steady expansion of trade with some of the developing countries, particularly the countries of East Asia. British exports to six leading countries (Hong Kong, Malaysia, Singapore, Korea, Taiwan and

Thailand) grew from 3.1 per cent of the total in 1983 to 4.7 per cent in 1992 and the proportion was continuing to rise fast.

As a member of the Community, Britain was bound by Community rules and increasingly restricted in the freedom with which it could devise and conduct an economic policy adapted to its own situation. At the same time the dominant position of Britain in world markets, whether as importer or exporter, had disappeared. As an exporter, Britain's share of world trade in manufactures had fallen from 25 per cent in the late 1940s to 7 per cent in the late 1980s. As for imports, these now consisted as to nearly 80 per cent of manufactures whereas in the 1940s imports of manufactures – nearly all producer goods – never exceeded 25 per cent. In the 1930s Britain was almost the only open market for many international commodities and had accounted for well over half total world trade in several of the more important. In 1990 Britain was only one importer of primary products among many.

The fundamental change was a loss of economic power: commercial power, bargaining power, financial power. Britain had become a much smaller fragment of the world economy with much less influence on the behaviour of that economy.

The standard of living

The rise in the standard of living may have fallen short of the rise in continental countries but it is still impressive. In 1989 spending in total had risen roughly threefold in real terms since 1939 (or alternatively since 1948 when the pre-war level was exceeded by a small margin). It had more than doubled since 1948 in all the main categories of spending except food and drink and had increased tenfold in the case of durable consumer goods. The consumption of food had gone up by just under a third and the consumption of drink by four-fifths. Since population has risen by about 15 per cent since 1948 these proportions slightly overstate the changes that have occurred in consumption *per head*.

Some part of the improvement represents over-spending in the 1980s financed by borrowing. If instead we take real personal disposable income as a measure of the rise in the standard of living, the rise between 1948 and 1989 was a little short of threefold and works out at an average of 2 per cent per annum. In more recent years, between 1979 and 1993, real personal disposable income increased at an average rate of 2.2 per cent annually.

The pattern of consumption has also changed greatly. Expenditure on food and alcoholic drink increased substantially while at the same time there was a large drop in the proportion of spending on these items. Food, for example, accounted for about 24 per cent of total consumer spending in 1948 but by 1971 this had fallen to 20 per cent and in 1993 to 11.6 per cent. Even the poorest 20 per cent devoted only 23 per cent of their spending to food – less than the average for the whole country in 1948. Between 1971 and 1993 the proportion of spending on alcoholic drink fell from 7.3 to 6.1 per cent, in tobacco from 4.8 to 2.7 per cent, on clothing and footwear from 8.5 to 5.9 per cent. The expanding elements (proportionately) have been housing (from 12.4 to 15.7 per cent), transport and communications (from 14.3 to 17.5 per cent) and, most of all, services, reflecting the growth of affluence, leisure and social services. Excluding rent, rates and water charges, expenditure on services grew from about 16 per cent of consumer spending in 1948 to 23 per cent in 1970 and 34 per cent in 1992. Apart from this, the most striking change has been in the expansion in durable consumer goods which now absorb about 10 per cent of total spending, motor cars usually absorbing over half of that. In 1993, 96 per cent of households had a colour television set, and 73 per cent a video recorder but only 16 per cent a dishwasher.[3]

Hours of work, health and welfare

The rise in the standard of living has been accompanied by a reduction in working hours and improvement in health and life expectancy. Normal working hours fell by about 15 per cent between 1945 and 1967 but hours actually worked increased at first and in 1967 had barely changed. In manufacturing the hours of male workers rose after the war from 47.6 in 1946 to a peak of about 48.7 hours a week in 1955. There was then a long slow downward trend over the next twenty years by about an hour every four years. Since the mid-1970s, however, there has been little further reduction. Working hours for men are the longest and for women the shortest in the European Community.

The improvement in health is most conspicuous in the fall in infant mortality from 55 per 1000 in 1938 to 6.6 in 1992. Life expectancy at birth in Great Britain, which had been 58 for males in 1931 and had risen to 66 by 1950, improved to 73 in 1989–91. For females the corresponding figures were 63 in 1931, 71 in 1950 and 78.5 in 1989–91. Much of this improvement reflected the fall in infant mortality. A better guide to the additional years of life that an adult could expect is provided by the change in the expectation of life at 20. For males this rose from 46.7 additional years in 1931 to 49.4 in 1950 and 54.1 in 1989–91 and for females from 49.7 in 1931 to 53.5 in 1950 and 59.3 in 1989–81.

Inequality

That the improvement in living standards has been widespread is not in doubt; real wages have more than doubled since 1948 and so also has the proportion of GNP expended by the state on social welfare, whether in cash transfers or in services such as health and education. But is the income of the country more equally divided than forty years ago?

To answer that question one has first to look at the trend in income distribution before taking account of the levelling influence of state taxes and benefits. The indications are that the trend in the first thirty years or so after the war was towards greater equality but that it has been in the opposite direction in later years. In 1949 the top 1 per cent of personal incomes, according to the Royal Commission on the Distribution of Income and Wealth, accounted for 11.2 per cent of the total, and the top 10 per cent for 33.2 per cent, while in 1976–7 these proportions had fallen to 5.6 per cent and 26 per cent. This trend was reinforced by the effects of taxation which had a particularly powerful effect on the top 1 per cent, cutting the proportion of after-tax income received by this group from 11.2 to 6.4 per cent in 1949 and from 5.6 to 3.5 per cent in 1976–7.[5] On the other hand, the lower half of income earners gained little additional share over this period; their share before tax fell from 27.3 to 24.5 per cent and their share after tax was increased only from 26.5 to 27.6 per cent. It was the intermediate group of income-earners who were the real gainers.

Later figures for the top 20 per cent of a sample of income earners suggest a reversal of the trend in distribution, with a rise in the share of this group from 44 per cent in 1975 to 51 per cent in 1987 before tax and from 38 per cent to 42 per cent after tax and benefits of all kinds. Similarly, the share of the lowest 40 per cent fell from 10.8 to 6.3 per cent before tax and from 20.1 to 17.2 per cent after tax and benefits.[6] It will be observed that the effect of tax and benefits is to reduce the rise in the share of the top group and the fall in the share of the bottom group.

The full effect of progressive taxation and welfare benefits is not brought out in these figures. For 1987 a sample of household incomes (adjusted for family size and structure) showed that the net effect of the tax-benefit system was to narrow the spread between the top 20 per cent of incomes and the bottom 20 per cent from a ratio of about 20:1 to a ratio of about 4:1.[7] The top group, starting with an average income of £25,470, paid nearly £10,000 on the average in direct and indirect taxes while the bottom group, starting with an average income of £1220 (and receiving £3170 in cash benefits and £2040 in benefits in kind) paid an average of £1620 in tax, about two-thirds of it indirect tax, ending up with a final income of £4820, nearly four times their original average. Unfortunately no similar figures exist for earlier years.

The biggest single factor in the improvement in the position of the poorest group in 1987 arose from the fact that nearly half the households in it were retired (as were also nearly half of the next poorest 20 per cent of the households) and retirement pensions accounted for a substantial part of the cash benefits they received. In 1949 state pensions of all kinds amounted only to about £360 million compared with £18,500 million in 1987. Allowing for the fall in the value of money, this represents a more than fourfold increase in less than forty years. Although pensions are paid regardless of income, they have undoubtedly done much to help many of the poorest families.

On the other hand, we have to take account of new sources of poverty. In the last twenty years, unemployment has multiplied and there is also a growing pool of families unable to seek regular employment: over a million lone parent families and the long-term sick. Many of the increased number who are self-employed earn relatively little. In the 1980s, while the incomes of the richest part of the community rose faster, the living standards of the poorest fell further behind the national average. It has been estimated by the Institute for Fiscal Studies that those who live in households whose incomes are less than half the national average have increased in number from about 5 million in the 1960s to over 11 million by the early 1990s. The result of the changes at work has been a growth in income inequality without precedent in recent times.

Changes in the machinery of policy-making

Economic policy in the United Kingdom is dealt with by the ministers in charge of economic departments either at their discretion or after discussion in Cabinet or in committees of the Cabinet. The key minister is usually the Chancellor of the Exchequer with the support of the Prime Minister, who may himself take an active interest in economic policy or may elect, as when Cripps was Chancellor under Attlee, to leave matters almost entirely to his Chancellor.

For most of the post-war period, the Treasury has discharged at least five distinct functions, each of which might be (and in some countries is) entrusted to a separate agency.

> It acts as a Ministry of Economic Affairs in charge of economic policy, a Ministry of Finance in charge of taxation, a Ministry of the Public Sector controlling public expenditure and the nationalized industries, a Ministry in control of monetary policy, and a Ministry responsible for the civil service, including pay, control of manpower, etc. Foreign economic policy, which might be thought to be a matter for the Foreign Office . . . is more likely to take shape in the Treasury.[8]

In the period after the war, an attempt was made to divide these responsibilities between the Chancellor (Dalton) as Minister of Finance and the Lord President (Morrison) as Minister of Economics. This division continued a war-time arrangement in which the allocation of resources through the various war-time controls was co-ordinated by the Lord President while the Treasury confined itself to matters of finance (particularly taxation and external finance).

In a world in which economic policy came to rest more heavily on financial instruments and less on allocations of labour and materials the arrangement proved unsatisfactory and was abandoned when Cripps took over at the Treasury.

A similar division was made in 1964 when a Department of Economic Affairs was established and charged with the creation of a National Plan. This too proved a failure, partly because the Treasury retained control over the key instruments of economic policy and partly because long-term planning in the middle of a major crisis is apt to come apart.

Other efforts have been made from time to time to split up the

Treasury. Responsibility for the civil service, for example, was entrusted in 1968 to a separate department but later reverted to the Treasury. In the 1990s there was much talk of an 'independent' central bank with complete control over monetary policy, as if monetary and economic policy could be torn apart with impunity. As for public expenditure, there has existed since the 1960s a second Cabinet Minister *within* the Treasury in the person of the Chief Secretary, whose main duties are to control public expenditure. The object of this arrangement, however, is not to split the Treasury in two but to lend additional support in Cabinet to the Chancellor when he has to confront the insatiable demands of spending ministers.

There have been changes from time to time in the responsibilities of the main economic departments and the ministers in charge of them, in the influence exerted by particular ministers and in the arrangements under which disagreements between them are resolved. New departments have been created, some have been merged or divided and others have disappeared in the years since 1945; the departmental and inter-departmental committees with which Whitehall is honeycombed have altered kaleidoscopically. Such changes have undoubtedly influenced the way in which economic policy is formulated. But the more significant changes have been in the way in which economic advice to ministers is prepared and injected.

The most striking change has been in the large number of economists in government service. In 1939 no economists were employed in their professional capacity in Whitehall (except in the Ministry of Agriculture) although some administrators had taken degrees in economics or even acquired, like Keynes and Hawtrey, professional standing during government service. There was, it is true, a Chief Economic Adviser, who might or might not be an economist and was rarely consulted on domestic issues of financial policy. His main job was to represent the government on imperial and international committees and at international conferences. There was also an advisory Committee on Economic Information, a survival from the Economic Advisory Council created in 1930 which prepared surveys of the economic situation until the outbreak of war and included among its members Keynes, Henderson, Stamp and (from 1936) Dennis Robertson.

Since then, economists have been recruited in increasing numbers until there are now some four hundred spread over the main government departments and another two hundred in the Bank of England. This is in addition to the large number of officials – several hundred throughout at least the last thirty years – with university or other qualifications in economics employed as administrators, executive officers or research assistants and not members of the Government Economic Service.

Professional economists first entered the Civil Service in large numbers in 1939–45 but few remained after the war except in the small group in the Economic Section of the Cabinet Office. This group, which was transferred to the Treasury in 1953, and rarely exceeded a dozen or so in number, exercised great influence on macro-economic policy, and to some extent also on micro-economic policy in the 1940s and 1950s. Amongst its main achievements were the development of modern economic forecasting and advising the Treasury on the preparation of budgets consistent with the management of demand on Keynesian lines. The Economic Section played a critical part in the various crises of the post-war years: for example, the loan negotiations in 1945, devaluation in 1949, rearmament in 1950–1 and the rejection of the Robot proposals in 1952. There were, however, no similar units or professional economists employed as such in other government departments with a few very limited exceptions. Some members of the Economic Section were assigned temporarily to other departments such as the Foreign Office and the Ministry of Overseas Development in the early 1960s and the practice began then of posting members of the Section to work with the expenditure divisions of the Treasury. But given the limited size of the staff (rarely exceeding fifteen) it was not possible to carry secondments very far.

Two important changes took place in 1962. One was the institution of a Centre for Administrative Studies to provide new recruits to the Civil Service with a six months' training in economics and allied subjects. This, although highly successful, was not expanded to undertake research in problems of government and provide a reserve of talent for government work but was merged with the Civil Service College a few years later. A second development was the building up of a large staff of economists at the National Economic Development Office. Many of these moved later to the Department of Economic Affairs.

The creation of this new department in 1964 after the return of the Labour government to office heralded a big expansion in the employment of economists. It led to the formation of the Government

Economic Service under the Director of the Economic Section (which remained in the Treasury). Initially the service was more a collection of private armies, sometimes recruited directly by ministers, than a unified service; but it gradually became more of a reality. By 1969 there were nearly two hundred members, all but a score or so in five major departments: the Department of Economic Affairs (and, under it, the Prices and Incomes Board); the Departments of the Environment and Transport; the Department of Trade and Industry; the Overseas Development Administration; and the Treasury (then employing fewer than the first four of these departments). By 1976 the total number had doubled and was now four hundred. In the next few years there was some fluctuation in the number before it returned to about the same total. By this time the Treasury employed about eighty economists and was the largest employer, with the Department of the Environment and Transport and the Department of Trade and Industry next in order and the Ministry of Overseas Development still a major employer; the economists in the Department of Economic Affairs had been absorbed into the Treasury in 1970.

A great many of the four hundred economists are in junior posts with a fairly high rate of turnover. At the same time, economists now often discharge administrative responsibilities and can ask to be transferred to the administrative grade. In the Treasury some divisions are headed by economists and in 1995 the Permanent Secretary is himself an economist; the Economic Section has ceased to exist as a separate unit. In 1993 the Chancellor instituted a new arrangement under which seven economists ('the seven wise men'), some of them in academic posts, others in the City or attached to a business, constitute a panel reporting at regular intervals on the economic situation. The reports, which are published and commented on in the press, give the separate forecasts of each member of the panel.

Economists, however, have no monopoly of economic advice. On major issues they may not even be consulted. The matters on which ministers need advice are rarely purely economic but may have political, diplomatic, technological, organizational and other aspects. They take advice from many sources and frequently bring in or turn to economists of their own political persuasion or advisers who know little or nothing of economics but offer advice on economic policy.

Of particular importance is advice to the Prime Minister (who traditionally has no department of his own) if, having put the Chancellor in charge of economic policy, he feels the need of a second opinion. He has always received briefs on the wide variety of issues coming before the Cabinet from the Cabinet Secretary or the various private secretaries loaned to 10 Downing Street by the Foreign Office, Treasury and other departments. Some prime ministers have supplemented official advice by calling in personal advisers as, for example, Churchill relied on Lord Cherwell, Harold Wilson used Lady Falkender and, at times, Lord Balogh, and Mrs Thatcher, Sir Alan Walters. Since 1974 the Prime Minister has also had a small policy unit, headed initially by Bernard Donoghue and including a few professional economists although rarely directed by one. The members of the unit, like policy advisers in other departments (whose numbers are limited) but unlike members of the Government Economic Service, give up their posts on a change of government. They can brief the Prime Minister, offer an alternative view to departmental advice and offer advice in which the political element is given fuller consideration. But it is not easy for them to enjoy the confidence both of the Prime Minister and of the departments on whose advice they pass judgment.

A somewhat similar difficulty can arise over advice from a body such as the Central Policy Review Staff which was established by Edward Heath in 1970 and abandoned by Mrs Thatcher. This was intended to advise the Cabinet on long-term issues such as the adequacy of research and development and the future of the motor-car industry. For some purposes a 'think tank' of this kind may be preferable to a series of interdepartmental committees. But it is liable to excite the suspicion of even hostility of the departments on whose work it encroaches and has to tread delicately in order to carry them with it. It is also likely to have a hard struggle to find a market for its output unless it is under the direction of a minister or can count on the continuing interest of a busy Prime Minister.

Changes in aims and policy instruments

We turn now to review some of the outstanding changes over the years since the second world war in the aims and instruments of policy.

The post-war period can be seen in retrospect as one of changing views on what the state should and can do. As the war ended, the involvement of the state in the functioning of the economy was at its height. It exercised control over the economy at many different points and in many different ways and spent about half the national income. Even more extensive control had been necessary in wartime; and the successful conduct of the war had done nothing to discredit the state as an agency for effective management of the economy in the difficult years of transition to a peace-time economy that lay ahead. On the other hand, the compulsions acceptable in war-time were bound to meet with growing opposition once the war was over and there was no longer a single unifying purpose such as winning the war that only the state could serve.

At that stage there was a presumption in favour of state intervention and control. It was accepted that the state had to intervene in order to deal with shortages, to prevent inflation and to ease adjustments in the balance of payments, particularly the balance in dollars. Control for those purposes could be assumed to be temporary. Other controls implied a more permanent extension of the boundaries of state action: for example, the series of nationalization measures, the expansion in the provision of welfare benefits, and whatever was necessary to prevent large-scale unemployment. Reliance on the state to put right whatever was thought to have gone wrong became an entrenched public reaction.

The change in attitude since then is no doubt exaggerated by the fading of war-time memories and by the switch in the political complexion of government from a Labour administration after 1945 to a Conservative administration in the 1980s. There has, however, been an unmistakable shift in public expectations of what the state can deliver.

The two most obvious illustrations of this are the wholesale privatization of industries nationalized after the war and the re-emergence of unemployment on a scale comparable with the 1930s. In the post-war years there was remarkably little opposition to nationalization except in the case of the steel industry and road haulage. In the 1980s there was remarkably little opposition to privatization except in the case of the main public utilities. On both occasions there was more rhetoric than reason in the arguments. The decisive factor was either faith in what the state could do or alternatively distrust of excessive state interference.

Similarly with unemployment. In 1945 it was largely taken for granted that when government committed itself to 'a high and stable level of employment' the thing was as good as done. By the 1980s the government's posture was back to that of the 1930s – depressions were made abroad and aggravated by excessive wage settlements – and the public once again was obliged to acquiesce in the unemployment of over 3 million workers.

Much the same applied to inflation: with this difference, that governments continued to make promises even when they failed to fulfil them. In the early post-war years governments had checked overt inflation by suppressing it through price control, rationing, etc. They had then had to face irresistible pressure in 1950–1 from enormous increases in the price of imported raw materials and had escaped with what now seems only a modest rise in domestic prices. By 1973–4 similar pressure produced a more dramatic burst of inflation that was checked but not curbed and burst out again in 1980–1. At the end of the 1980s it was only too apparent that governments had still to find a way of controlling inflation without plunging the economy into recession.

Thus the state still professed to control inflation while withdrawing from ownership – and to some extent also control – of a large tract of industry. It had abandoned its commitment to a high level of employment and was even willing to destabilize employment as an anti-inflationary move. In other directions there was a similar withdrawal: regional policy was largely abandoned or left to the European Commission; and efforts to achieve a more equal distribution of income through the tax system, or alternatively to put much heavier tax burdens on the rich, either ceased or were reversed. These changes, however, were very much the work of the party in power at the end of the period and may not prove enduring. The Welfare State, on the other hand, has shown great resilience. Expenditure on the various welfare benefits financed by national insurance or from public funds has increased as a proportion of GDP at market prices from about 12 per cent in 1950–1 to about 22 per cent in 1987.

When we turn to policy instruments it is the contraction in the range of instruments that is most striking. The loss of faith in the state is compounded by a loss of capability. All the war-time controls have gone. So, too, have some, such as restrictions on hire purchase and limits on bank credit, that were introduced after the war and repeatedly used to influence demand. The tax regulator introduced in 1961, the selective employment tax and the regional employment premium have been abandoned. Incomes policy is out of favour. The budget, which proved to be much the most powerful weapon at the government's disposal, now serves more traditional purposes. The budget judgment, once cast in terms of the change in effective demand likely to result, is now limited to the borrowing requirement implied – a criterion formerly thought to be almost completely irrelevant. The one major instrument still retained, control over short-term interest rates, is itself of diminishing value as international financial markets become increasingly closely linked. International economic management remains rudimentary.

What became increasingly clear was that national governments with few exceptions had only limited control over their domestic economy. The increasing integration of the world economy was steadily narrowing their ability to pursue a policy of their own choosing. As Sir Douglas Wass, then Permanent Secretary of the Treasury, pointed out in 1978 the trend towards international economic integration was 'the single most important structural change in the world economy in the second half of the twentieth century'.[9]

The United Kingdom was no exception to the trend. From about 20.5 per cent of GDP in 1948, and again in 1964, imports of goods and services grew to over 27 per cent in 1988. In exports there was a parallel growth from about 18.5 per cent to 23.5 per cent. The growth in trade, moreover, was heavily concentrated on the European Community and so beyond government control. In 1948 British trade with the original six member of the Community was under 10 per cent of the total in the case of both imports and of exports; by 1964 this had grown to 20.4 per cent in the case of exports and 16.5 per cent in the case of imports. These proportions in turn had grown to 44.6 and 43.7 per cent by 1989, much of the increase occurring before 1973 when Britain joined the Community.

An important aspect of economic integration was increased import penetration. For foodstuffs and raw materials this was nothing new. The big change was in manufactures which by 1989 accounted for nearly 80 per cent of all imports and exceeded exports of manufactures by 25 per cent. Finished manufactures alone had grown from under a tenth in 1959 and just over a quarter in 1969, to more than half total imports in 1989.

There was also closer integration of capital markets. At the long end, British investments abroad grew rapidly in the 1980s and reached £100 billion. At the short end, the money markets of the world were joined by currency flows on a vast scale beyond the power of governments to control, although not to influence. Neither trade nor investment abroad was subject to direct limitation across the board although various forms of protection were maintained against imports from outside the European Community.

Changes in the System of Policy-making

Since the early 1970s, increased importance has come to be attached to monetary policy, to opinion in financial markets, and to the views of the Bank of England as the operator of monetary policy. Partly this represents greater confidence in the power of monetary weapons, partly it reflects the greater vulnerability of national economic policy to uncontrolled capital movements, and partly it corresponds to mistrust of the competence and integrity of government. There is correspondingly less reliance on short-term budgetary influences, especially under a government seeking to reduce the level of taxation: less faith in the power of demand management to regulate the volume of employment and more confidence in the power of monetary policy to control inflation. In short, there has been a wholesale retreat from what were taken to be the doctrines of Keynes.

One consequence of these changes has been a move to give greater weight and independence to the central bank. The Governor of the Bank of England is freer to express his views, to press them on the Chancellor, and to make public any disagreement with the Chancellor. Minutes of their meetings are released after an interval so that the views of both are known.

A second consequence has been a greater readiness to surrender responsibility for monetary policy to an international agency – a European Central Bank. If governments are not to be trusted with such responsibilities, and monetary policy is nevertheless of key importance, then it may seem reasonable to enlist the services of a new financial agency, free from political domination, to frame monetary policies for the whole of Europe. With a common currency the possibility of conducting a separate monetary policy in each country would disappear; but given the free movement of capital between countries, one may ask how much freedom to pursue a separate monetary policy now survives in each country.

It is not, however, a matter of monetary policy only. With a common currency the freedom to use other instruments of economic policy would be subject to increasingly tight limits and the end-result would be likely to be a single economic policy for the whole Community. Eventually a single currency would require a single government. To some this prospect may be welcome but others will hesitate to surrender control to a new political arm of the Community and monetary policy to a non-elected Central Bank.

Structural change

Table 8.6 shows some of the major structural changes in the economy since 1948. Unfortunately the industrial classification used has changed from time to time so that for many industries there is no continuous series. The most important breaks were in 1948 and 1959 and there have been other minor changes since then of which no account is taken. It is possible, however, to gain a general impression of the main trends from table 8.7, bearing in mind that it relates to employees only (excluding the self-employed) and to Great Britain (not the United Kingdom).

It will be seen that between 1948 and 1993 employment in total changed remarkably little but that while male employment fell by 3.7 million, female employment increased by nearly as much – in fact by 50 per cent. Of the jobs held by women in 1993 4.8 million were part-time and 1.2 million men were in part-time jobs. Most of these jobs were in the service industries – all but about 500,000 jobs in all. About 800,000 workers – mainly self-employed – had two jobs.

The most striking change in employment since 1948 has been the decline in the manufacturing sector. Since productivity grew faster in that sector than in the rest of the economy, the decline was more apparent in employment than in output. Indeed, in absolute terms, manufacturing output rose considerably. In the first twenty years after the war manufacturing employment, too, increased and it was only after 1965–6 that a gradual decline set in. The most rapid contraction was in 1980–1 when over a million jobs were shed. By 1993 less than one employee in five, was employed in manufacturing and employment had contracted by over 50 per cent from the peak in 1965–66.

Within manufacturing there has been a particularly heavy fall in employment in the textiles, clothing, and footwear group. Some of the contraction shown in table 8.6 is due to re-classification but it seems certain that over a million jobs have gone since 1948. Heavy industry has also suffered severely: shipbuilding, locomotive building, steelmaking and other branches of the metal and engineering industries have contracted greatly.

Perhaps the biggest reduction in employment has been in coalmining where the number on the books has fallen from over 700,000 in 1948 to 36,000 in 1993 and under 10,000 in 1995. Agriculture is another example of a heavy fall in employment, although since the figures in table 8.6 relate only to farm workers and do not include farmers, the overall reduction has been a good deal less steep.

These falls in employment have been more than offset by a large expansion in service industries. Again the figures are inexact and the picture given is incomplete. They point to a growth in the services sector by 5 million jobs since 1959. It is this sector that has absorbed most of the additional women workers since 1964. Of the 15.2 million workers in service industries in 1993, 8.7 million were women – more than were employed in all sectors in 1964. There were four times as many women in the services sector as in the rest of the economy whereas there were only about 30 per cent more men.

Recent changes in the labour market

The structural changes affecting industry in particular have been accompanied by big changes in the labour market (see table 8.7). These include the continuance of high levels of unemployment, which has never fallen below 1.5 million since 1980 but had never reached that total in the previous forty years. There have been changes also in the kind of employment available. Full-time jobs for men have shrunk and part-time jobs for women have expanded. There has been a growth in the number of self-employed, often at low rates of pay, and in the number of workers holding two jobs. Part-time jobs offer an average of about 15 hours a week and second jobs would seem to average under ten. The changes occurring are best illustrated by a comparison between the spring of 1984 and the spring of 1994, unemployment being somewhat higher in 1984 than in 1994 and rising, not falling as in 1994.

Table 8.6 Distribution of employment in Great Britain, 1948–1993 (June)

(000)

	1948 Old series	1959 Old series	1959 New series	1964	1993
Agriculture, forestry, fishing	1178	999	642	528	256
Coalmining	724	658	658	498	36
Construction	1450	1509	1523	1617	814
Manufacturing industry	8137	9169	8314	8731	4218
of which					
Textiles, footwear, clothing	1662	1563	1451	1382	401
Food, drink and tobacco	750	939	783	805	459
Service industries, of which	9928	10255	11359	15239	15239
Electricity, gas, water supply	321	374	374	402	247
Distributive trades	2484	3000	2697	2937	3283
Transport and communication	1787	1676	1685	1637	1328
Banking, finance, insurance	–	–	–	–	2557
Education and health services	–	–	–	–	3398
Public administration	–	–	–	–	1815

Total employees in civil employment	21569[a]	21565	21565	22892	21368
Males	14549[a]	13984	13984	14611	10861
Females	7020[a]	7581	7581	8281	10507
Unemployed	282	385	385	317	2865
Self-employed and employers	1673	1677	1677	1673	2989
Total (incl. HM Forces and govt trainees)	22780	24196	24196	25306	27814

[a] Including employers and self-employed.
Source: Annual Abstract of Statistics; Employment Gazette, September 1993.

Table 8.7   Changes in the labour market, 1984–1994 (000's)

	full-time	Men part-time	self employed	two jobs
Spring 1984	11111	426	1978	211
Spring 1994	10335	735	2389	295
	–776	+309	+411	+84
	full-time	Women part-time	self employed	two jobs
Spring 1984	4966	3952	639	234
Spring 1994	5538	4664	819	494
	+572	+712	+180	+260

Thus the number of full-time jobs for men dwindled – as they did for the greater part of the decade – while in all other forms of employment there was a net increase. The biggest increase was in women in part-time employment: in their case this corresponded to their own preference. Nearly all part-time jobs were in services. Over the decade the total number of jobs for men fell slightly but changed in character while the total number of women's jobs increased no less than 1.7 million. With the decline in manufacturing employment the pressure in the labour market was concentrated on male labour.

Regional change

At the end of the war great hopes were invested in measures to improve the prospects of what in the 1930s had been the 'depressed areas' of the country. These measures developed into regional policy which had a similar but broader aim: to promote a more even development of the different regions of the country.

A symptom of uneven development was the spread in unemployment rates between the more prosperous and less prosperous parts of the country.

Table 8.8   Regional pattern of unemployment, 1949–1993

Region	% Unemployment in second quarter of					
	1949	*1965*	*1974*	*1979*	*1986*	*1993*
Northern	2.5	2.4	3.4	6.5	15.5	11.9
Yorkshire and Humberside	0.7	1.0	2.0	4.1	12.6	10.5
East Midlands		0.8	1.6	3.3	10.0	9.6
East Anglia	1.1	1.2	1.3	3.2	8.5	8.3
South East		0.8	1.2	2.6	8.3	10.3
South West	1.3	1.5	1.8	4.1	9.5	9.7
West Midlands	0.7	0.6	1.7	3.9	12.9	11.1
North West	1.6	1.5	2.5	5.0	13.8	10.9
Wales	3.9	2.4	2.8	5.5	13.2	10.3
Scotland	2.8	2.8	3.0	5.7	11.1	9.8
Northern Ireland	6.4	6.0	4.1	7.9	17.2	14.0
United Kingdom	1.6	1.4	2.0	4.1	11.2	10.4

Source: Economic Trends Annual Supplement 1990; British Labour Statistics: historical abstract 1886–1968; Economic Trends

Unemployment rates reflected differences in the pressure of demand for labour in the different regions and the pattern of unemployment rates maintained a remarkable constancy until the 1980s. The employment pattern, however, did undergo gradual change. Employment increased in the regions with low unemployment and was constant or fell in regions where unemployment was high. The unemployment figures might suggest that changes in job opportunities, whether resulting from government measures or the discovery of North Sea oil or other developments, were powerless to affect the relative position of the different regions.

It would seem, however, that job opportunities operated on out-migration rather than unemployment. North Sea oil, for example, was a more powerful job creator than anything governments did. It did not prevent Scotland from continuing to have the highest or one of the highest rates of unemployment in Great Britain: what it did do was to cut net emigration from Scotland.

Table 8.9   Changes in regional income in the UK, 1971–1992
(United Kingdom = 100)

| | Personal Income per head | | Proportion of total | |
| | 1971 | 1989 | 1992 | 1992 |
			in %	
Northern	87.1	86.9	90.6	4.8
Yorkshire and				
Humberside	93.2	88.1	93.2	8.0
East Midlands	96.5	95.0	94.3	6.6
East Anglia	93.8	99.3	100.4	3.6
South East	113.8	120.6	114.9	35.1
South West	94.7	95.6	95.0	7.8
West Midlands	102.7	91.7	93.1	8.5
North West	96.1	91.5	93.3	10.3
Wales	88.4	83.6	84.1	4.2
Scotland	93.0	93.1	99.1	8.7
Northern Ireland	74.3	76.1	84.1	2.3

Source: Economic Trends November 1975, November 1990 and May 1994.

Between 1949 and 1965 little change took place in the regional pattern of unemployment. The main change was an improvement in the relative position of Wales. Between 1965 and 1993 there were larger changes in the relative position of the different regions (table 8.8). Three regions showed a marked improvement: Scotland, East Anglia and Wales. East Anglia by 1993 had the lowest percentage of any region, starting from a middling position; Wales fell from near the top to about the middle; and Scotland, once well about the average was below it in 1990. On the other hand, three regions suffered a relative change for the worse. The West Midlands, which once enjoyed the lowest unemployment rate, was a little above the average in 1993. Yorkshire and Humberside suffered a comparable change. The Northern Region, at first below Scotland, ended well above it but well below Northern Ireland where unemployment was continuously well above the national average.

There were also changes in the relative prosperity of different regions. The estimates of regional GDP, which do not go back beyond 1971, show an increasing gap between the South East, including Greater London, and the rest of the country (table 8.9). By 1989 income per head in the South East was more than 20 per cent (and in Greater London nearly 30 per cent) above the national average whereas in 1971 the margin had been under 14 per cent. In 1992 the depression had narrowed the gap again. No other region in 1989 was above the national average, East Anglia coming closest; in 1971 only the West Midlands had been above, standing out as nearest in prosperity to the South East. In the eighteen years between 1971 and 1989 the one region apart from the South East that registered a conspicuous improvement was East Anglia. Four regions showed a marked drop in relation to the others: the West Midlands, Wales, the North West and Yorkshire: i.e., the industrial heartland of the country. In 1992 all four showed a relative improvement, the biggest loser being the South East.

Conclusions

Could British policy have been better directed and if so, how? If one looks at the whole panorama since 1945 there are plenty of crises, false starts, failures and reversals of policy, misconceived ideas and matters that might have been better managed. On the other hand, there were powerful constraints limiting the government's freedom of manoeuvre. In external economic policy these included the large external debts inherited from the war; the orientation of Britain's trade towards markets that expanded relatively slowly and to which preferential access was being gradually withdrawn; the increasing integration of the world economy that set limits to the powers of national governments. In domestic policy the constraints included the high expectations of the public in relation to the true weakness of Britain's competitive position; the failure to develop a restraint in wage bargaining to match the experience of full employment; the inadequacies of industrial management and training; poor industrial relations.

In evaluating the policies of successive governments one has to ask how far a more skilful conduct of policy would have helped towards the main economic objectives such as faster economic growth, more stable prices, and a more even and more equal development of the country's resources. In framing an answer it can be of some help to make comparisons with other countries, remembering that their policies, too, were not beyond criticism and took shape also within constraints.

If, for example, we look at the rate of growth in the United Kingdom and in OECD (table 8.3), it is striking to see how the rate declines in each successive period from 1945 to 1989 in continental Europe whereas it fluctuates within comparatively narrow limits in the United Kingdom. It is true that the rate on the continent remains consistently above the British rate until the 1980s. But from 1970 it is either within reach of past British experience or below the current British rate. Continental experience suggests that one element in the rapid growth of post-war years was the existence at the end of the war of large reserves of idle capacity and labour in contrast to the pressure on capacity and the shortage of man-power in Britain. As the pressure increased on the continent, productivity rose with fuller utilization of capactiy and a momentum developed in which further resources were sucked in from the countryside and abroad with a prolongation of increasing returns. There was thus a long period in which resources grew, output expanded, productivity increased and fresh resources were created or attracted. The United Kingdom, on the other hand, started off fully employed and never worked up the momentum of expansion (and increasing returns) enjoyed by the continent for thirty years.

What is impressive is the comparative steadiness of the British rate under different governments and different policy regimes. British policies may not have succeeded in raising the rate of growth from what was felt to be a relatively disappointing level but neither did they reduce it disastrously in comparison with neighbouring countries. It is perhaps not unreasonable to conclude that the influence of government policy on the underlying rate of growth in an industrial country is of less consequence than is popularly supposed.

To this there is one major reservation which emerges clearly from the experience of the 1970s and 1980s. What matters more to growth than anything else – both GDP and labour productivity – is expanding employment and, in various ways also, full employment. When the need to curb inflation or balance the international accounts obliges governments to pursue restrictive policies, it is not only GDP that suffers – and suffers more than from obvious inefficiencies – but the growth of productivity as well. There used to be a tendency to lament full employment as a cause of labour hoarding and slow growth. No doubt there is some waste of labour when fluctuations occur around full employment. But unemployment can be an even greater waste; and scarcity of labour is itself a force for economy in manpower and for progress towards higher levels of output per man. The pressures that it sets up within the economy make it easier to attack restrictive practices and effect the adjustments that rapid innovation requires. The greatest failure in post-war policy has been large-scale, continuing unemployment; and it is of little comfort if other countries have failed as badly.

There has also been a tendency to deride demand management as neglecting the medium and long term for the sake of immediate employment and neglecting also the supply side of the economy in order to concentrate solely on demand. Neither criticism has more than limited force. It is true that if it proves impossible to contain cost increases, and/or balance of payments deficits, for lack of any instrument of policy operating directly on costs and the balance of payments, it may prove necessary to restrain demand and generate slack in the form, for example, of unemployment. But this has nothing to do with the time horizon. The government continues to plan its expenditures against different time horizons and in managing demand can give effect to long-term considerations in its selection of cuts or additions just as it can select tax changes that take account both of their immediate impact on demand and their longer-term consequences. Similarly, while it may be true that the government has given insufficient attention to the supply side of the economy, this can hardly be laid at the door of its concentration on demand management, which not only has more immediate and more far-reaching effects on production but makes very little demand on government manpower.

It can be argued that in the 1950s and 1960s full employment was pushed too far and that it would have been wiser to run the economy under less pressure. Germany might be able to raise the pressure even higher without producing more inflation. But Germany had a public fully alive to the dangers of inflation and an elastic supply of labour from the countryside and from abroad. In Britain, there were spurts in consumer prices from time to time in the first twenty post-war years, usually when demand was clearly excessive. There was, however, no enduring acceleration. It was only at the end of the 1960s, when unemployment was already higher, that there seemed a danger that inflation would move into a higher gear. In the years before 1970 inflation had been little greater, and for some of the time appreciably less than on the continent (table 1.2). It was the 1973 boom and the oil shock that first produced a wide margin between inflation in Britain and the rest of Europe. Since then there has been no mistaking the greater proneness to inflation in Britain, and this in spite of levels of unemployment far higher than in earlier years.

British governments have undoubtedly tried hard to keep inflation under control; but they have obviously not been very successful and it is the lack of success that has made them seek desperate remedies. Incomes policy had mixed results and the successes were confined almost entirely to Labour governments. Monetary policy never matched the prospectus of those who underwrote it, and it was only by producing recessions that it caused inflation to fall off. The problem remains of expanding employment to full potential on a secure footing without being made to slow down by inflation or an external deficit.

For much of the period the British public was given the impression that all that stood in the way of faster growth was some external constraint: either a fixed rate of exchange, or the role of sterling as a reserve currency, or some obscure obstacle called 'the balance of payments'. There were certainly times when sterling was over-valued or when the reserve currency role was an embarrassment; and the balance of payments before the days of North Sea oil was a constant threat to the continuity of policy. But over-valuation nearly always reflected over-expansion or domestic inflation; sterling remained a reserve currency largely because Britain was in no position to liquidate the balances in which other countries' reserves were held; and the difficulties with the balance of payments reflected the failure to match these same balances by adequate reserves. Although there was much talk in the 1950s of a balance of payments target, little was ever done before 1977 to accumulate larger reserves and cater for a less violent response to balance of payments pressure.

Whatever may have been the situation in earlier decades, at the end of the 1980s it was indeed dominated by external difficulties. A large current account deficit, even when unemployment stood at 1 million or more, made a resumption of growth extremely hazardous. The deficit had to be financed from abroad, and this in turn dictated high rates of interest to attract the necessary finance, pushing the economy still further into recession. To the deflationary influence of the balance of payments deficit was added the sluggishness of the forces making for change, innovation and adjustment that had long been characteristic of the economy. It was not easy to see how a deterioration that had occurred with North Sea oil at or near its peak could be quickly reversed as the revenue from North Sea oil continued to fall. The problem of restoring external balance seemed as formidable in 1990 as it had been in 1945. Nevertheless when the pound was allowed to float again in 1992 after two unhappy years of fixed exchange rates, the external deficit dropped rapidly to manageable proportions.

Could the forces making for growth have been given more momentum by government intervention? There are many who feel that governments neglected the supply side of the economy and could have intervened more decisively to improve industrial efficiency and lend support to innovation. They dismiss the efforts of Labour governments to raise industrial productivity in 1945–50, or to restructure industry in 1964–70, or to develop industrial policy in the 1970s, as half-hearted or misdirected and argue for a more determined, planned effort of modernization. There are plenty of good reasons why governments intervene in industry but most of these reasons relate to infrastructure, health, the environment, monopolistic influence, and so on, not to innovation and productivity. There are also circumstances in which governments exercise great influence over industry through their control over scarce materials, their much greater command over finance, their control over research facilities and over markets like that for defence equipment where they are important buyers. But in an industrial economy with free access to materials markets and finance and a diversified industrial structure it is not at all clear that governments can do much to make industry more efficient and more innovative. It is not easy to make better decisions from outside an organization than the decisions taken from inside: and to make them in relation to sufficient businesses to change the trend in industrial productivity. Governments may boast of higher productivity; but their power to contribute to it is usually not so apparent.

The more hopeful line of advance has generally been seen in improved management education, in better industrial training, in more widespread facilities for consultancy, and so on. There may also be scope for more government assistance in industrial reconstruction such as was envisaged for the Industrial Reconstruction Corporation or the National Enterprise Board. Perhaps, too, there is need for a closer *rapprochement* between government and industry, with greater circulation between them such as occurred in war-time, so as to ensure that industrial policy, whatever shape it takes, can draw on an expertise that has not in the past been very abundant in Whitehall.

For most of the years since 1945 there was widespread agreement on the aims of government and some agreement also on how they should be pursued. Keynes and Beveridge had provided the elements of a public philosophy governing political action. There is no such public philosophy in the 1990s. The consensus of earlier decades has faded away and there is now no general acceptance of fundamental principles to regulate the activity of the state. Yet on the other hand disagreement seems to go less deep. Economic factors have assumed more importance but are less firmly embedded in political ideology.

As we look back on the past, we tend to interpret events in the light of the policies professed by governments as if what occurred was largely attributable to government policy. We are easily persuaded that things would have been different if government had acted differently and we find in government a convenient scapegoat for outcomes of which we disapprove. Looking to the future, national governments will occupy less and less of the stage and so far as we continue to look to government policy for an explanation of events, it will have to be increasingly to institutions that are international in character. The economic history of the future will need a wider focus and will have to give more prominence to international factors, whether they derive from the world-wide influence of the market or from policies devised at the international level.

Notes

1   D. T. Jones, 'Output, employment and labour productivity in Europe since 1955', *National Institute Economic Review*, August 1976, pp. 72–85.

2   For the most recent analysis see A. D. Smith, D. M. W. N. Hitchens and S. W. Davies, *International Industrial Productivity*, 1982, Cambridge: Cambridge University Press.

3   *Economic Trends Annual Supplement 1990*, table 6; *Social Trends 1995*, p. 102.

4   Institute of Fiscal Studies, *Update*, Autumn/Winter 1994.

5   Royal Commission on the Distribution of Income and Wealth, 1979, Report no. 7, Cmnd 6999.

6   *Economic Trends*, May 1990, p. 118.

7   Ibid., p. 86

8   Joseph A. Pechman, (ed.), *The Role of the Economist in Government*, Harvester Wheatsheaf Press, 1989, p. 25.

9   Lecture to the Johnian Society, St John's College, Cambridge, 15
     February 1978, para 9.

Appendix 1 Main Economic Events

1945	*July*	General election won by Labour with majority of 146
	September	Japan surrenders
	December	Anglo-American financial agreement
1946	*July*	Loan agreement ratified by Congress
1947	*February*	Fuel crisis begins
	June	General Marshall suggests US aid to Europe
	July	Beginning of convertibility crisis
1948	*April*	European Co-operation Act becomes effective
	July	Berlin air lift
1949	*September*	Devaluation of the pound to $2.80
1950	*February*	General election: reduced Labour majority of 5
	May	Announcement of Schuman Plan
	June	War in Korea
	July	Agreement on European Payments Union
1951	*April*	Resignation of A. Bevan, H. Wilson and J. Freeman
	October	General election won by Conservatives, majority of 17
	November	Bank rate raised to 2.5 per cent: 'new monetary policy'
	December	London foreign exchange market re-opened
1952	*January*	Commonwealth Finance Ministers Conference
	February	Cabinet sets aside 'Robot' plan to let pound float and make it convertible
1953	*March*	Steel industry de-nationalized
1954	*July*	Food rationing ends

1955	*February*	Government allows Bank of England to support rate for transferable sterling
	May	General election: Conservative majority of 58
	July	Beginning of credit squeeze
	October	Autumn budget
1956	*October*	UK announces plan for European Free Trade Area; Anglo-French invasion of Egypt
1957	*August*	Council on Prices Productivity and Incomes established
	September	Bank rate raised to 7 per cent
1958	*January*	EEC inaugurated
	November	France rejects EFTA proposals
	December	Convertibility of European currencies
1959	*October*	General election: Conservative majority of 100
	November	EFTA Convention signed in Stockholm
1961	*July*	'Pay pause'; first use of tax regulator; National Economic Development Council to be established
	November	Negotiations in Brussels for UK entry to EEC
1962	*April*	End of pay pause
	July	Cabinet reconstruction: seven ministers asked to resign
1963	*January*	UK application to EEC rejected
1964	*April*	Resale Price Maintenance abolished
	October	General Election: Labour majority of 4; 15 per cent import surcharge
	December	Statement of intent on prices, productivity and incomes signed by TUC and employers' organizations; IMF lends $1 billion to UK
1965	*February*	National Board for Prices and Incomes established
	April	Import surcharge cut to 10 per cent
	May	UK draws $1.4 billion from IMF
	September	National Plan announced aiming at 25 per cent increase in GNP by 1970
1966	*March*	General election: Labour majority of 96
	July	Prices and Incomes (early warning) Bill; six months wage freeze; deflationary measures
	November	End of import surcharge

1967	*May*	Formal application to join EEC
	August	Relaxation of hire purchase restrictions
	September	Dock strikes in London and Liverpool
	November	Devaluation of £ to $2.40; Chancellor and Home Secretary exchange places
	December	France vetoes UK application to EEC
1968	*January*	Cuts in public expenditure
	March	Closure of gold pool; dual price system adopted
1969	*June*	Government drops plans for legal restraints on unofficial strikes
	October	Department of Economic Affairs abolished
1970	*December*	EEC agrees to negotiations for British entry
	January	General election: Conservative majority of 30
	December	Industrial Relations Bill introduced
1971	*December*	Smithsonian agreement on exchange rates
1972	*February*	State of emergency declared: large-scale power cuts
	June	Pound allowed to float
	November	Ninety-day freeze on prices, pay, and dividends
1973	*January*	The UK joins the EEC
	April	Phase 2 of counter-inflationary policy
	October	Phase 3 of counter-inflationary policy
	Oct.-Dec.	First oil shock
	November	Bank rate raised to 13 per cent
	December	Prime Minister announces three-day week from 1 January
1974	*February*	General election; no party has majority
	March	Labour government under Harold Wilson; end of three-day week and miners' strike
	April	UK demands renegotiation of EEC entry
	July	Repeal of Industrial Relations Act; abolition of Pay Board
	October	General election: Labour majority of 3
1975	*February*	Margaret Thatcher succeeds Edward Heath as leader of Conservative Party
	June	Referendum on EEC: 2 to 1 majority in favour
	July	Anti-inflationary policy; £6 a week limit on wage increases till August 1976

1976	*April*	James Callaghan succeeds Harold Wilson as Prime Minister
	May	Stage 2 of anti-inflationary policy endorsed by TUC
	June	£3 billion standby from US and European banks
	July	Government announces monetary target of 12 per cent
	October	Pound falls to $1.57; bank rate increased to 15 per cent; negotiations with IMF for a loan begin
	December	Letter of intent submitted to IMF
1977	*March*	Lib–Lab Pact
	July	Stage 3 of incomes policy: 10 per cent limit on earnings
	November	Firemen strike for 35 per cent wage increase
1978	*May*	Government suffers defeats on budget
	July	Government proposes 5 per cent pay guideline
	October	Guideline rejected by Labour Party Conference
1979	*March*	Government defeated on vote of no confidence
	May	General election won by Conservatives: majority of 43; major tax changes in budget
	October	Exchange control discontinued
	Oct.-Feb.	Second oil shock
	November	Bank rate raised to 17 per cent
1980	*March*	Medium-term financial strategy announced
	November	Pound peaks against the dollar at $2.45
1981	*March*	364 economists protest in *The Times* against government policies
1982	*April*	Argentine invades Falkland Islands
	July	Abolition of hire purchase controls
	November	Pound begins fall against the dollar
1983	*May*	General election: Conservatives re-elected with majority of 144
1984	*March*	Miners' strike begins
1985	*February*	Unemployment reaches 3 million; pound falls to $1.10
	September	Plaza accord on lowering dollar exchange rate

	December	European Council of Ministers agrees on a Single European Act for European Community by 1 January 1993, and eventual monetary union.
1986	*July*	Unemployment reaches peak of over 3.1 million (seasonally adjusted)
1987	*February*	Louvre accord on exchange rates
	June	General election: Conservatives re-elected with majority of 101
	October	Sharp fall in stock exchange prices
1988	*May*	Bank interest rates fall to 7.5 per cent
1989	*October*	Nigel Lawson resigns as Chancellor; base rates of commercial banks raised to 15 per cent
	November	Dismantlement of Berlin Wall begins
1990	*October*	Britain enters Exchange Rate Mechanism
	November	Margaret Thatcher resigns as Prime Minister
1991	*January*	Start of Gulf War
	April	Community charge to be replaced by Council Tax
	August	Attempted coup in Russia
	October	Agreement between EC and EFTA on creation of a European Economic Area by January 1993
1992	*February*	Treaty of Maastricht signed
	April	Conservatives win General Election with majority of 21
	September	Italy and the UK suspend membership of the ERM
1993	*January*	Single European Market established
	February	First Report to Chancellor of 'seven wise men'
	May	Norman Lamont succeeded by Kenneth Clarke as Chancellor
	November	First winter budget uniting revenue and expenditure plans
1994	*March*	First fall in unemployment for three years
	July	Inflation rate of 1.2 per cent lowest for 30 years
	August	All ERM currencies except guilder and DM to have wider bands of 15 per cent

Appendix 2 Key Figures in Economic Policy, 1945–1990

Date	Prime Minister	Chancellor of the Exchequer	Minister of Economic Affairs	Governor of the Bank of England
July 1945 (Labour govt)	C. R. Attlee	H. Dalton	–	Lord Catto
November 1947		R. Stafford Cripps	–	
1949			H. Gaitskell	C. F. Cobbold
February 1950		H. Gaitskell		
November 1950				
October 1951	W. S. Churchill	R. Butler	–	
April 1955	A. Eden		–	
December 1955		H. Macmillan	–	
January 1957	H. Macmillan	P. Thorneycroft	–	
January 1958		D. Heathcoat Amory	–	
July 1960		J. Selwyn Lloyd	–	
January 1961			–	Lord Cromer
July 1962		R. Maudling		
October 1963	Sir Alec Douglas Home			
October 1964	J. H. Wilson	J. Callaghan	G. Brown (First Secretary of State)	
July 1966				L. K. O'Brien
August 1966			M. Stewart (First Secretary of State)	
August 1967			P. Shore (Secretary of State)	
November 1967		R. Jenkins		
June 1970	E. Heath	{ I. MacLeod / A. Barber	–	
July 1973				G. Richardson
March 1974	J. H. Wilson	D. Healey	–	
April 1976	J. Callaghan		–	
May 1979	M. Thatcher	G. Howe	–	
June 1983		N. Lawson		
July 1983			–	R. Leigh Pemberton
October 1989		J. Major		
November 1990	J. Major	N. Lamont	–	
May 1993		K. Clarke		
July 1993				E. George

Appendix 3
Definitions of Money

Until the rise of monetarism in the 1970s, most economists in the United Kingdom were content to use, as a measure of the stock of money, deposits with the London clearing banks plus notes and coin in circulation. Since 1970 a variety of measures have been used, some based on narrow definitions and some including an increasingly wide range of financial instruments. They include:

Narrow money

M0 The wide monetary base. Notes and coin in circulation with the public plus banks' till money and balances with the Bank of England.

M1 M0 plus sight deposits held by the private sector with UK banks.

Broad money

M2 Notes and coin in circulation with the public plus sterling 'retail' deposits held by the UK private sector with UK banks and building societies and in the National Savings Bank ordinary account. Bank 'retail' deposits include all non-interest bearing deposits plus 'chequable' sight or time deposits regardless of maturity.

£M3 Notes and coin in circulation plus all sterling deposits (including time deposits and certificates of deposit) held by UK residents in both public and private sectors.

M3 £M3 plus private sector deposits held by UK residents in other currencies.

M4 £M3 plus all sterling deposits (including certificates of deposit) held with building societies by the private sector (excluding banks and building societies).

M5 M4 plus private sector holdings of various money-market instruments (bank bills, Treasury bills, local authority deposits), certificates of tax deposit and national savings instruments.

Of these, £M3 and M3 were discontinued in the course of the 1980s.

Bibliography

Statistics

The first requirement of any student of the post-war period is access to the facts, particularly the statistical magnitudes. Readers should be warned that statistics are not, in principle, any more accurate and reliable than other 'facts' about the past and that official statistics may be changed, sometimes quite radically, both shortly after and long after publication.

Three sources giving long runs of figures are particularly valuable:

Economic Trends Annual Supplement published annually by the CSO.

Feinstein C. H. 1972. *Statistical Tables of National Income, Expenditure and Output of the United Kingdom 1855–1965* Cambridge: Cambridge University Press.

The British Economy: Key Economic Statistics 1900–1970, 1972, Cambridge; London and Cambridge Economic Service.

For *labour* statistics there is a useful collection of data up to to 1968 in:

British Labour Statistics: Historical Abstract 1886–1968, 1971. Department of Employment and Productivity, London: HMSO.

Statistics of the leading industrial countries for the past twenty years are given in *OECD Economic Outlook* and *OECD Historical Statistics*, Paris: OECD.

For current statistics the most useful sources are:

Monthly

Monthly Digest of Statistics
Economic Trends
Employment Gazette
Financial Statistics
Main Economic Indicators (OECD)

Quarterly

Bank of England *Quarterly Bulletin*
National Institute *Economic Review*

Annual

Annual Abstract of Statistics
Financial Statement and Budget Report
Autumn Statement
Social Trends

Books

The fullest treatment of the entire post-war period is in the succession of studies published by the National Institute of Economic and Social Research:

Dow, J. C. R. 1964. *The Management of the British Economy, 1945–60*, Cambridge: Cambridge University Press for NIESR.
Blackaby, F. (ed.) 1978. *British Economic Policy 1960–74*, Cambridge: Cambridge University Press for NIESR.
Britton, A. J. 1991. *Macroeconomic Policy in Britain 1974–87*, London: NIESR.

These are very different in treatment but written from a common standpoint. Dow's interest is in discovering how the economic system really works and his book gives more space than the others to the lessons of historical experience for economic theory.

Blackaby's volume is a symposium on different aspects of policy and is not confined like Britton's to macro-economic policy.

Two recent volumes contain contributions covering the whole period and full bibliographies:

Crafts, N. F. R. and Woodward, N. (eds) 1991. *The British Economy since 1945*, Oxford: Oxford University Press.
Floud, R. and McCloskey, D. (eds) 1994. *The Economic History of Great Britain*, vol. 3, Cambridge: Cambridge University Press.

Two useful short histories of the period are:

Alford, B. W. E. 1988. *British Economic Performance 1945–1975*, London: Macmillan.
Wright, John F. 1979. *Britain in the Age of Economic Management*, Oxford: Oxford University Press.

A more extended treatment covering a longer period is in:
Pollard, S. 1983. *The Development of the British Economy 1914– 1980*. London: Edward Arnold.

Tomlinson, J. 1990. *Public Policy and the Economy since 1900*, Oxford: Clarendon Press.

In addition to the references given at the end of each chapter, readers may wish to consult works on different aspects of policy. A selection appears below.

Economic policymaking

There are full bibliographies in:

Cairncross, A. 1989. 'The United Kingdom', in J. A. Pechman (ed.), *The Role of the Economist in Government*, Hemel Hempstead: Harvester Wheatsheaf.
Cairncross, A. and Watts, N. 1989. *The Economic Section 1939– 1961: a study in economic advising*, London: Routledge.
Coats, A. W. (ed.) 1981. *Economists in Government: an international comparative study*, Durham, N. Carolina: Duke University Press.

To the references given in these volumes should be added:

Cairncross, A. (ed.) 1989 and 1991. *The Robert Hall Diaries*, vol. 1 1947–53; vol. 2 1954–61, London: Unwin Hyman.

Mosley, Paul 1984. *The Making of Economic Policy: theory and evidence from Britain and the US since 1945*, New York: St Martin's Press.

Pliatzky, Leo 1989. *The Treasury under Mrs Thatcher*. Oxford: Blackwell

Employment, the Labour Market and Industrial Relations

Blackaby, F. (ed.) 1980. *The Future of Pay Bargaining*, London: Heinemann for NIESR.

Donovan Report 1968. *Report of Royal Commission on Trade Unions and Employers' Associations 1965–68*, London: HMSO, Cmnd 3623.

Dow, J. C. R. 1990. 'How can real wages ever get excessive?', London: British Academy.

Fishbein, W. H. 1987. *Wage Restraint by Consensus: Britain's search for an incomes policy agreement 1965–79*, Boston: Routledge.

Hart, Peter (ed.) 1986. *Unemployment and Labour Market Policies*, Aldershot: Gower.

Jones, Russell 1987. *Wages and Employment Policy 1936–1955*, London: Allen & Unwin.

Layard, R., Nickell, S., and Jackman, R. 1991. *Unemployment*. Oxford: Oxford University Press.

Matthews, R. C. O. 1968. 'Why has Britain had full employment since the war?', *Economic Journal*, September.

Oxford Review of Economic Policy 1991. *Labour Markets*, Spring. Oxford: Oxford University Press.

Phelps Brown, E. H. 1983. *Origins of Trade Union Power*, Oxford: Clarendon Press.

Sargent, J. R. 1995. 'Roads to Full Employment', National Institute *Economic Review* February.

Tomlinson, J. 1987. *Employment Policy: the crucial years 1939–1955*, Oxford: Oxford University Press.

Worswick, G. D. N. 1991. *Unemployment: a problem of policy*, Cambridge: Cambridge University Press for NIESR.

Fiscal Policy and Public Expenditure

Clarke, R. W. B. 1978. *Public Expenditure: Management and Control*, London: Macmillan.

Cripps, F., Fetherston, M. and Godley, W. 1976. 'What is left of "New Cambridge"?', *Cambridge Economic Policy Review*, 2.

Else, P. K. and Marshall, G. P. 1979. *The Management of Public Expenditure*, London: Policy Studies Institute.

Goldman, S. 1973. *The Developing System of Public Expenditure Management and Control*, London: Civil Service College.

Hansen, Bent 1969. *Fiscal Policy in Seven Countries 1955–65*, Paris: OECD.

Heald, D. 1983. *Public Expenditure: its defence and reform*, Oxford: Oxford University Press.

Hicks, J. R. 1948. *The Problem of Budgetary Reform*, Oxford: Oxford University Press.

Kay, J. A. and King, M. 1986. *The British Tax System*, (4th edn), Oxford: Oxford University Press.

Levitt, M. S. (ed.) 1987. *New Priorities in Public Spending*, Aldershot: Gower.

Levitt, M. S. and Joyce, M. A. S. 1987. *The Growth and Efficiency of Public Spending*, Cambridge: Cambridge University Press.

Meade Committee 1978. *The Structure and Reform of Direct Taxation*, London: Allen & Unwin.

Pechman, J. A. 1986. *The Rich, the Poor, and the Taxes They Pay*, chapter 21, Brighton: Wheatsheaf Books.

Pliatzky, L. 1984. *Getting and Spending: public expenditure, employment and inflation*, (revised edition), Oxford: Blackwell.

Pliatzky, L. 1985. *Paying and Choosing*, Oxford: Blackwell.

Plowden Committee 1961. *Report on Control of Public Expenditure*, London HMSO, Cmnd 1432.

Royal Commission on the Distribution of Income and Wealth 1979. Report no. 7, Cmnd 1999, London: HMSO.

Wright, M. (ed.) 1980. *Public Spending Decisions: growth and restraint in the 1970s* (especially chapter 6), London: Allen & Unwin.

Growth

Abramovitz, M. 1989. *Thinking about Growth*, Cambridge: Cambridge University Press.

Allen, G. C. 1976. *The British Disease*, London: Institute of Economic Affairs.

Arndt, H. 1978. *The Rise and Fall of Economic Growth*, Melbourne: Longman Cheshire.

Bacon, R. and Eltis, W. 1976. *Britain's Economic Problem: too few producers*, London: Macmillan.

Beckerman, W. (ed.) 1979. *Slow Growth in Britain: causes and consequences*, Oxford: Oxford University Press.

Blackaby, F. (ed.) 1979. *Deindustrialisation*, London: Heinemann for NIESR.

Cairncross, A. 1988. 'Britain's industrial decline', *Royal Bank of Scotland Review*, September.

Denison, E. F. 1967. *Why Growth Rates Differ: post-war experience in nine western countries*, Washington: Brookings Institution.

Denison, E. F. 1979. *Accounting for Slower Economic Growth*, Washington: Brookings Institution.

Department of Economic Affairs. 1965. *The National Plan*, Cmnd 2764, London: DEH.

Elbaum, B. and Lazonick, W. (eds) 1987. *The Decline of the British Economy*, Oxford: Oxford University Press.

Feinstein, C. H. 1972. *National Income, Expenditure and Output of the United Kingdom 1855–1965*, Cambridge: Cambridge University Press.

Feinstein, C. H. 1988. Economic Growth since 1870: Britain's performance in international perspective', *Oxford Review of Economic Policy*, Spring.

Feinstein, C. H. and Matthews, R. C. O. 1990. 'The growth of output and productivity in the United Kingdom: The 1980s as a phase of the post-war period. *National Institute Economic Review*, August.

Jones, D. T. 1976. 'Output, employment and labour productivity in Europe since 1955, London: *National Institute Economic Review*, August.

Kaldor, Lord 1966. *Causes of the Slow Rate of Growth of the United Kingdom*, Cambridge: Cambridge University Press.

Kindleberger, C. P. 1967. *Europe's Post-war Growth: The role of the labour supply*, Cambridge, Mass: Harvard University Press.

Maddison, A. 1982. *Phases of Capitalist Development*, Oxford: Oxford University Press.

Maddison, A. 1989. *The World Economy in the 20th Century*, Paris: OECD.

Matthews, R. C. O. (ed.) 1982. *Slower Growth in the Western World*, London: Heinemann for NIESR.

Matthews, R. C. O., Feinstein, C. H. and Odling-Smee, J. C. 1982. *British Economic Growth 1856–1973*, Oxford: Oxford University Press.

National Economic Development Office 1963. *Conditions Favourable to Faster Growth*, London: NEDO.

Olson, Mancur 1982. *The Rise and Decline of Nations*, New Haven and London: Yale University Press.

Oxford Review of Economic Policy, 1988. *Long-Run Performance in the UK* Spring, Oxford: Oxford University Press.

Pavitt, K. (ed.) 1982. *Technical Innovation and British Economic Performance*, (revd edn), London: Macmillan.

Smith, A. D., Hitchens, D. M. N. N. and Davies, S. W. 1982. *International Industrial Productivity*, Cambridge: Cambridge University Press.

Weiner, M. J. 1981. *English Culture and the Decline of the Industrial Spirit 1850–1950*, Cambridge: Cambridge University Press.

Industry

Aaronovitch, S. and Sawyer, M. C. 1975. *Big Business. Theoretical and empirical aspects of concentration and mergers in the UK*, London: Macmillan.

Barnett, Correlli 1986. *The Audit of War*, part II, London: Macmillan.

Blackaby, F. (ed.) 1979. *Deindustrialization*, London: Heinemann for NIESR.

Burn, D. L. (ed.) 1958. *The Structure of British Industry: a symposium*, (2 vols), Cambridge: Cambridge University Press.

Carter, C. F. (ed.) 1981. *Industrial Policy and Innovation*, London: Heinemann for NIESR.

Central Policy Review Staff 1975. *The Future of the British Car Industry*, London: HMSO.

Chester, D. N. 1975. *The Nationalization of British Industry*, London: HMSO.

Hannah, L. and Kay, J. A. 1977. *Concentration in Modern Industry: theory, measurement and the UK experience*, London: Macmillan.

Hart, P. E. and Clarke, R. 1980. *Concentration in British Industry, 1935–75*, Cambridge: Cambridge University Press.

Kay, J., Mayer, C. and Thompson, D. 1986. *Privatization and Regulation*, Oxford: Clarendon Press.

National Institute of Economic and Social Research 1990. *Productivity, Education and Training: Britain and Other Countries Compared*, London.

Prais, S. J. 1976. *The Evolution of Giant Firms in Britain*. Cambridge: Cambridge University Press.

Prais, S. J. 1981. *Productivity and Industrial Structure: a statistical study of manufacturing industry in Britain, Germany and the US* Cambridge: Cambridge University Press.

Pratten, C. F. 1976. *Labour Productivity Differences Within International Companies*, Cambridge: Cambridge University Press.

Pryke, R. 1981. *The Nationalized Industries: policies and performance since 1968*, Oxford: Martin Robertson.

Williams, K., Williams, J. and Thomas, D. 1983. *Why are the British bad at Manufacturing?*, London: Routledge & Kegan Paul.

Inflation, Money and Finance

Bank of England 1984. *The Development and Operation of Monetary Policy 1960–1983*, London.

Brown, A. J. 1955. *The Great Inflation 1939–51*, Oxford: Oxford University Press.

Brown, A. J. 1985. *World Inflation since 1950: an international comparative study*, Oxford: Oxford University Press.

Dow, J. C. R. and Saville, I. D. 1990. *A Critique of Monetary Policy*, (2nd edn) Oxford: Oxford University Press.

Fellner, W. *et al.* 1961. *The Problem of Rising Prices*, Paris: OECD.

Flemming, J. 1976. *Inflation*, Oxford: University Press.

Forde, J. S. (1992) *The Bank of England 1944–58*.

Hicks, J. R 1990. *A Market Theory of Money*, Oxford: Clarendon Press.

Howson, Susan 1993. *British Monetary Policy 1945–51*. Oxford: Oxford University Press.

Kaldor, Lord 1982. *The Scourge of Monetarism*, Oxford: Oxford University Press.

Krause, L. B. and Salant, W. S. 1977. *World-wide Inflation*, Washington: DC: Brookings Institution.

Laidler, D. 1981 'Monetarism: an interpretation and an assessment', *Economic Journal*, March.

Oxford Review of Economic Policy, 1990. *Inflation* Winter, Oxford: Oxford University Press.

Radcliffe Committee 1959. *Report on the Working of the Monetary System*, Cmnd 827, London: HMSO

Wilson Committee 1980. *Report to the Committee to Review the Functioning of Financial Institutions*, Cmnd 7937, London: HMSO.

International Trade and Finance

Bordo, M. and Eichengreen, B. (eds) 1993 *A Retrospective on the Bretton Woods System* Chicago: University of Chicago Press.

Bryant, R. C. 1987. *International Financial Intermediation*, Washington DC: Brookings Institution.

Cairncross, A. and Eichengreen, B. 1983. *Sterling in Decline*, Oxford: Blackwell.

Cripps, F. and Godley, W. A. H. 1978. 'Control of imports as a means to full employment and the expansion of world trade', *Cambridge Journal of Economics*, September.

Day, A. C. L. 1954. *The Future of Sterling*, Oxford: Oxford University Press.

Eichengreen, B. 1994 *International Monetary Arrangements for the 21st Century* Washingtonh, DC: Brookings Institution.

Gilbert, Milton 1980. *Quest for Monetary Order*. New York and Chichester: John Wiley and Sons.

Kaplan, J. and Schleiminger, G. 1989. *The European Payments Union: Financial Diplomacy in the 1950s*, Oxford: Clarendon Press.

Kenen, P. (ed.) 1994 *Managing the World Economy*, Washington, DC: Institute for International Economics.

Krause, L. B. and Salant, W. S. 1973. *European Monetary Unification.* Washington DC: Brookings Institution.

Major, R. L. 1979. *Britain's Trade and Exchange Rate Policy,* London: Heinemann for NIESR.

Oxford Review of Economic Policy 1987. *International Trade and Commercial Policy Spring,* Oxford: Oxford University Press.

Oxford Review of Economic Policy 1990. *Balance of Payments* Autumn, Oxford: Oxford University Press (especially the article by Coutts and Godley).

Solomon, R. 1977. *The International Monetary System 1945–1976: an insider's view,* New York: Harper & Row.

Strange, Susan 1971. *Sterling and British Policy,* Oxford: Oxford University Press.

Tew, J. H. B. 1985. *The Evolution of the International Monetary System 1945–85,* (3rd edn), London: Hutchinson.

Thirlwall, A. P. 1982. *Balance of Payments Theory and the UK Experience,* London: Macmillan.

Regional Policy

Armstrong, H. and Taylor, J. 1987. *Regional Policy: the way forward,* London: Employment Institute.

Brown, A. J. 1972. *The Framework of Regional Economics in the United Kingdom,* Cambridge: Cambridge University Press for NIESR.

Economic Trends 1975. 'Regional Income Accounts 1971', November.

Economic Trends 1990. 'Regional Income Accounts 1988', November.

Economic Trends 1994. 'Regional Income Accounts 1992', May.

Law, C. M. 1981 *British Regional Development since World War I,* London: Methuen.

MacLennan, D. and Parr, J. (eds) 1979. *Regional Policy: past experience and new directions,* Oxford: Martin Robertson.

Moore, B. and Rhodes, J. 1973. 'Evaluating the Effects of British Regional Policy', *Economic Journal,* March.

Parsons, D. W. 1985. *The Political Economy of British Regional Policy,* London: Routledge.

Social Policy

Atkinson, A. B. 1969. *Poverty and The Reform of Social Security,* Cambridge: Cambridge University Press.

Barr, N. 1987. *The Economics of the Welfare State,* London: Weidenfeld & Nicholson.

Beveridge Report 1942. *Social Insurance and Allied Services,* Cmd 6404, London: HMSO.

Dilnot, A. W., Kay, J. A. and Morris, C. N. 1984. *The Reform of Social Security,* Oxford: Clarendon Press for Institute of Fiscal Studies.

Digby, A. 1989. *British Welfare Policy: workhouse to workforce,* London: Faber.

Goodin, R. E. and Le Grand, J. 1987. *Not Only the Poor,* London: Allen & Unwin.

Hannah, L. 1986. *Inventing Retirement: the development of occupational pensions in Britain,* Cambridge: Cambridge University Press.

Johnson, P. 1986. 'Some historical dimensions of the Welfare State "crisis" ', *Journal of Social Policy,* October.

OECD 1985. *Social Expenditure 1960–1990,* Paris.

Walker, A. and Walker, C. (eds) 1987. *The Growing Divide: a social audit,* London: Child Poverty Action Group.

Wilson, T. and Wilson D. 1982. *The Political Economy of the Welfare State,* London: Allen & Unwin.

Economic Trends 1990 'The effect of taxes and benefits on household income in 1987', May.

International Comparisons and Foreign Assessments

Boltho, Andrea (ed.) 1982. *The European Economy: growth and crisis,* Oxford: Oxford University Press.

Cairncross, A. (ed.) 1971. *Britain's Economic Prospects Reconsidered,* London: Allen & Unwin.

Caves, R. and associates 1969. *Britain's Economic Prospects,* Washington, DC: Brookings Institution.

Caves, R. and Krause, L. B. (eds) 1980. *Britain's Economic Performance,* Washington, DC: Brookings Institution.

Chick, M. 1990. *Governments, Industries and Markets: aspects of government—industry relations in the UK, Japan, West Germany and the United States since 1945*, Aldershot and Brookfield, Vermont: Edward Elgar.

Dornbusch, R. and Layard, R. 1987. *The Performance of the British Economy*, Washington, DC: Brookings Institution.

Graham, A. with Seldon, A. 1990. *Government and Economies in the Post-War World: economic policies and comparative performance 1945—85*, London and New York: Routledge.

Jones, D. T. 1976. 'Output, employment and labour productivity in Europe since 1955', *National Institute Economic Review*, August.

National Institute of Economic and Social Research 1990. *Productivity, Education and Training: Britain and Other Countries Compared*, London.

Panic, M. (ed.) 1976. *The UK and West German Manufacturing Industry 1954—72*, London: National Economic Development Office.

Van der Wee, H. 1986. *Prosperity and Upheaval. The world economy 1945—1980*, Harmondsworth: Penguin Books.

Memoirs and Diaries

Barnett, Joel 1982. *Inside the Treasury*, London: André Deutsch.

Benn, A. N. W. (Tony) 1987. *Out of the Wilderness: diaries 1963—67*, London: Hutchinson.

Benn, A. N. W. (Tony) 1988. *Office without Power: diaries 1968—72*, London: Hutchinson.

Benn, A. N. W. (Tony) 1989. *Against the Tide: diaries 1973—1976*, London: Hutchinson.

Cairncross, A. (1995) *A Treasury Diary 1964—69*, London: The Historian's Press.

Callaghan, James 1987. *Time and Chance*, London: Collins.

Castle, Barbara 1980. *The Castle Diaries 1974—76*, London: Weidenfeld & Nicolson.

Castle, Barbara 1984. *The Castle Diaries 1964—70*, London: Weidenfeld & Nicolson.

Crossman, R. H. S. 1975—77. *The Diaries of a Cabinet Minister*, vols 1—3, London: Hamilton and Cape.

Dalton, Hugh 1962. *High Tide and After: memoirs 1945–60*, London: Frederick Muller.

Donoghue, Bernard 1987. *Prime Minister*, London: Jonathan Cape.

Healey, Denis 1989. *The Time of My Life*, London: Michael Joseph.

Jay, Douglas 1980. *Change and Fortune: a political record*, London: Hutchinson.

Lawson, Nigel. *The View from No 11*, London: John Murray.

MacDougall, Donald 1987. *Don and Mandarin*, London: John Murray.

Macmillan, Harold 1969. *Tides of Fortune 1945–1955*, London: Macmillan.

Macmillan, Harold 1971. *Riding the Storm 1956–1959*, London: Macmillan.

Macmillan, Harold 1972. *Pointing the Way 1959–1961*, London: Macmillan.

Macmillan, Harold 1973. *At the End of the Day 1961–1963*, London: Macmillan.

Meade, James (eds. Howson and Moggridge) 1990. *Collected Papers*, Vol IV: *the Cabinet Office Diary 1944–46*, London: Allen and Unwin

Plowden, Lord 1989. *An Industrialist in the Treasury: the post-war years*, London: André Deutsch.

Robbins, Lionel 1971. *Autobiography of an Economist*, London: Macmillan.

Roberthall, Lord 1989, 1991. *The Robert Hall Diaries*, Vol. 1 1947–53; Vol. 2 1954–61. London: Routledge.

Wilson, J. Harold 1971. *The Labour Government 1964–1970: a personal record*, London: Weidenfeld & Nicolson and Michael Joseph.

Wilson, J. Harold 1979. *Final Term: the Labour government 1974–76*. London: Weidenfeld & Nicolson and Michael Joseph.

Index